I0795453

PRAISE FOR

SURVIVING BULLY CULTURE

"Behind every polished workplace façade lies the quiet cruelty no policy can prevent without human dignity and empathy. Through real stories and hard-earned insight, Andy Regal's book reveals how bullying on the job corrodes trust, confidence, profits and, ultimately, individual lives."

—STEVE HANNAH, former CEO of *The Onion*

"A fearless, unfiltered journey behind the cameras and conference tables of America's media empires. *Surviving Bully Culture* pulls back the glossy veneer of broadcast glamour to expose the egos, betrayals, and psychological toll hidden in newsrooms and studios. From toxic mentors to tyrannical executives, Andy Regal's work offers a rare, firsthand account of ambition colliding with cruelty and of one man's determination to reclaim dignity in an industry built on power plays."

—JAY SAMIT, bestselling author of *Disrupt You!* and *Second Act Advantage*

"In *Surviving Bully Culture*, Andy Regal bravely shares his harrowing journey through workplace degradation. Andy's story is not just one of personal hardship but a powerful testament to resilience in the face of adversity.

Andy's work is as enlightening as it is heart-wrenching. With each page, we witness the toll that workplace bullying takes on individuals and families. What sets *Surviving Bully Culture* apart is its exploration of the problem and its unwavering commitment to seeking solutions. Andy's journey is not one of resignation but of empowerment. This is more than a book—it's a call to action, a manifesto for change."

—DR. GARY NAMIE, social psychologist and founder of the Workplace Bullying Institute

"As the costs of workplace violence, bullying, threats, and harassment grow ever more severe, Americans are deeply concerned about the dangers of our increasingly toxic culture to their safety and well-being. Despite the awareness of its impact on vulnerable communities, Andy Regal's emotionally harrowing experiences—even as a successful straight white man in a series of impressive jobs—offer powerful testimony to the pervasiveness of destructive behavior patterns and the damage they cause. No one is immune to the toll. Just in time, *Surviving Bully Culture* provides a practical, constructive, engaging, empathetic, and much-needed guide to dealing with bullying culture, repairing its destructive impact, and raising awareness for the urgent public goal of changing the ways we treat our fellow human beings, both on and off the job."

— LESLIE BENNETTS, journalist and author of *The Feminine Mistake*

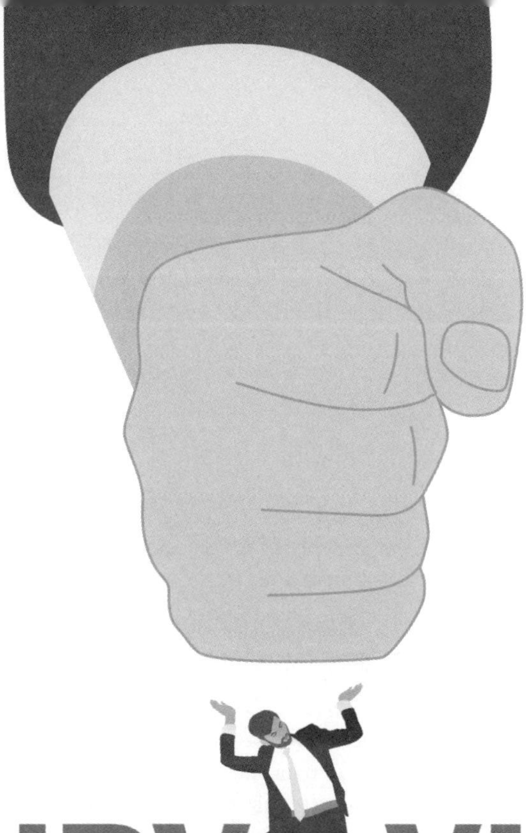

SURVIVING BULLY CULTURE

A CAREER SPENT NAVIGATING WORKPLACE BULLYING AND A GUIDE FOR HEALING

ANDREW REGAL

amplify
an imprint of Amplify Publishing Group

www.amplifypublishing.com

Surviving Bully Culture: A Career Spent Navigating Workplace Bullying and a Guide for Healing

©2026 Andrew Regal. All Rights Reserved. No part of this publication may be reproduced, stored in a retrieval system, or transmitted in any form by any means electronic, mechanical, or photocopying, recording, or otherwise without the permission of the author.

This book reflects my personal experiences, perceptions, and recollections of events as I remember them. Some names, job titles, physical descriptions, and identifying details have been changed or omitted to protect privacy. In some cases, certain events have been condensed, for narrative clarity. Nothing in this book is intended to negatively characterize any institution.

My account is presented in good faith and is not intended to assert objective fact about any person's motivations, or conduct, nor is it intended to allege misconduct by any employer or organization. The views expressed here are my own and should be understood as my personal interpretation of my experiences.

For more information, please contact:
Amplify Publishing, an imprint of Amplify Publishing Group
620 Herndon Parkway, Suite 220
Herndon, VA 20170
info@amplifypublishing.com

Library of Congress Control Number: 2025925972

CPSIA Code: PRV1025A

ISBN-13: 979-8-89138-947-2

Printed in the United States

To all who seek to share their light with those around them.

If you do not tell the truth about yourself,
you cannot tell it about other people.

—VIRGINIA WOOLF

Writers, Woolf believed, must tell all their truths, including the ones that describe themselves as unfavorable, unkind, unsympathetic, vindictive, and unsuccessful.

CONTENTS

SECTION 3: I GET MY OWN SHOW . . . UNFORTUNATELY

SECTION 4: BULLIES AND BOOSTERS

SECTION 5: YOU CAN GO HOME AGAIN . . . IF THE BULLY HAS MOVED OUT

SECTION 6: LIFE AND DEATH IN THE NEWSROOM

SECTION 7: GENIUSES TO THE LEFT OF ME, BULLIES TO THE RIGHT . . . HERE I AM (AGAIN)

SECTION 8: REACHING THE APEX . . . AND I WAS SCARED OF HEIGHTS

PROLOGUE

Some people try to be tall by cutting off the heads of others!
—SRI YUKTESWAR

I have locked myself into our home office. I'm too ashamed to be seen by Melissa, the young woman who will be here shortly to drive my kids to their after-school activities. I'm not supposed to be home. I should be at work. What will I say to my wife, Jennifer, and my kids, Sophie and Lucas, when they come home from school? Should I simply tell them what my boss said to me a couple of hours ago?

"We've decided to make a change at the top of your department."

Until that moment, I'd *been* the top of my department.

I've fallen to the floor in despair, not having the strength to even sit at the desk. I'm so, so weary. I lie there for I don't know how long. When I start to think I'm strong enough and capable enough to fend off the bullies, I remember that the bullies have triumphed once again.

It's 2017. But it could be 1987, 1993, 1997, 2003, 2010, 2017, or 2022. I have experienced and observed bullying throughout my career.

And now, I don't think I can get up off the floor.

I may not deserve your sympathy. Who am I to complain? I have a great wife who supports me and copes with my failures much better than me. I have good kids, and my mother-in-law doesn't hate me. I've got loyal friends too. But despite a gratifying homelife, the way I have been mistreated throughout my career in the media has left me feeling anxious, alone, full of shame, often unable to sleep, exhausted, sleep deprived, frequently throwing up, and at times contemplating suicide.

In the workplace, a bully doesn't have to beat you *up* to beat you *down*.

In the following pages, I will be describing counterproductive bully behaviors in the workplace, such as:

- Sending an angry text or email or speaking in a harsh and demeaning tone
- Perceiving someone's talent as a threat and removing that "threat" by holding back funding and approvals for key projects
- Failing to include a targeted employee in appropriate meetings and off-site events
- Demonstrating a complete lack of communication between the manager and employee
- Setting up a targeted employee for failure

My colleagues and I talked incessantly about the bullies and what they'd said or done. But we never considered what *we* could say or do in response. Taking any action was dangerous and, therefore, taboo.

I felt trapped. I stayed and took it. Does that make me a victim? I'll let you decide.

I want to be clear. I was fairly, sometimes generously, compensated for the work I did, and I never complained to human resources.

That was not a viable option. The bully often signed their checks.

There's a zero-tolerance bullying policy at my kids' school. But in my thirty-year career, I found a 100 percent tolerance for bullying in the places I worked. It's still rampant in the newsroom, and I know from talking to people in a variety of disciplines that bullying is *prevalent* everywhere because it's *legal* everywhere.

The Workplace Bullying Institute (WBI) in an online survey found that 27 percent of those working in healthcare reported being bullied, 23 percent in education, 16 percent in public service / social welfare, 10 percent in the service industry, 14 percent in "other," 5 percent in IT, and 5 percent in manufacturing.*

I have found that targets of bullying, in general, seek to support, guide, assist, and collaborate with their colleagues. In most cases, those who are likely to be bullied are the types of employees who disregard office politics and gamesmanship.

Bullying is not against the law, and very few businesses have guidelines prohibiting the workplace aggression that causes so much misery.

It's an abuse based on an imbalance of power. That's what makes it so insidious.

I've experienced and witnessed bullying in twenty-seven of my thirty years working in television newsrooms. And during those years, I stood up to the bully once, as I recall. Maybe twice.

Pathetic.

Your career may parallel mine, in which you were gaslit, backstabbed, interrupted repeatedly, derided, excluded from email chains and pivotal meetings, and ostracized. Maybe you just kept your mouth shut and took it like me.

In all those years, I never saw anyone else stand up for themselves or for any other good, hardworking employee who was being intimidated.

Stories of the righteous underdog emerging triumphant against the all-powerful archnemesis are found in the Bible, fairy tales, and certainly Hollywood movies.

In the office, not so much.

The WBI also discovered in its 2024 survey that 32 percent of all American workers report being direct targets of bullies. That's more than fifty-two million people. If you include the 14 percent of people in the poll who reported witnessing workplace aggression, then nearly 75 million people acknowledge being affected by psychological harassment while at work. Bullying affects women, African Americans, Hispanics, and LGBTQ individuals at higher rates,

---

* Gary Namie, *Bullying by Industry: Workplace Bullying* (Workplace Bullying Institute).

and men comprise the vast majority of perpetrators at 71 percent.*

This is true across all businesses—large and small, public and private, profit and nonprofit.

Now, for my story, I want to make a clear distinction between a *jerk* and a *bully*. A jerk cuts you off and gives you the finger at an intersection. He offends you for the next five minutes.

Bullies in the office abuse the influence they wield over our emotional well-being, our self-esteem, our finances, and the trajectory of our careers. Bullies cause physical and emotional harm.

My definition of a *workplace bully* is someone who has power and authority over you and uses that dominance unreasonably.

You can't *reason* with a bully.

Of course, I am not suggesting that a workplace bully engages in bullying full-time. Bullies are often the most engaging people in the room. They love to be the center of attention. I am describing their characteristics when they are in full bully mode, which is far too often.

When there's a conflict, disagreement, misunderstanding, or a problem of any kind, the bully with the power refuses to have a reasonable conversation to resolve it. In my experience, they'll intimidate, threaten, and connive. Or they'll punish you.

They won't listen or engage in a civil discussion to understand and resolve the issue and examine ways to enhance communication and performance.

Perhaps it's naive to hope bosses will appreciate and understand the extent of their power over our welfare and sense of self.

But is that too much to expect?

The bullying behaviors I experienced never solved a problem, never improved production, and certainly didn't increase revenues.

According to the Center for Workplace Mental Health, "People who work in hostile environments are likely to leave the company, be absent from work,

---

* Workplace Bullying Institute, *2024 WBI US Workplace Bullying Survey: The National Study*, October 22, 2024, https://workplacebullying.org/2024-wbi-us-survey/.

and feel dissatisfied with their job. These factors seriously impact a business's bottom line in multiple ways."*

Consider this alarming fact from a 2024 Fast Company article titled "How Workplace Bullying Affects Your Bottom Line":

"The American Psychological Association estimates that bullying costs US businesses $300 billion each year through direct and indirect effects, such as lower productivity, absenteeism, turnover, and legal costs.

There are two main reasons this happens. First, bullying has a massive detrimental effect on people's mental health and well-being, which then affects their ability to perform in the job."†

So why do the bullies bully? Ego. And narcissism, and sadism, and insecurity, and fear. I've seen it all and finally understand it—though I don't excuse the behavior. As a witness to it and its effects and a student of its underpinnings, I seek here to illuminate the reality of bullying to empower other bullying victims to better cope and heal. And perhaps some bullies will recognize their management style and change their behavior.

I am not here to expose my bullies or shame them. That is not my mission. To that end, I have changed some names in the following pages, including the bullies and the bullied.

I am advocating an end to this pervasive and pernicious abuse of power and status.

Bosses need to stop killing our spirit. We're not the competition, and we are certainly not the enemy. We're on the same team!

There are no benefits to bullying in the workplace, not to the people suffering it or the employees witnessing it, and not to the company's bottom line. It does not make organizations more competitive, weed out the weak or mediocre, or give anyone an edge. It cannot be justified as "just the way things

---

* "Workplace Bullying Is Costly," Center for Workplace Mental Health, https://workplacementalhealth.org/Mental-Health-Topics/Bullying?utm_source=chatgpt.com.

† Anna Eliatamby, "How Workplace Bullying Affects Your Bottom Line," *Fast Company*, August 5, 2024, https://www.fastcompany.com/91167308/how-workplace-bullying-affects-your-bottom-line?utm_source=chatgpt.com.

are done" or by the idea that because the bully is a rainmaker, their behavior should be tolerated.

In an article published in the *MIT Sloan Management Review*, titled, "Why Every Leader Needs to Worry About Toxic Culture," researchers analyzed data from 34 million online employee profiles in the US Bureau of Labor and Statistics database, as well as 1.4 million Glassdoor reviews, and determined that "toxic corporate culture" was the single biggest predictor of employee attrition, ten times as significant as compensation.*

If I knew how to avoid, or better yet, how to chasten bullies, they wouldn't have repeatedly knocked me down. I saw the bully coming, like an old steam locomotive rising over the hill, then bearing down on me from a distance. Even with all that time and perspective, I could never figure out how to get out of the way before getting run over.

I often wondered, *What about me attracts or provokes bullies?* As a young person, I was never a target of bullies. My parents were loving and supportive, and they rarely, if ever, raised their voices. At school, I was well-liked by my classmates and teachers. I was a strong student, a three-sport athlete, and a first-chair trumpet player in the high school band.

I had friends.

But as an employee, did I suddenly become particularly annoying, cloying, overly self-involved, overtly ambitious, or highly sensitive and weak and vulnerable?

Maybe.

Why was I mistreated for most of my career? I have always considered myself hardworking, productive, a team player, and an innovator.

If you're the boss, why would you bully someone like me?

And why did I arrive at work every day to seek the bully's approval, or dare I admit it, their love? (Yes, I thought if I did a great job, my boss would love me like a parent loves a child.)

---

* Donald Sull et al., "Why Every Leader Needs to Worry About Toxic Culture," *MIT Sloan Management Review (2022)*, https://sloanreview.mit.edu/article/why-every-leader-needs-to-worry-about-toxic-culture/.

Perhaps you've asked similar questions. These thoughts have disturbed me for three decades. I wanted to know how many people shared the trauma I experienced, and I wondered if there were any people out there who could explain why this happens so frequently to so many of us.

I've found that there are such experts. You will meet them in these pages. Speaking with them has changed my life. I have understanding and relief. I no longer blame myself. The shame has diminished. I no longer feel like a failure. I have reclaimed my self-worth. I find joy in life and have purpose in my life and work.

If you have been or are a target of bullying, I trust this information will do the same for you. And if you or someone you know is suffering from the effects of workplace degradation,

please skip to:

Chapter 53: Good Advice, Then Really Bad Advice, Then the Best Advice on page 385.

There, you'll find extensive coping and healing methods and expert advice, including my six tenets of self-care, which are critical to finding joy even in crisis.

While no animals were harmed during the events described herein, I certainly was, as were many of my colleagues.

So, this is my attempt at letting the bullies know the adverse effect they've had on me and all the people—hundreds, if not thousands, of staffers—who worked for them.

You know, as I do, that if you were bullied as a child or as an adult, it stays with you—in some cases, for decades.

Bosses have the authority to validate us, to make us popular and respected, or to crush us. In my experience, they often crush us.

I'm no hero. No whistleblower. I'm safe from the bullies now. I no longer hide in my home office in shame. I can pay my bills. You could certainly accuse me of cowardice for waiting to write this book. Fair. The bullies can no longer berate, belittle, disregard, and discard me. But I now have a voice. I can speak up and speak out. And that's what I want for all bully victims.

This isn't a work of fiction. These are my best recollections.

This is a call to action to managers, supervisors, and bosses across the globe to stop harming your employees; it damages them and can destroy your business.

It's my coming-of-age journey, a twentysomething who moved from Chicago to New York for a career in television. This is my life inside the newsrooms of CNBC, Court TV, MSNBC, and the *Wall Street Journal,* among others. These are my specific memories of the characters I met, the newsmakers and celebrities I encountered, the women I loved, the captivating news stories I covered, and the mean-spirited, uncaring bullies I endured.

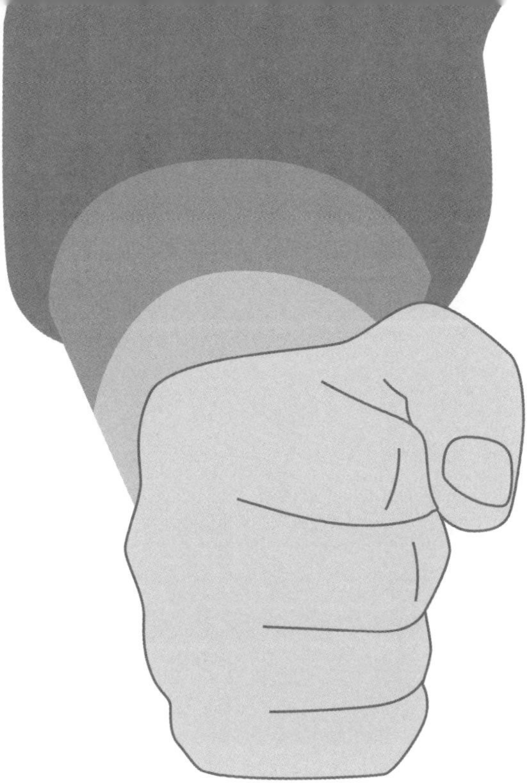

SECTION 1

THE BULLY WHO ROARED

A good leader inspires people to have confidence in the leader.
A great leader inspires people to have confidence in themselves.
—ELEANOR ROOSEVELT

CHAPTER 1

LET THE BULLYING BEGIN

It was 1985. I'd decided to apply for a producer's job at WMAQ Radio, a big-time, big-market station in Chicago. It was in the famed Merchandise Mart building and was the sister radio station to WMAQ-TV, the powerhouse NBC-owned and -operated station in Chicago. I was twenty-four years old, out of work after losing my job at a smaller Chicago station, WIND, which was transitioning to a Spanish language format. I was still living at home. My friends had received their JDs, MBAs, and even their marriage licenses.

I didn't question my career choice—covering the news, writing about it, and communicating it to the broadest audience, that was for me.

"So, Andy, what interests you in working for WMAQ Radio?"

"Well, you have a job open, and I need a job."

No, that's not what I said to Siobhan, the senior producer of WMAQ Radio. But that's what I was thinking.

"Have you heard that we're going through a format change?"

"I have," I said. "I understand you're moving to a talk format. I've got a lot of experience, having just come from WIND."

"Yes, I'm aware." Siobhan peered up from my résumé. She smiled. "How are you with conflict?"

"I don't cause conflict. I'm a total team player."

Siobhan seemed amused, as if she thought I was making a joke.

"No, I mean, do you like heated debate?"

"Oh, you mean on the air?"

I watched politically charged shows like *Crossfire* and *The McLaughlin Group*. They entertained me from the comfort of my parents' couch.

At home, I was both uncomfortable and unfamiliar with acrimony. My parents never fought, at least not in front of us. There was never a raised or critical voice in our home, and expletives were expressly forbidden—unless my dad was watching the Chicago Bears.

My grandfather, however, broke the peaceful domesticity rule when I was about eight. We were visiting his home in Sarasota, Florida, at Christmas, and one of his favorite activities was to take me out fishing.

I hated fishing.

My grandfather had a penchant for running up on sandbars, but we made it safely to our destination on this occasion. The worst part of our fishing trips was reaching into the bait bucket. There were a dozen slimy shrimp in that wet pail of repugnance. And they were alive! My grandfather could tell I was reticent.

Repulsed was more like it.

"Oh, for heaven's sake, Andy," he wailed while shoving my wrist into the shrimp's temporary home. "Grab one!"

I did as I was told but kept my eyes shut tight. I pulled one out and could feel it wriggling in my palm. I could sense my grandfather's rising irritation.

"Now, take the hook and put it right through its heart. It will stay on the hook better that way," he said without compassion for me or the shrimp.

I couldn't do it. I tried but couldn't quite go through with it.

"Jesus Christ. Just give it to me."

He secured the shrimp. There was a crunching sound as the hook went through its heart.

"You are such an egghead," my grandfather scolded.

I felt a hook go right through my heart.

Nobody in my family had ever called me a "mean" name before. In my family we didn't speak that way to one another. And I prided myself on being a good kid, who deserved compliments and love, not insults.

To this day, it's the only conversation with my grandfather I can recall.

Dr. Leah Katz, author of *Gutsy: Mindfulness Practices for Everyday Bravery*, told me, "The messages we receive as young children penetrate deeply, all the way down to our very core, and feel like truths."

"Have you worked with tough talent?" Siobhan asked.

I had the perfect answer to that question. Not only had I worked with difficult talent, but I'd also worked with a certifiably crazy talent—former baseball star Jimmy Piersall. Jimmy was infamous for his antics on the field when he played for the Boston Red Sox in the 1950s. He was institutionalized due to a psychological breakdown, which was chronicled in a book (*Fear Strikes Out: The Jim Piersall Story*) and movie (*Fear Strikes Out*). Anthony Perkins was cast as Piersall in the movie. Jimmy disavowed the film for two reasons. First, he said it was too harsh in its portrayal of his father. Second, Jimmy explained, "Perkins throws like a girl."

I was assigned to be Jimmy's producer for a nightly sports talk show titled *Calling All Sports* on WIND Radio. Jimmy was tense and intense, shuffling his papers as he prepared for the show. He had a penchant for being highly critical of the players on the field, which didn't ingratiate him with the athletes, but the Chicago radio sports fans adored him for his candor and outspoken nature.

Jimmy had no filter. He said and did pretty much whatever he wanted. He was a bull of a guy and tough on those he felt had done him wrong. He acknowledged, "Going crazy was one of the best things that ever happened to me. Nobody knew my name before that."

His reputation for being unsteady allowed him to get away with bullying anybody and everybody in his path. Nobody knew what he might do next or what he was capable of. Jimmy was given wide latitude, and the bosses left him alone . . . for me to manage.

Jimmy never bullied me.

I was *his guy*.

But Jimmy was a bully.

"Andy, I need to have some minor surgery," Jimmy said to me one day. "No big deal. I'm not telling the bosses. And don't you tell them either. Just find a sub for the show. I don't want to give the suits any reason to start thinking they can replace me."

I did what I was told.

After the show, in which every caller asked about Jimmy's whereabouts, Cheryl Morton, my boss, came into the control room screaming. "Where's Jimmy, and why wasn't I informed he wasn't hosting tonight?!"

After profusely apologizing, I went to the hospital to see how Jimmy was doing.

He'd called me a couple of hours earlier saying that although he was a bit groggy, he'd like me to come visit.

I got to the hospital and asked for Jimmy's room, headed down the hallway, and found his door was slightly ajar. I knocked gently.

Jimmy was lying in bed with just a sheet over him. "How ya doin', buddy?" he said affectionately. "I bet the show was a boring piece a shit tonight. And all the callers wanted to know where I was. That'll show them how valuable I am. Want to see my little scar?"

I was thinking he had simple shoulder or knee surgery. He lifted the sheet and wasn't wearing anything underneath. Literally nothing—no gown, no underwear, no anything. In between his legs, his scrotum was the size of a grapefruit and all bruised and purple. Jimmy looked at me with pride and joked, "Everybody always said I had big balls!"

You had to agree with Jimmy there. He did have big balls.

"I worked with Jimmy Piersall," I said to Siobhan. "He was tough, but we got along great. We had a ball. Err, um, we had a great time together, even if he was a bit nutty."

"Well, that experience might help you in this role. Have you ever heard of Morton Downey Jr.?"

Up to this point, I had suffered only one bullying episode in my life. In the spring before my freshman year at the University of Illinois, I received a bid from Zeta Beta Tau (ZBT) fraternity. Rush was to occur well before the fall semester. I accepted with great anticipation.

I had the assurance that when I arrived in late August, I would have fifty big brothers looking out for my welfare as I adjusted to life away from home. I'd receive tutoring from the older guys who'd already taken my classes and sorely needed guidance on how to talk to college girls.

As it turned out, I got fifty bullies instead of brothers; nobody ever helped me with my coursework, and my fraternity "brothers" not only *didn't* help me talk to girls but outright ruined the only date I was able to get my freshman year.

Instead of being nurtured and cared for as promised, I was physically and emotionally abused at ZBT by a collection of sadistic, toxic young men.

As first-year students, we lived in the fraternity house. The brothers of the house would often wake up the pledges at two or three in the morning, screaming obscenities and banging ferociously on our doors with thick, varnished wood paddles that rattled our rooms and sent my heart pounding.

They'd line us up in the downstairs foyer, demanding we keep our heads down and our eyes on the floor at all times, remaining completely still and silent. Then they would make us crawl on the ground like dogs as they screamed invectives at us.

This thirty-minute nightmare occurred about once a week in various forms, but we never knew when, which meant I went to sleep every night dreading what might happen before sunrise.

On the Sunday night that officially launched Pledge Dance Week, which doubled as our hell week, the entire fraternity—some twenty-five pledges and seventy-five brothers—was called to a special conclave in the fraternity house dining hall.

Once there and seated, the brothers closed all the curtains and dimmed all the lights. We were told that this gathering had been brought to order to initiate Pledge Dance Week.

"It's time to reveal the most reviled, most hated pledge in this year's ZBT class," the fraternity president rose to say. The brothers in the room stood and cheered like a bloodthirsty, angry mob.

I paid little attention. I detested all this faux macho ferocity. I just wanted to get out of there and go to the library. It was a couple of months into the semester, and midterms were approaching.

I had a full course load and a paid job writing sports articles for *The Daily Illini* newspaper. My schedule was exhausting. I had no interest in who the "most hated pledge" was. I felt sorry for whichever weak, nerdy, or apathetic member of my pledge class they intended to humiliate.

I was a devoted and loyal pledge who dutifully cleaned up the spilled beer and vomit during and after our late-night keg parties. I even gave away my coveted tickets to the highly anticipated Illinois versus Indiana basketball game to a brother whose best friend was visiting from out of town.

Sophomore brother Brody Lennox rose to address the plebes and brothers alike.

Lennox walked around the house with a swagger and proudly showed off his stunning girlfriend and rock-hard physique every chance he got. The former high school wrestler still looked like he could compete for a state title.

He also came across a little . . . unhinged.

"We are here tonight," he began, "not to honor you losers but to identify the worst of you. And that's saying something. You are all pathetic, and this brotherhood has voted one low-life, worthless pledge as the most hated of all—and I hate all of you, so that's saying something."

The brothers laughed like hyenas.

"Therefore, it is my distinct burden to condemn this year's Most Hated Pledge, Andy Regal."

I remember trying to smile as if to acknowledge the joke of it all. But inside I was stunned, hurt, and humiliated. The brotherhood roared its approval. The dining hall shook from the pounding on the tables and walls.

I hadn't noticed before, but to Lennox's left was a carved-out pumpkin for the festivities. He picked it up off the nearby table, walked over to me, raised his arms, and slammed it down onto my head.

I stumbled from the weight of it. I became nauseous from the smell. I was in shock. Even though the pumpkin covered my ears, I could hear the derision, the mocking, the delight of the older guys.

As my head swung uncontrollably around the room, I spied through the tiny eyeholes a number of my fellow pledges relishing in my ignominy. They were relieved it was me and not them.

I finally got my bearings and exited the dining hall to the sounds of the brothers hooting and jeering. What had I done to deserve this? Was it because I was a mama's boy, weak and homesick in the first weeks of living on my own? What was wrong with me, and even worse, why was I so feeble that I allowed this abuse?

With the entertainment for the evening concluded, we were given five minutes to get in line and march down into the unfinished basement of our fraternity house. We were told this would be our home for Pledge Dance Week. It was filthy. We brought our mattresses from our cozy rooms and set them down one next to the other on the chilly, dank, musty floor.

The nonsensical logic was that sleeping together would further bond us as we suffered together. I never bought into the ridiculous notion that being abused somehow brings people together, making them more loyal and devoted.

According to the brotherhood, it would also serve us well, to be imprisoned together in the basement so we could write and rehearse the sketches and build the sets for the pledge dance comedy show. We were mandated to make fun of the brothers in our skits. It was our chance to gently roast them in a good-natured way. This was a bit of "permissible revenge" for all the revilement we'd suffered at the hands of the older guys.

Just as we were all settling in for bed around midnight in our cramped new digs, the brothers placed a six-foot speaker at the top of the stairs and blasted "My Sharona" by The Knack at the highest decibel level the speaker was capable of, in what turned out to be an endless loop all night. And if that wasn't enough, the following day, while we were in class, the older guys in the house pulled a hose around to the stairs and flooded the basement, soaking our mattresses, blankets, books, and clothes.

Despite the torment, we worked tirelessly to put these clever, biting skits together.

We were ecstatic at the opportunity to lampoon those who had attacked us all semester. Of course, it would all be in good fun. We knew the brothers would love laughing at themselves and appreciate our comedic efforts, and we'd laugh along with them, as would our dates.

We were told that this night, this dance, and the pledge skit were among the most sacred traditions of the ZBT fraternity and that this night was the final step before we would become full-fledged brothers with all the rights, privileges, and prestige that came with it.

In other words, the brothers would no longer treat us like crap.

Claire, who lived in my sister's sorority, had agreed to be my date to the dance. She was nice. We had never spoken much, but she had a beautiful smile and a sweet disposition. I was feeling great anticipation for my first college date and dance. The night was going beautifully. I was having a great time with Claire and wondered if she would become my first college girlfriend. In the seventh grade at Edgewood Jr. High School, my first "real" girlfriend, Cyndi, took pity on me and taught me how to make out.

It was time for the pledge skit. We were all on a high. Many of my pledge mates were already drunk or high or both, and we were ready for our comedic star turn. The older guys were going to love this. Our parody scripts were hilarious.

I remember watching the first set of five to six guys in my class go out onto the makeshift stage with great glee and anticipation for the first skit. We were going to start strong with one of our best scenes. From the wings, I could hear the assembled crowd's hearty laughs and see their broad smiles. The women in attendance didn't understand all the inside jokes, so they just followed along.

By the second and third comic sketches, the mood took a decided turn as we playfully mocked the various upperclassmen in the house. The laughs were harder to come by, and you could see the body language and facial expressions among the fraternity's executive membership in the front row becoming clearly uncomfortable and even contemptuous of our comedic stylings.

And then the laughs completely stopped. The expressions were uniformly stern, and almost every male audience member had crossed arms. Our energy wilted on- and offstage.

At first, we were killing. Now, we were bombing. Backstage, we were aghast. Something was going horribly wrong. After the fourth or fifth disastrous skit, the house president abruptly stepped toward the stage and halted the show.

In front of everyone, all our dates, he said, "You've humiliated yourselves enough, and worse, you've maligned the brotherhood and sullied this hallowed tradition." He was so sorry, but he had to ask all our dates to go home. "Pledge dance is over," he said sorrowfully and forcefully. The girls, including Claire, were ashen-faced and silent as they filed out of the ZBT house.

We were shell-shocked, not just by this night's humiliating and ugly turn of events but also by the accumulated sleep deprivation here at the end of hell week. How could we have so missed the mark, especially when we'd been encouraged to have some fun at the older guys' expense?

After all the invited guests departed, we were lined up and ordered back into the dining room.

The brothers were solemn, some shaking their heads, not yelling at us, because they weren't so much angry with us as disgusted by us. They were calling each of us out as to how we could have done such a thing to them and the fraternity.

We were each instructed to take a seat at any one of the six tables in the dining hall. One brother stood directly behind each pledge. Then, we were told to push out our chairs, put our heads under the table, and stretch our arms across the top of the table with only our fingertips touching it. All we could see was the ground, the legs of the table, and the legs of our fellow pledge brothers.

The brothers proceeded one at a time to methodically rebuke us. We had disgraced ourselves and the ZBT fraternity. We were told over and over our behavior was an outrage that had never happened before in the storied history of this heretofore-hallowed annual event.

This went on for well over ninety minutes as every brother took his turn to express his dismay at our disgraceful display.

The last exalted brother spoke his mind. My neck had stiffened from looking down from under the table, my back ached, my arms were cramping, and my fingertips were raw from digging into the table top.

Finally, and I would argue unmercifully, a massive bang like a gunshot shook the entire room and all the tables, inches above our heads. Each brother, standing behind one pledge, slammed down on the table what turned out to be a twenty-four-ounce bottle of beer.

Following this emotional and physical torture, these entitled, heartless young men suddenly started whooping and shouting in joyous celebration.

The brothers, every ruthless one of them, took our outstretched arms gently off the tables and helped us remove our heads carefully from beneath the tables so as not to hit our heads.

It must have been 1:30 or 2:00 a.m., and my bleary eyes tried to focus on the now-surreal surroundings. I saw all the brothers holding big twenty-four-ounce bottles of beer, pouring glasses for all of us, high-fiving and hugging us. I shoved away anyone who even moved to approach me. I was trying to understand what the fuck had happened and what was happening now.

"It's the Big Pimp!" I heard one of the brothers say with a clownish grin.

"And we pulled it off. It was all a joke, and you guys fell for it," said another, laughing deliriously.

"But you guys got through it. Congratulations. You are brothers now. You made it through hell week."

The entire thing had been a con game. The plan all along was for the brothers to be appalled at our comedy show, no matter what we said or did.

Apparently, the "Big Pimp" was something that hadn't been done in five years, and this group of miscreants who would go on to become doctors, lawyers, engineers, financiers, dads, and, yes, bosses decided to resurrect it for their perverse enjoyment.

Adding to my disbelief, I looked around the room and saw many of my classmates partaking in the now-ebullient atmosphere. They had endured, even *enjoyed* the experience. Making it through hell week and the "Big Pimp" was somehow an accomplishment, something of value, something meaningful and fun.

They were already talking about how they couldn't wait to unleash the Big Pimp on next year's pledge class.

I saw it differently. What was going on in this emasculating power dynamic? As the high-fiving continued, I walked unnoticed out of the dining room. I made it back to my room, locked the door, threw myself on my bed, and cried.

How could anyone do this to me? These were the people I thought would be my best friends, my big brothers, my protectors, and my family. And why was I such a wimp? The other guys were celebrating their (toxic) masculinity and their ability to endure while I hid in my room weeping.

Months later, I was still wearing the stigma of being the Most Hated Pledge, like an orange letter sewn on my university sweatshirt (The University of Illinois' colors are orange and blue). My best college buddy, Bruce, who remains a great friend to this day, ran toward me. His older brother was a senior in ZBT. "Regs. My brother swore me to secrecy, but he told me why you were picked as Most Hated.

"They selected you because you're an excellent pledge. You do everything they ask. You are a loyal pledge. You may not be the most popular guy, but you aren't despised in any way. They couldn't pick someone like me who has a blood relative in the house. And they wouldn't choose a weak or nerdy guy they really don't like. And they didn't dare pick someone like Neumann or Goldberg [the biggest and toughest guys in our class] because they'd fight back and cause a riot.

"They knew you would take the abuse and go right back to being a good, loyal pledge. Doesn't that make you feel better about the whole thing?" Bruce said hopefully.

It didn't. I couldn't convince myself that I wasn't somehow to blame for my mistreatment, and this became a distressing theme throughout my career.

Years and years later, I recognized that for much of my adult life, I had been my worst bully. The things I said to myself about my experiences of workplace degradation, harsh criticism, and ostracism were as bad as anything a boss has ever said to me.

Self-blame is a typical response by bully targets.

I wanted to understand my response to the bullying and why so many bully targets turn their anger inward.

Dr. Kenneth Yeager, director of the Stress, Trauma and Resilience Program at the Ohio State University Wexner Medical Center in Columbus, treats bully victims in his private practice. He said this to me:

"Here's the deal, Andy. Do you talk to yourself? Of course you do. Do you answer yourself? You do. We all do. Do you argue with yourself? Of course you do. Do you beat yourself up? Resilient people learn that self-talk is so very important. And what you say to yourself about any situation has the ability and the power to change the response to the situation. If you talk to yourself harshly throughout your life, when someone else talks to you in that way, it reinforces your self-image. You feel you deserve it. You have to change how you talk to yourself; otherwise, you will accept other people talking to you that way."

My fraternity brothers had power over me, like a boss over an employee. I lived in the fraternity. I couldn't just move out.

I felt I had no recourse.

It was made clear to we former pledges that this ritual was never to be spoken of outside the fraternity.

From that moment on I only walked in and out the back door of the fraternity. I was ashamed that I lived with people who could do this to me and enjoy it. But more, I was guilt-ridden that I allowed it to happen.

I wasn't strong enough or man enough to fight back. I vowed that if anyone at ZBT tried this in any form the following year, I would report them to the university. I made that clear. The Big Pimp was never "played" on any hopeful and unsuspecting freshman at ZBT while I was on campus. I stuck around the fraternity enough to be certain.

Maybe you think this kind of hazing doesn't happen anymore. I was talking to my nephew, who graduated from college six years ago. I told him about my interest in adult bullying. When I shared my hell week tale of woe, his eyes widened in dismay. "Uncle A., you will never believe this. I was voted Worst Pledge by the brothers in my house my freshman year. In our fraternity, there were two guys whose sole job was to run the hazing program."

This abasement is still ubiquitous on college campuses.* Freshmen pledges are being urinated on and forced to eat cat food and jalapeno peppers and vinegar until they vomit, all the while being shouted at with invectives. They are being forced to take part in physical stress tests until they throw up or bleed. And then there are the most heart-wrenching stories, like the 2025 death of twenty-year-old Caleb Wilson, a student at Southern University and A&M College. According to reports, the young man was pledging Omega Psi Phi fraternity but ended up dumped at a nearby hospital by a group of men who claimed he had been injured playing basketball. Staff at the hospital called the police, who later told reporters Wilson died "as a direct result of a hazing incident."†

And in years to come, some of these sadistic perpetrators will end up in the corner office.

It occurs to me that jobs are often like pledging. You can't just decide you've had enough and walk out.

I thought bullying was pretty simple. I didn't know there was much to it at first. Then, I reached out to Dr. Gary Namie, a social psychologist. He began his pioneering study of workplace degradation with his wife, Ruth, also a clinical psychologist, after a supervisor tormented her. From that horrible start, they created the Workplace Bullying Institute.

Dr. Namie told me, "Andy, all bullying begins with a singular instigator. It's trauma by intentional human design. Bullying is someone else controlling your life and your thoughts, and therefore, it is a loss of control."

"But what about the object of the aggression?" I asked. In other words, me. "There's no bully without the victim, right?"

"Sure. But in our world, we don't call them *victims*; we refer to them as *targets*. Targets are the fuel of the bullies' ambition."

---

* Katie Reilly, "College Students Keep Dying Because of Fraternity Hazing. Why Is It So Hard to Stop?" *TIME*, October 11, 2017, https://time.com/4976836/fraternity-hazing-deaths-reform-tim-piazza/.

† Walter M. Kimbrough, "Caleb Wilson's Hazing Death Is a Familiar Cautionary Tale," MSNBC, March 14, 2025, https://www.msnbc.com/opinion/msnbc-opinion/hazing-death-caleb-wilson-southern-university-black-greek-life-rcna196350.

"I like that a little better," I replied, "thinking of myself as a target rather than a victim."

"Andy, we've discovered that targets are typically nice people. And good people. Targets are altruistic and highly sensitive. They're well-liked. They dare to be independent and refuse to be subservient. They're often more competent and the veteran go-to person. They're ethical and honest."

These were the exact reasons I was told I'd been picked as the most hated pledge. Hearing this explanation was somewhat comforting.

"But, Gary, that sounds so facile. Bullies bad, targets good."

"Bullies aren't bad all the time, nor are targets good all the time. But they each always have a worldview that is totally in conflict. Targets believe in a benevolent world. They make assumptions that if you work really, really hard, good things will come. But that is naive in a cutthroat workplace."

My naivete was about to be tested.

CHAPTER 2

HOW REGAL BECAME WEASEL

"Hiya, pal," Mort Downey said when we first met. He had a cigarette burning in his hand. His grin was wide. His capped teeth were shiny white. He had good hair for a guy just past fifty. He was wearing tan pants, a blue blazer, and what became his signature bright red socks. He wore red socks every single day.

"I understand we're going to be a team," he said with the enthusiasm of a car salesman saying hello to a prospective customer. "What's your name?"

"Andy Regal," I said meekly.

"What was that? Andy Weasel? Okay, from this moment on, you'll be known as 'the Weasel,'" he exclaimed regally.

Mort's radio show would air locally in Chicago on WMAQ-AM from 2:00 to 6:00 p.m. daily. Mort and I shared a tiny office, our desks facing each other. We couldn't have been more than three feet apart in this five-by-eight-foot space as he smoked his six packs a day. My job was to book politicians, journalists, authors, and occasionally celebs, all wrapped in a debate format.

We had one phone line, and Mort would be on the phone all the time talking to old friends, creditors, jewelry store owners, and an assortment of relatives who might be pejoratively described as hangers-on. These phone conversations often started out quite cordially and then devolved into bitter arguments.

I'd be sitting there patiently waiting to use the phone to book guests for the show until Mort was done with his calls. Oh, what I would have done for a cellphone.

The worst was when he was on the phone with Kim, wife number three. The conversation would often start sweetly. "Hi, honey peepsy poopsie," Mort would say in an amorous, infantile voice. But then the call would begin to degenerate. Mort would start to pull harder on his cigarette. His left eye would close just slightly as he puffed and his ire started to rise.

I couldn't hear what she was saying on the other end of the line, but I heard Mort's reply loud and clear when he screamed into the phone, "I hope you choke on a chicken bone and die!"

I'd never seen this level of vitriol in my entire life. And I'd certainly never heard anyone speak in that tone to anyone else, let alone a spouse.

I couldn't imagine how Kim must have felt on the other end of the line. How could anyone recover from that type of attack? If Mort loved his wife but still treated her in this fashion, what was I in for? I could only hope that if I worked hard and made Mort a star, he would appreciate me, treat me with respect, and spare me his wrath.

On the day of our premiere, just about an hour from air, I heard the *clap, clap* of high heels coming down the hallway. "Mr. Downey, you've received a beautiful arrangement of flowers," the front desk receptionist said breathlessly.

"That is so nice of my wife," Mort said as he was reaching for the little envelope. He tore open the card carefully and started to read aloud.

"'Dear Mort. Congratulations on your premiere. With love, Ron and Nancy.' Oh, that is so very considerate of them, given how busy they must be."

This was 1985, and the only Ron and Nancy I knew were the Reagans, and "Ron" was the sitting president of the United States.

I'd love to tell you that Mort's radio show premiere was big news in the Chicago area. News that even reached the White House. Not a chance. It was a well-kept secret.

At that point, I'd known Mort for only a few weeks, and a strange and somewhat troubling (but highly entertaining) behavior pattern was already emerging. Mort seemed to be telling quite a few fanciful stories.

He told me he grew up with the Kennedys. He fought in the Biafran War. His father was "the Frank Sinatra of the 1930s before there was a Frank Sinatra." His mother and aunt were also celebrities. He participated in the civil rights movement marches and was very close with the Reverend Jesse Jackson. He wrote the 1960s hit song "Wipe Out" (Much later, I was told he didn't actually write the song, but he sang backup).

I didn't have the benefit of Wikipedia in those days, so I just shrugged my shoulders, shook my head, and went on with my day. But I was determined to prove the veracity of one or more of these tales.

I learned that Mort did indeed come from Hollywood royalty. His father, John Morton Downey, was a renowned Irish tenor. His mother, Barbara, and aunts, Joan and Constance Bennett, were film stars in the 1930s and '40s. And Mort had all kinds of stories about growing up with the Kennedys and summering with them in Hyannis Port.

As I noted earlier, the radio station office and studios were located at the Merchandise Mart, a historic Chicago site coincidentally owned by the Kennedy family at the time. Soon after Mort arrived, we started calling our home the Merchandise Mort because his outsized ego and electric personality seemed to match the massive Chicago landmark.

On the air, every weekday for four hours, he argued, debated, railed, mocked, insulted, laughed, interrogated, and opined on a wide array of topical subjects. To this day, Mort remains the best pure-talk performer I've ever seen or heard. He was a performance artist—both on and off the air.

Mort often treated me with kindness and respect—unless he was furious with me for something going wrong with the show, which happened frequently.

His anger and bullying weren't limited to his on-air performance, though. He was confrontational off the air too. I found there was no way to separate Mort the performer from Mort the person. I couldn't discern the fantastic stories from the fanciful lies. I couldn't tell if Mort loved me like a son, which he often seemed to, or hated me like a son of a bitch, which he appeared to when he was bullying me. That's the paradox of being a target. You think you are doing great work for the bully, and yet, you never know when the next attack is coming.

When he wasn't calling me Weasel, he called me "pal." I can see him now, a cigarette in his mouth. "Hey, pal," or "Hey, Weasy," he would say if he was in an especially good mood. "You got a good show set up for me today?" he would ask as he walked into our tiny office. I liked—no, I *loved*—being Mort's guy, and I'd have done anything for him. But then, without warning, he'd direct all his wrath at me. He'd rail about a guest I booked or didn't book. He'd be furious if I wasn't listening to every word he said on the air.

Pleasing Mort, no matter how hard or productively I worked, was an impossible task.

That's the tyranny of the bully.

After thirty years of study, Dr. Namie concludes that adult "bullies are born with brains that don't work in the empathy sector. They have very little ability to experience their feelings—at best, they are muted—and they can't experience empathy." There was no reasoning with Mort when he was irate.

It was soul-crushing.

Mort's angry outbursts became more frequent, more voluble, and more anxiety-provoking. I regularly vomited into the control room's trash can during the show, anticipating his next tirade.

Mort fired me three times during our five years together. Why do I remember that number? Because every time he fired me, he bought me a watch a few days later as an attempt to apologize. I have three Cartier watches. I'm wearing one now.

There is a term for this behavior and the resulting type of relationship. Ivy Kwong, a licensed marriage and family therapist specializing in healing trauma and author of *Healing from Codependency*, explains that a *trauma bond* develops in relationships "where there is a power imbalance and a cycle of reward and punishment. The abuser is in a position of power over the person being abused and alternates between hurting and soothing them."*

Almost everyone at the radio station had at least one Cartier watch.

* Ivy Kwong, "Do You Really Know About the Peril of Trauma Bonding?" Medium, April 13, 2023, https://medium.com/no-shame/do-you-really-know-about-the-peril-of-trauma-bonding-5264e1ce5383.

CHAPTER 3

RADIO NERD NO MORE

One day, Mort said somewhat conspiratorially, "Hey, Weasel, don't tell anyone, but I'm going to New York City to discuss a television project. Bob Pittman is involved," he added nonchalantly, which was Mort's signature move when he had a good hand. Bob Pittman, who had started his career in Chicago radio as a teenager, had become a true media mogul. Bob was known as a wunderkind, and he had become a radio programming executive by his midtwenties. He went on to help launch MTV and become the CEO of MTV Networks. He is now chairman and CEO of iHeartMedia.

Given what I knew of Mort's proclivity toward hyperbole and that we weren't even near the top of the Chicago radio ratings, I was dubious. Why would anyone want to do a TV show with Mort? WGN Radio had a stranglehold on first place and had for a couple generations. However, Bob Pittman's involvement was an interesting detail that really got me thinking about the possibilities. And despite Mort's histrionics and often-abusive behavior, my ambition was getting the best of me.

Might this be my chance to get into television?

Our radio station was directly across the hall from WMAQ-TV. The TV side had glass doors leading into a vast newsroom with bright, shiny, intimidating cameras, lights, and editing equipment. I often peered in, seeing all the beautiful TV people in their tailored clothes. I was like those teens in *Saturday Night Fever* at the time, looking longingly toward Manhattan, wondering what life was like there.

I'd walk back into the radio station with the other radio nerds, dressed in ill-fitting jeans and T-shirts, working in what I thought was a dying medium.

Perhaps Mort was my way out and my way in.

He returned midweek from his business trip and couldn't wait to share information about his new venture. "This show is going to be big, Weasel. We'll preempt the Knicks and Rangers games in New York."

Yeah, right, I said to myself as I looked at Mort with my usual anticipation and requisite enthusiasm.

Could someone as smart as Bob Pittman want Morton Downey Jr. to host a talk show in New York? Was my life about to change forever? Nah. It's Mort.

But then again, *it was Mort*. Who could say for sure?

About three weeks later, Bob Kritt, my best friend since first grade, told me his wife had just told him that her best friend's husband was the leading candidate to be the executive producer of *The Morton Downey Jr. Show*, which Bob Pittman was developing.

That's when it hit me for the first time. This was independent, corroborating evidence. Mort was going to have a television show in New York. This *was* happening.

"Weasel," Mort said to me, "I can't make this journey without you."

It was true. If Mort was going to have a television show, he'd need the person who understood him best—understood what he needed, understood how to give it to him—the person who had dealt with his craziness, unpredictability, and bombast over the last nearly three years.

I was his company clerk, and he was my sergeant.

Mort often talked on air about "the Weasel." My persona, as created by Mort, was of a nerd who was not altogether competent. Often, we did personal appearances together; hundreds of his fans would show up, and invariably they would express surprise that I was in no way, dare I say, an egghead.

I cared for Mort more hours each week than anyone else in his life.

"Jack Sussman, the executive producer, is coming here, and you'll need to interview with him," Mort continued.

I was slightly insulted that I needed to audition, but I knew I had an incredible *in*. This guy Jack had no idea what it took to deal with Mort and his anger issues. He needed me more than he knew.

Jack arrived at WMAQ in February 1987 with the show's launch set for September or October. He was in his thirties and had a raspy New York accent. He inspired me. I was thrilled to hear about the exciting plans for the program.

Mort's show would be shot at WWOR-TV, Channel 9, in Secaucus, New Jersey. We'd have an entire production team and studio crew. The program would start with a thirteen-week commitment and air solely on Channel 9 at 9:00 p.m. If it was successful, there'd be an effort to sell the show nationally. I would get only a four-month deal. I'd have to give up my job in Chicago, and there were no guarantees beyond the four months. The show would likely fail and be canceled after one thirteen-week cycle. Most shows end after one season.

"Is this something you really want to do?" Jack asked me. "It's going to be a big commitment and likely quite a bit of pressure."

"Believe me, I'm used to it. Working with Mort is pressure every day." Though true, I tried to say it with a smile, not wanting to scare him off.

"Congratulations, you're moving to New York. You're now a *Morton Downey Jr. Show* producer," Jack exclaimed. It was a very short interview.

I was thrilled. It would no longer just be Mort and me. I had a strong boss now to work with and protect me.

And so, at twenty-six, I'd made it to television in New York.

I just *knew* this job would be different.

CHAPTER 4

NEW JERSEY IS MY ELLIS ISLAND

I'll never forget the first time I visited New York City. I was sixteen. I remember thinking the city was so packed with people that you could get knocked into the East River or the Hudson and nobody would notice. It felt like a never-ending struggle to get to the "safer" center of the city and a fight against all the evil people looking to force you farther and farther out until you were pushed into oblivion.

I also remember visiting Ellis Island with my family. In those days, they'd herd you into an auditorium to watch a twenty-minute documentary hosted by famed NBC broadcaster Tom Brokaw. The film chronicled the heartbreaking and heartwarming stories of immigrants arriving on our shores over the last 125 years. About two hundred of us sat transfixed, thinking about all that had transpired right here on these grounds.

At the end of the film, a young man who'd ushered us in at the start stood up at the front of the theater and calmly said, "Is there anyone in attendance today who perhaps landed at Ellis Island many years ago?"

Heads swiveled to the left and the right. Eyes darted to the front row and back.

To my left and about six rows up, an elderly man sheepishly raised his hand.

"Hello, sir. Welcome back to Ellis Island. How long has it been?"

"I arrived here seventy years ago. I was eight years old. I have not been back since."

The man had a thick accent. I was guessing Greek or Turkish.

"Well, much has changed since you were last here. Would you be willing to tell us what it was like back then?"

The gentleman stared straight ahead. He was squinting as if trying to look through the walls of Ellis Island into his past. The theater went silent.

"It was 1907. My parents believed a better life awaited me in America. I remember it was a Sunday because we went down to the boatyard right after church. It was a dreary, drizzly, gray, and chilly day. That's when my mother and father told me I was going on a wonderful journey to America. I was so excited . . . until they told me they would join me soon, but they weren't coming with me *that* day. I would be going alone."

The man seemed lost in thought.

"I don't remember all that much, but I do remember my father telling me it was time for me to grow up and that this was a test for me. He then handed me my little duffel bag, which included a few changes of clothes, a comb, a toothbrush, and my favorite teddy bear. I'm quite certain my mother packed the bag.

"I remember the horn of the ship blowing loudly and people rushing onto the deck. My father shook my hand, and my mother gave me a tearful hug. She then handed me a note with the names of my relatives. The word *Cleveland* was written on the note in what I later learned was English. 'Show this note to anyone who asks you where you are going,' she said to me in Greek. 'Cleveland. Cleveland.' And then she let me go.

"I stuffed the note in my pocket, and with my ticket in hand, I walked up and onto that boat. I looked back for my parents, but others had followed me on, and I could no longer see behind me. I hugged my teddy bear and was herded onto the boat."

While the gentleman was talking, nobody in the room was moving. It was as if nobody else was even breathing.

"I don't remember much about the voyage across the Atlantic. I remember sleeping on the floor of the ship down below. I remember people throwing up into buckets. I remember playing marbles with some kids and learning for the first time to play cards. I remember shivering on the damp floor at night, not so much from the frigid cold but from the fear. And I remember crying myself to sleep but muffling my cries so nobody would think I was sick. The other kids told me if you came to America and you were sick, they'd put you in jail.

"Oh! And I remember the day our ship chugged into the harbor right here."

He started to cry. Taking his glasses off, the old gentleman grabbed a handkerchief from his breast pocket, wiped his eyes and glasses, and tried to compose himself.

"Everybody started running for the upper deck. I had no idea why. There was screaming, and as I ran toward the main deck, I saw people hugging and weeping and pointing. It was the most magnificent thing I had ever seen, although I wasn't even sure what it was. Then, I heard people saying, 'Statue of Liberty.' All I knew was that she was majestic, strong, and most of all, welcoming. She gave me strength and confidence that I could survive."

I looked around the theater. People were moving just a bit now, wiping tears from their eyes, blowing their noses, putting their arms around loved ones.

"The boat docked, and we were rushed off the ship. I had my bag over my shoulder, and my teddy clutched to my heart. I followed the rush of people down the gangplank. I remember we were loaded into a vast room with thousands of other people. I had no idea about Ellis Island. I kept remembering my mother's instruction to show the people my note.

"I vaguely remember people poking me and prodding me and looking in my mouth and ears. I just wanted to lie down and cry. But I told myself, if I can get through this, my life will never be this difficult again. At that moment, a woman came up to me. She was talking to me, but I had no idea what she was saying.

"Then, it struck me: *Give her the note; give her the note*. She had brown hair, a green dress, and a smile that said, *I'm going to make things better*. She read the note and said, 'Hello, Anatole.' She stuck out her hand. I hesitated and then took it. I don't remember much after that. We held hands and walked a long way. I remember the sun shining through dirty windows. And when I looked up at the lady, the sun was shining on her. She looked like an angel to me.

"'Cleveland?' she said. I nodded. She smiled. Somehow—I have no idea how—she got me to the right bus," he said, wiping his eyes once again. "I remember she kneeled and hugged me before I boarded. I never saw her again. And sadly, I never saw my parents again." He hung his head for just a moment and then looked up and around him as if he was once again aware of us listening with rapt attention.

"But I have had a very good life in Cleveland. Four children and ten grandchildren. I love this country, and I am very proud to be here today to tell my story."

At that moment, the entire theater stood up and gave the man a standing ovation. He just sat there, not knowing quite what to do other than dab his eyes.

I, too, had to go. It was the gravitational pull of Morton Downey.

I wasn't thinking about *leaving* so much as *going*. My mom, Barbara, whom I cherished and who loved me with all her heart, was focused on me *leaving*.

As my mom and I were driving to O'Hare International Airport, it occurred to me I was about to be on my own for the first time. I thought, if that man at eight years old could cross the Atlantic on a ship and make it to Cleveland, I should be able to, as an adult, make it to New York on a plane.

And I speak English!

My mom was having a tough time. Despite having driven to O'Hare hundreds of times in her long life in and around Chicago, she got lost on the way to the airport. I'd been lost in thought and had no idea where we were.

We pulled over. And then my mom started to sob. Grabbing the steering wheel tightly, she looked over at me and said, "I'm sorry, my darling. I really do want you to go to New York. At least, I think I do. I will so miss you, though."

She smiled and laughed a bit, wiping away her tears.

We finally found the right exit and reached the airport. We shared another tearful goodbye.

I remember at the time thinking how silly she was—how silly moms are. But she knew something I was still too young to appreciate.

She knew I was leaving and never coming back.

I figured I'd be in New York for only a few months.

Mom was right. I was gone for good . . . and bad.

Okay, the boat is leaving the dock, and I have no teddy bear for support.

CHAPTER 5

30 ROCK WITH NONE OF THE LAUGHS

I got up early for the five-mile drive to WWOR-TV, Channel 9, in Secaucus. It was about forty-five minutes outside Manhattan in northern New Jersey, surrounded by marshlands and swamps, office parks, and outlet malls. Channel 9 was an imposing two-story white structure with massive satellite dishes all around the exterior of the building.

I was eager to meet the people I'd be working with to create *The Morton Downey Jr. Show*.

I walked through the front doors, and suddenly, there was Mort bounding down the stairs, his signature red socks leading the way.

"Weasel!" he exclaimed louder than I would've liked. I'd really hoped we'd leave that moniker back in Chicago. "Hiya, pal! Welcome. Isn't this spectacular?" Mort looked all around. "Wait until you see the studio. But you should meet the team first. They're all up in the production office."

I felt a great sense of anticipation as Mort and I approached the production office. I was about to embark on my television career.

Jack Sussman, our executive producer, was first to approach me. "Andy, great to finally have you here. Let me introduce you to *The Morton Downey Jr. Show* team."

It suddenly occurred to me that I'd been the only Morton Downey team member for the last three years until that moment. It also wasn't lost on me that this group knew I was "Mort's guy."

I had zero television experience, and I wondered and worried how much that would hinder me and affect my relationships with more experienced television talk show colleagues.

The room was maybe twelve by twenty feet. There were six desks along each wall, one behind the next going to the back of the room: no cubicles, no windows, and absolutely no privacy. Unadorned, whitewashed walls gave the place a bit of a psych ward feel.

The show's debut date was early October. So we had just over two months to figure out exactly what the show was supposed to be, how it would look and feel, how it would work in the WWOR-TV studio, and how we'd incorporate a live audience into the program.

We had to begin thinking about topics and guests for the show. It was set for an hour, so we also had to determine how many segments, how many topics, and whether Mort would do an opening and closing monologue.

Jack held frequent meetings on all these issues with the producers and members of the production team while keeping the studio execs apprised of our progress. Jack was always upbeat, enthusiastic, and very optimistic about our chances of going beyond the thirteen-week trial period.

I was getting to know Jack, and while I was still adjusting to the stresses of my new home and job, he gave me a sense of stability and calm to which I was unaccustomed.

Now I had someone I could rely on to shoulder the burdens. And knowing Mort the way I did, I was happy to hand those over, knowing full well that as much as I owed Mort for altering the direction of my life, the tirades, the chaos, and the histrionics would come soon enough. I didn't want to be responsible for Mort or his untethered behavior. In Chicago, I spent most of my time trying to produce the best radio show possible—but that included spending countless hours trying to calm Mort down, keep him focused, rein him in, and ultimately keep him from self-destructing.

I hoped I was done with all that.

I wanted Jack to succeed.

I wanted Mort to succeed too.

Aside from the occasional TV interview, Mort had never done television. In this case, he'd be hosting a national, hour-long talkfest with all the scrutiny that would come with it.

The idea for the show's bully pulpit came from Bob Pittman.

The unique approach for Downey was that shows like Phil Donahue's and Oprah's, while popular, didn't reflect the often-heated, even vitriolic, discourse revolving around the day's issues. Bob told us, "Nobody pays attention to two people conversing pleasantly and politely as they walk down the street. But if those same two people begin a heated argument, get in each other's faces, and start pointing fingers at one another, you can bet a crowd will gather."

That is the idea that spawned *The Morton Downey Jr. Show*.

Plus, if those two people happened to use invectives or even throw a punch, an even bigger crowd would gather to see what all the commotion was about.

Mort treated me well during these early days. He was on his best behavior, but I was waiting for the madness to begin. I was no longer Mort's guy. He had lots of people vying for that position: PR people, marketing people, chauffeurs, members of Mort's extended family. Some things remained the same. He continued his tradition of wearing red socks every day, smoking six packs of Kent cigarettes a day, and being the most charming man in the building.

The premiere was approaching. The staff would meet and discuss possible topics. Iran was a big issue in the late '80s, as were the cost of car insurance, taxes, the death penalty, abortion, pornography, gun control, and the environment. It wasn't dissimilar from today's headlines. On the radio, Mort always took a more conservative position; he would do the same on this show. Pro-life, pro-gun, less government regulation. He loved Reagan, and he hated "pablum-puking liberals," porn, and feminists.

The weeks went by, and we put cards up on the board to suggest topics and guests we might book for the first set of dress rehearsals.

During these weeks, I saw glimpses of the Mort only I knew. He would order lunch in the WWOR-TV café and never pay. Every Friday at lunch, Jimmy, the cafeteria manager, would ask, "Hey, Mort, do you want to settle your bill today?" And Mort would say, "Just add it to my tab, pal."

Mort was the budding star of the station. Jimmy wasn't about to press him.

Pittman and his partners occasionally came around, but Jack prepared the show for prime time. We were all hunkered down in a small office, watching the days go by, knowing full well that our launch was just weeks away. I knew the show had three months to attract an audience once it debuted or face the dreaded c-word.

Cancellation.

We got into the studio and practiced with a few sample segments. Members of the staff played the role of guests. We were learning how to research a topic, formulate questions for Mort, and find guests who would take opposing sides of an issue.

We even invited local New Jersey folks to sit in the studio to see how Mort might play to a live audience. He was a natural showman but hesitant in these first run-throughs. It was more of a Ping-Pong match: Mort would ask a question, the guest would answer in full, and then Mort would move on to his next question. It just went back and forth but with no natural energy or spark.

I wondered if Mort could muster the bravado if not all-out anger and incivility that he'd tapped doing our daily radio show in Chicago.

He had always been more cordial to those in our radio studio than those who appeared by phone. When he wasn't face-to-face with the guest, he felt free to call them a scumbag, moron, or pig at the top of his lungs. Then he'd scream, "Let's go to a break! I can't take these left-leaning idiots!"

As soon as the commercial rolled, he'd get on the intercom system. "Hey, Weasel, how about that?" he'd say, laughing with delight, a cigarette hanging precariously from his mouth. He'd end his cackling with a long, self-congratulatory drag.

But now, he was being asked to summon a brashness not yet seen on television. Mort was meant to be the blue-collar talk show demigod who didn't take any bull from anybody but slung quite a bit of it himself. Mort certainly wouldn't let the usual spin get spun—not on his watch, not on his show.

But it just wasn't happening. The rehearsal shows were fine, but there was no heat. Mort was studying his material and following the general script and segment plan we devised for each topic. He just wasn't . . . well . . . *performing.*

I sometimes saw Bob Pittman and his partners huddling but didn't think much of it. It seemed to me that Mort just needed more time. Frankly, I never liked it when he went ballistic anyway. Conflict is not in my nature, so I was happy that he was toning it down.

After our fourth rehearsal run-through, Jack called us into our production office for an all-staff evening meeting. I assumed it was to discuss the show and the next rehearsal. I remember he didn't have the usual sparkle in his eye when he walked into the room.

Jack closed the door. Our office was already small; now it was claustrophobic.

Jack looked down and looked up. "I wanted to tell you guys I've just been let go as executive producer. You're a great group, and this can be a great show, but they want to make a change. They want to start fresh." Jack always had this youthful look, this youthful exuberance. Now he looked sullen and old.

I was in absolute shock, and tears started streaming down my face. I wept quietly at my desk. I was embarrassed and tried to hide my face but couldn't hold it in. I dared not look around the room for fear of embarrassing myself further. I had no idea how my colleagues reacted or if they considered my response overwrought and childish.

Jack had been my protector, my oasis from the bedlam that followed Mort like dirt followed Pigpen in the *Peanuts* cartoons.

Jack then turned and walked out the door.

All I could think was, *What will he do now? How will he recover from this? If we have a hit show, won't he be tortured with angry, vengeful, hurtful feelings?*

Mort walked in after Jack walked out. I couldn't even look at him. Pittman and Brian Bedol, one of Bob's chief lieutenants, followed. They had no idea what they'd done, leaving Mort in charge. He was talented, and erratic at that, and had neither the interest nor temperament to oversee the show, nor any interest in doing it.

I sat up, took a deep breath, and tried to focus on what was next for me, my colleagues, and the show.

In Pittman's best professorial tone, he said, "We had to make a change now. Jack has done a fine job, but it's not the show we want. It lacks spontaneity and, most of all, controversy. We hired Mort to take on the issues of our time, the only way Mort can. We aren't interested in polite discourse. We want to throw bombs and ask questions later. Does everyone understand that? Good. Please get back to work on the show I just described."

Bob and Brian walked out and took their limousine back into New York City.

It was all on us now. We were without a leader and had just weeks to prepare for our live national debut in front of a studio audience the first week of October 1987.

We had no confirmed topics and no booked guests.

We couldn't depend on Mort for any production support. He was the star quarterback. Mort was roaming the hallways of Channel 9, smoking his cigarettes, making friends, and hiding from bill collectors.

Bob Pittman and Brian Bedol demanded a verbal heavyweight fight every night. The debut was only six weeks away.

My heart was pounding just thinking about it.

We were caged animals in our production office, and it smelled like it. The pressure was building, and the tension was overwhelming. It was a talk show sweatshop.

Over the couple of months of preproduction, we'd become characters in a dysfunctional workplace sitcom. Twentysomething production assistant Amy Rosenblum was just too sweet and nice for this show and this environment. Producer Rebecca Johnson was the haughty East Coast intellectual feminist so miscast for this testosterone-infused, ultra-conservative shout fest.

Associate producer Michael Weinberg was smart and capable and somehow able to keep his sense of humor during these frantic, sixteen-hour days. Jill Blackstone, another associate producer, helped me keep from having panic attacks on my show days when a guest was threatening to cancel and my carefully crafted show was falling apart. Star producer David Sittenfeld, always droll and sardonic, thrived in all the chaos. Our brash senior producer, Peter Goldsmith, always made us laugh with silly anecdotes about his life in our most distressing moments. Peter was keeping us sane enough for the moment.

Despite our differences, the *Downey* show staff developed a bunker mentality and grew very close. I was devoted to this wacky group.

If you have never seen *The Morton Downey Jr. Show*, you might wonder if it is the precursor to *The Jerry Springer Show* and Maury Povich's parade of hair pulling and paternity tests. Well, yes and no. We did plan to deal with sexually charged topics, but there was more to the show than sex.

Mort's persona was that of the staunchly conservative, moral, angry man of the people. You may recall a movie from the 1970s titled *Network*. It satirized our trust in the media and the "ratings at any cost" mentality of the time.

It's from that movie's main character, down-and-out news anchor Howard Beale, that we get the infinitely quotable line, "I'm mad as hell, and I'm not going to take this anymore!"*

That was Mort. Or at least that was supposed to be Mort's character on the show. Mort was indeed angry much of the time, both on and off the air. He was very angry—at his wife, ex-wives, children, attorneys, creditors (of which there were many), members of the TV production team, and me. Mort was involved in his own life drama. He was conversant with the day's issues with our help, but he wasn't at all invested in those matters.

We decided that in the first show we had to put Mort in a position where he could show his outrage while representing and perhaps even defending the values and morals of "regular Americans." We were looking for a foil—a yin to Mort's yang—who would draw eyeballs but not be sympathetic when Mort went after them.

I had an advantage from booking and producing two years' worth of guests for our Chicago radio show. I had a pretty good list of people who were great at interacting with Mort.

---

* *Network*, directed by Sidney Lumet, produced by Metro-Goldwyn-Mayer, and released by United Artists, 1976.

I suggested, with some trepidation, Seka, the still well-known porn star from the 1970s and '80s. She was at the end of her career, still statuesque with bright platinum-blond hair. She'd appeared on our radio show. And while Mort had taken her to task for her line of work, he'd never ridiculed or demeaned her.

Unbeknownst to her, the plan this time was to go after her for "immoral behavior."

Our premiere was October 19, 1987. Coincidentally, it became known as Black Monday, not because of what we unleashed on the American television audience that day, but because it was the biggest one-day drop in the stock market's history.

CHAPTER 6

HOT LIGHTS AND HEATED ARGUMENTS

Our team sat at the production table the night of the first show. We had Mort's rapt attention.

We'd put together precise information on blue cards about each guest appearing on the show for Mort to hold in his hands. This information was Mort's playbook, created from extensive preinterviews.

Each blue card also provided Mort's responses to the main points that guests would make during the program. We did precise preinterviews with the guests, so we knew exactly what would be covered and exactly what they would say.

For this and future shows, we would book four to six people: Often one or two primary guests were diametrically opposed, and ancillary guests represented various sides of a particular debate.

The show was like a professional football game in which the quarterback wears the entire set of primary plays displayed on a wide wristband but still has several audibles he can call. In the early days, Mort followed our game plan detailing which questions to ask, in what order, and what answers those questions would elicit.

The show was meant to look free-form and spontaneous, but it was highly scripted. That was our producing sleight of hand. My colleagues were great producers, and together we crafted each show, line by line.

The stage was set. We'd concluded our production meeting. Mort was ready. But he was always ready. He was always on. I just was never sure when, if ever, the performer would take a bow and the real Morton Downey Jr. would reveal himself.

I was proud of Mort—and proud that he brought me along on this journey. I didn't think anyone else could do what was being asked of him. It required a high level of narcissism, and Mort had that. On a nightly basis, he was called to go into verbal warfare.

Neither television nor radio had ever seen or heard anything like this before.

There had been argumentative hosts, but never a combative and confrontational one. We were about to unleash Morton Downey Jr. on New Jersey and the world. It was not going to be a polite introduction.

The live audience was filing in. About 150 folks from northern New Jersey had received advance tickets. They had little idea what they were in for, even if they'd seen the promos running on WWOR-TV.

We met with Mort one last time.

He took me aside backstage just a few minutes before he went out. He hugged me and said, "Thanks for everything, Weasy. I love you, pal. You got us here. How do I look?"

"You look great, Doc," I called him Doc because Mort had told me he had earned his doctorate at some unfamiliar university. "You look just great, Doc."

And he did. He was in his usual uniform. Blue sport coat, khaki pants, and his signature red socks. His hair was styled. He was tanned and trimmed.

He took a long drag on his cigarette. The smoke was wafting into the lights. He looked at me for a moment. Did he love me? Did he care about me? I so much wanted to believe it. He put his arms on my shoulders, hugged me again, looked me directly in the eyes, hesitated, smiled, and walked toward the set.

There were times when I truly loved the man. This was one of them.

And now it was showtime.

I don't remember whether this evolved or whether it was planned from day one, but if you saw the show at the time (or watch clips on YouTube), you see staff members walking out with Mort from backstage and stopping just before the audience sees him for the first time.

This idea emerged from the boxing world, in which the heavyweight champ walks slowly toward the ring with his entourage behind him. Then, alone, he steps into the ring with his fellow combatant.

The audience didn't know it yet, but Mort had a pretty good verbal jab, and he was very canny and knew just when to throw a crushing right.

On that first night, Mort came onto the stage to a nice, polite, courteous, enthusiastic round of applause. That wasn't going to cut it.

He introduced adult actor Seka and got into it with her pretty quickly once the bell rang: about her life, lifestyle, and morals. The first segment was Mort moving around the stage, feeling out the guest, throwing a few verbal jabs but keeping his distance. We went to break, and the applause was more urgent, certainly more vocal. You could see the audience members looking at each other in amazement, sensing they were watching something unexpected and unpredictable.

The audience was starting to understand that Mort was the home-team bully, and their role was home crowd.

Early in the second segment, Mort got right in Seka's face. He called her a slut. Seka wasn't prepared for these low blows. As we went to break again, after a heated exchange between the two, you can see her taking off her mic and walking off the set. She walked right by me in the wings and kept going out the studio doors. I felt a twinge of self-doubt, or maybe it was abject guilt for how shabbily Seka had been treated.

The term *slut shaming* was not part of the vernacular yet.

I was watching the audience, seeing it on their faces. They were pumped up. They were getting the point of the show, and they wanted in. *Okay, if this is the game, we're playing too.*

When we came back from break, the applause was much louder. People were high-fiving each other and raising their fists in the air, shouting, "*Way to go, Mort! You showed her! Tell it like it is, Mort!*"

Onlookers like to watch a bully in action.

Mort had his home-crowd advantage.

We went right back to work after our premiere. We had produced one good show, and now all we had to do was produce 150 more just like it.

CHAPTER 7

BOB PITTMAN SHOULD BE THRILLED

We were under pressure to make sure we served up topics and people that Mort could tear into and that could and would provoke the audience to do the same.

We did a few more sexually oriented topics, such as "Strippers for God." Still, in the show's first year, we covered such sobering topics as animal testing for medical research, the high cost of car insurance, vigilantes, the feckless United Nations, legalizing drugs, and children's beauty pageants.

We did a show on the rights of cigarette smokers, and Mort walked right over to the seated anti-smoking guest, puffing on his always-lit cigarette, turned his back to him, bent over from the waist, and screamed, "If you don't like my butt, you can kiss my ass!"

The crowd went wild, hooting and cheering gleefully and pumping their fists.

We had an avowed racist on the show. He came ready. As the debate became more heated, he shouted at Mort, "Do you love your race?"

"Of course I love my race."

"Then you're a racist."

"I love the human race, you jerk!" Mort fired back with all the righteous indignation he could muster, to the audience's utter delirium.

Mort then took the American flag that was ever present on our stage, wrapped it around his torso, and turned his back on the guest.

"You can kiss my flag."

At that point, the guest called Mort a prostitute. I could see the glee in the faces of our audience members as they awaited Mort's next erudite retort in this highly sophisticated tête-à-tête.

"Don't call me a prostitute, you fat, ugly slob!"

Now the crowd was on its feet. The guest slowly got out of his chair. I had no idea what he was going to do. We always had a few burly security guards near the stage just in case an overzealous crowd member stormed the set. We'd never had a guest physically attack Mort, but I thought this guest was about to lunge at him.

Instead, he stood straight up, shot his arm straight out at Mort, and yelled, "Heil Hitler!" before goose-stepping off the stage.

With the crowd in a frenzy, Mort threw to a commercial.

We produced a show titled "Women in the Military." To Mort's frustration, our primary guest wouldn't answer his fundamental question, "Should women be on the front lines?"

"Well, define *front lines*."

Mort was becoming increasingly agitated at her unwillingness to engage in the debate.

So, he finally turned from the guest and looked into the camera, scowling. "I'll tell you something. I don't want all that's between me and a Russian tank to be 36Bs and designer combat boots. We'll be right back."

And then there was the show we did on the vegan lifestyle. Veganism was about as far from how Mort lived his life as possible.

A woman came up to the podium toward the end of that show. We had one podium on each side of the studio, where audience members could walk up and ask Mort or the guests a question. We always invited our guests to bring like-minded friends and colleagues to sit in the audience.

In a condescending tone, the audience member chastised Mort for his cigarette-smoking, meat-eating, unhealthy lifestyle, which she said was bad for both him and the environment. She had a downtown grunge look—part hippie, part hipster. Mort came right up to her face and slowly looked her up and down. And with all the venom he had, he said, "Honey, I eat raw meat, I smoke six packs a day, and I'm twenty-five years older. And you know what? I look a helluva lot better than you."

The faithful went wild with cheers and hoots and high fives.

I have to give Mort credit. His put-downs were all his doing, and they made him a star.

We explored other topics like the legality of bounty hunters, diplomatic immunity, cryonics, Jewish racism, atheism, and men's rights.

We were three months in, and it appeared we had a burgeoning hit. Almost every major periodical in the country wrote a piece—some of them cover stories—on "The Bully Taking the Country by Storm." The show was being seen live nationally every night on cable superstation, WWOR-TV, and new viewers who came across it had to stop and watch this "angry everyman" and the "accident waiting to happen."

WWOR's execs were hell-bent on making sure that other New York–based news operations wouldn't scoop them on a story about their own show taking place in their own building.

Things were getting so raucous that the WWOR-TV news division had an entire battle plan, assigning specific reporters to cover the show in case a riot broke out inside the studio or outside the building.

The live, anything-might-happen element of the show added extra suspense and even a sense of danger. Mort was playing his role, and the New Jersey crowd came (often drunk) looking for a good fight from their newfound leader and provocateur.

At the end of each episode, we'd write a parting message on the teleprompter for Mort to deliver to his guests and both the in-studio and national prime-time viewing audiences. We planned a program exploring the issue of child abuse. On that particular night, Mort ad-libbed as he looked into the camera, enraged, and said, "Hey, you kids out there, if any scumbag molests you, find the nearest gun."

We never went live again.

We had two choices: encourage Mort to tone it down and be a bit more judicious in his tirades, or edit the outrageous showdown later in case Mort said something that could lead to a lawsuit or an incitement of violence. The latter was the easy choice for Pittman and WWOR, to avoid costly litigation because of what Mort might do or say.

During the first season, when I'd meet people socially and tell them what I did, they'd say to me playfully, "You seem like such a nice guy; how could you work on a show like that?"

It was simple. I had little time to consider our effect on the guests, the national audience, or the zeitgeist. Each producer had to construct one great show every week, and that was our only focus as we toiled away in our little asylum.

Despite the show's growing notoriety, I don't remember having even one conversation with another producer about what it was like working on a growing phenomenon. Not one. The pressure to produce was so intense that it took away any sense of accomplishment or enjoyment for creating something people were watching and talking about.

As producers, that's precisely what was demanded of us, and we delivered nightly. Mort, for his part, was always yelling—on and off the set.

We still had no real leader, nobody to serve as any buffer to mitigate the overwhelming pressure. It was getting to us. David, one of our producers, spent much of his time writing all over the walls. Rebecca would say to no one in particular, "I can't believe I work on this show." Amy looked bewildered and scared. Michael giggled nervously. Peter strutted around the office, mocking all of us: his wife, our guests, and anyone else he could think of.

I was throwing up regularly, as I had during my radio days with Mort.

Now that we were on the air and everyone knew about Mort, you could no longer invite unsuspecting guests on the program. That made booking the show even more difficult, if not impossible.

The honest pitch to prospective guests would've gone something like: "Hi, this is Andy Regal, a producer at *The Morton Downey Jr. Show*. I know you're an esteemed expert on this topic. Would you like to come to Secaucus, New Jersey, to get screamed at, belittled, and insulted by the host in front of a rowdy crowd who is likely to ridicule you, harass you, and shout you down?"

Well, that wouldn't work. I had to find people who would relish the opportunity to go toe to toe with Mort and, at times, go face to ass.

I remember sitting in my little living room in Jersey City on the furniture set my parents bought me as a housewarming gift. They had been thrilled at the deal: "Three pieces for just seven hundred and fifty dollars!" I was nearly catatonic that my latest episode was falling apart because a colleague of my key guest had warned him not to go anywhere near that "disgraceful show," and he had just canceled and hung up on me.

I sank deeper into the couch and felt the copper coils poking me. Not such a great deal after all. I could find no comfort, no solace, anywhere in my life. I was nearly crippled with anxiety.

But the news wasn't all bad. Pittman, Bedol, and the other execs begrudgingly acknowledged that the long hours and emotional strain were killing us. That didn't seem to worry them as much as the concern that any of us might quit, thus disrupting the already chaotic production schedule.

So they decided to give us all a raise.

As the producer of a hit national show, I made $29,500. The newfound generosity took that all the way up to $32,500.

I knew exactly what I was going to do with that money.

I hated doing laundry. It wasn't just the colorless, drab, depressing laundromat in Jersey City. It was taking the few hours of rest I could find during a weekend and spending them washing and folding. With my extra $3,000 before taxes, I decided I'd no longer join my neighbors at the local laundromat on Saturdays. I used my raise to drop off my laundry and pick it up the next day clean and folded.

I vowed never to do laundry again.

CHAPTER 8

LOVING HIM, MORTS AND ALL

A modicum of relief came when Bill Boggs was hired as our new executive producer. Bill is soap opera handsome. He was a local celebrity due to his many years hosting the New York television talk show *Midday with Bill Boggs* on the Fox affiliate.

Boggs had been watching our show and had written a fan letter to the Downey production office. Bill appreciated the WWE-style theatrics. The execs contacted him and asked if he might be interested in the vacant executive producer role. Bill had no idea what he was walking into. Mort, by this point, was more notorious than famous. While the New Jersey crowds adored him, numerous columnists and pundits were opining that he was responsible in significant part for the decline of civility in our culture.

Bill saw all of this with more humor than I ever did, and he was a steadying influence on our ragtag team. He proved to be a caring, effective boss. He listened. He understood the toll producing this show was taking. When things went wrong—and they always did—he tried to make them right. Bill appreciated each of us and spent a lot of time trying to rein Mort in.

As time went by, Mort's attention span for things related to the show diminished. In the show's first year our production meetings were never rushed and always focused on each precise question to be asked and the desired answer.

Now they moved quickly to match Mort's impatience and avoid his rancor.

"Let's go, Weasel! Keep it moving," Mort would say after ten minutes as I was going through a show that had taken me sixty hours of painstaking work and anguish to put together. "Do you think I'm a fucking idiot? How many of these shows have we done already? I think I get it by now."

Bill did his best to keep Mort's head in the game, but Mort was doing it his way now.

He was a lightning rod, and becoming one of the most recognizable people in America. *Live with Regis and Kathie Lee* invited Mort to their program, as did *Nightline* with Ted Koppel. Mort was everywhere.

The show continued to influence the culture. *Saturday Night Live* parodied Mort and our show. While the attention was great for ratings and Mort craved the publicity, he didn't appreciate how he was portrayed on *SNL*. Jim Downey (no relation) played Mort in the *SNL* sketches with warts all over his face. You've heard the expression "You have to take him, warts and all"?

Mort did have a few raised moles on his face, and I never knew him to be particularly self-conscious about them. But he was embarrassed by the caricature and decided to do something about it.

One Monday, Mort showed up with at least six circular Band-Aids on his face. He had removed the moles on a whim, without telling any of us or thinking about the impact it would have on the show. Pittman was aghast. He canceled that night's show and sent the disappointed audience home.

Despite the ridiculous histrionics, we were renewed for a second season, and soon we'd be syndicated on local stations in markets across the country. I wouldn't be going back home a failure. At least not yet.

This was great news, but there was no announcement or celebration. No party. No appreciation. Not even a thank-you. We had more shows to produce. So we just kept grinding.

As we launched headlong into our second season, my relationship with Mort deteriorated. I was no longer "his guy." He no longer confided in me. The loving feelings were gone. We had a business relationship. I was one of his producers, not his "pal."

Mort brought in a few friends to help work on the show. Most of us saw them as parasites. He started spending more time with them during work hours and after hours in bars and strip clubs. They kept Mort occupied. There was some benefit to that.

And Bill, to his credit, brought in some excellent production help. He called our new hire, Ed Glavin, "the secret weapon." Ed was tenacious and a great producer. One of the best I ever worked with. Bill also brought on Jill Goehringer, a terrific associate producer. She was a bright, crunchy, fun-loving Jersey girl with a quick wit. Jill, Ed, and I became close friends.

We also added another Andy. Andy Lassner. He was fun and funny. Mort loved him. Everybody loved Andy. He became known affectionately as "Little Andy."

With the staff at full strength, we decided to take *The Morton Downey Jr. Show* on the road to support a few of our top markets and give some of Mort's growing ardent fan base across the country a chance to attend the show and meet their new blue-collar bully.

We would shoot on location in Atlantic City, Detroit, Kansas City, and Houston, and from the historic Apollo Theater in Harlem.

I'll forever remember one of the several shows we produced at the Showboat Hotel and Casino in Atlantic City—but not because we produced it brilliantly or addressed a crucial issue of great civic significance.

We shot the episode in the heat of summer, and it aired in mid-August 1988. The topic was bathing suit–optional beaches. To add to the visuals, we invited audience members to come in their finest Jersey Shore beach attire.

Like all the casinos in Atlantic City, the Showboat Hotel was right on the Atlantic Ocean, so many audience members walked straight over from the beach. The crowd was great, and the nudists (who were clothed to some degree) played their parts as foils for Mort's faux anger about this free, easy, and "repulsive" lifestyle.

I wasn't producing this episode, so I had plenty of time to survey the audience from backstage on the monitors. Right in the first row were three women in their early twenties. They were having the time of their lives. It wasn't unusual for young women to come to the show, but they were often accompanied by their boyfriends or husbands, who tended to be Mort's biggest fans. The show appealed to a predominantly male audience. When we had attractive women attend the show, our audience coordinators sat them in the front row where Mort and the rest of America couldn't miss them.

As I watched the taping, I could tell these three women were avid Morton Downey fans. I quickly saw that I wasn't the only one to notice these women. Mort spent almost every commercial break talking them up, making it impossible for the producer to prep him for the next segment.

After the spirited show ended and Mort was shaking hands with the adoring studio audience, I walked up to him as I often did after shows to congratulate him on another outstanding performance.

"Weasel, let's make sure these girls get invited to the wrap party later tonight. Ladies, this is Weasel, my producer, and he can make sure you get in."

"Hi. I'm Andy. Mort calls me Weasel. It's a long story. Thanks for coming to the show."

The women were beaming.

"Can we really come to your party?" one of them asked.

"We're sisters!" the other shouted, pointing to her sibling on my right.

"And I'm their best friend," said the third.

I watched them head off with absolute glee and then turned my head only to see Mort smiling lecherously. He took the cigarette out of his mouth.

"Weasel, I just paid you back for all you've done for me, believe me."

This was much better than another Cartier watch.

I wasn't even aware of it, but a wrap party was planned to celebrate the end of our successful, albeit brief, two-day, four-episode run at the Showboat Hotel. The bash would be held in Mort's massive and opulent hotel suite. The room was reserved for the headliners who performed at the Showboat, and if no celebrities were present, the suite was used by the highest of high rollers.

Mort was very single at this point, having divorced Kim. So you might wonder why he quickly introduced me to these women. He wasn't being altogether magnanimous.

During our stint in Atlantic City, Mort somehow found time between all the meetings, media interviews, and tapings to be introduced to Lori Krebs, an Atlantic City showgirl. She was to become Lori Krebs Downey, Mort's fourth wife, the love of his life, and his soulmate for the remainder of his days.

So, on this day, he was preoccupied with his own budding romance.

I met the women backstage after our final taping. I wish I could remember their names. It was early evening, and they still had their beachwear on but had brought along wraps.

They were from New Jersey and had decided to spend a few days in Atlantic City once they had secured tickets to the show. They asked me all kinds of questions: "What's it like to work on the show? What's Mort really like? How did you get into television?"

I always wanted—no, I *yearned* for—this kind of attention. My parents told the story that when I played the trumpet in the grade school band, at the end of the concert our music teacher would have the band members stand in unison to the applause of our adoring parents, who had endured yet another assault on their ears. My bandmates would finally take their seats, and I would remain standing, soaking up the remaining applause as if it were all for me.

I was finally getting recognition and appreciation for the untold sleepless hours and tension-filled days researching topics, cajoling guests to come on the show or pleading with them not to cancel, and throwing up daily in the nearest waste can.

If I wasn't mistaken—and this kind of thing happened, like, never—these women were interested in me. All three of them! In the moment, I thought I must be drunk with my own self-importance. Or maybe they were just plain drunk. Either way, I didn't care.

As we walked, the girls put their arms around me and each other. We headed up to the penthouse. I could feel the eyes of my colleagues on me. It wasn't just Mort and the guys who'd noticed these Downey fans; it was also the women on our staff—Rebecca, Amy, and Jill—who glared at me as if to say, *These women have been invited to our wrap party? Why? And by whom? We don't remember seeing them in our office hour after hour, having to deal with all the crap necessary to get this show on the air.*

They were justified. I paid no attention.

I started drinking, and the three women continued drinking. The suite was filled with food and alcohol. There must've been fifty people there. Mort was holding court.

As the evening wore on, staff and crew began to peel off. I didn't even notice that the crowd was dwindling. I was entranced.

We were laughing and partying.

More surprisingly, none of my male colleagues tried to crash my little party.

Suddenly, I looked around, and everyone had gone—even Mort.

We had the entire suite to ourselves.

It was as if God had just parted the Red Sea for me, and I would stroll to the promised land. This was a miracle.

It did occur to me that Mort might return anytime, and I had no idea who else had keys to his room.

The four of us looked around and said, "Now what?"

There was one way to ensure privacy if anyone returned to the suite. The bathroom was like nothing I'd ever seen before. It was about the size of my living room.

It had a Jacuzzi tub with room for four. How convenient. My new BFFs were already in their bathing suits anyway, so we all looked at each other, ran in, and locked the door.

I remember laughing and drinking as the water was turned on, the jets started pulsing, and the massive tub was filling up.

One by one, the three women got in the tub, easing their way into the rising warm water. I hesitated momentarily, stripped to my boxers, and jumped right in.

One of the sisters and the best friend sat across from me. The other sister was to my left. We were splashing, laughing, and drinking from various bottles we'd dragged into our party room.

The two across from me looked at each other and took their tops off as if on cue. And the other, to my left, followed suit . . . or lack of suit.

At any other time, the real Andy Regal would've fainted, but this was "the

Weasel," the producer of a hit (okay, notorious) entertainment show (okay, the broadest definition of and furthest reaches of *entertainment*).

And when in a gambler's town like Atlantic City, I decided for once to up the ante. *I see your tops fall, ladies, and I raise, or should I say lower, my boxers.*

Now, they're topless, and I'm bottomless. The two women across from me started making out, and not to be outdone, the girl to my left and I locked lips.

It's not that I was unaware of what was happening here and how unlikely it seemed. I was grateful for the experience. Another guy would've grabbed a bottle of vodka and suggested moving the party to his room. But that wasn't me. This series of events was enough.

I was pretty wrinkly when we finally got out of the tub and toweled off. We must've been in there for over an hour, and I may have started to sober up. It was the early hours of the morning.

I remember opening the bathroom door with some trepidation. To my relief, there was nobody in the suite. My room was on another floor. I'll never know why I didn't suggest inviting my newfound friends in. Still, I was satisfied. Not sexually but personally. For me, this was a triumph.

I vaguely remember thanking the women for coming to the show, hugging each of them, and heading into my room.

Occasionally, years after, I'd watch that episode on videotape and see my three hot tub pals right there in the first row and shake my head. My heart would start to beat a bit quicker. A surreal home movie of sorts. It's become a fantasy in my mind, like a sex dream, as I reconstruct and recollect these events.

You know, some successful producers have Emmys. I've got my VHS tape.

CHAPTER 9

THE WAR OF WORDS GETS PHYSICAL

The publicity both locally and nationally elevated Mort to the peak of his popularity. The show was attracting increasing attention and consequently securing better time slots on local stations across the country.

It came at a cost, though. Mort became more belligerent, angry, impatient, and distracted as his infamy grew.

One night, he informed us that we had to start the show a little early because he had tickets to a Broadway show in the city with Lori. He rushed me through the preproduction meeting.

"Jesus fucking Christ, Weasel, you don't have to prove to all of us you can produce a show. Give me the blue cards, and let's get on with it. And don't you dare hold up the show, over-preparing your guests in the greenroom. Just get them out to the fucking studio."

As often happened, a few guests ran late because of traffic, and it took a while to get the audience seated. The taping started at about the usual time. As Mort and I walked out toward the set with his faithful audience roaring at seeing their hero, he turned to me and said, sneering, "I'll kill you if I miss the curtain."

We had one more segment to tape. But a seven-minute segment could take twenty minutes to shoot. Mort looked at his watch, glaring at me standing offstage. He took off his mic and walked away. Bill ran after Mort and confronted him in the lobby. "You can't leave. The show isn't done. You have to get back in there. Now!"

With that, Mort lunged at his neck. Bill grabbed Mort by the shoulders. Mort loosened his grip and stumbled toward the revolving doors. Lori and his limousine were waiting. Off they went.

Bill took several minutes to compose himself before reentering the studio to an impatient audience.

He hosted the final segment of the show.

The hostile atmosphere and these antics made me less proud of the program I'd helped create and nurture. I was worn down by the repetitive talk show assembly line—and more so by the contrived outrage. And I was exhausted from being beaten down by Mort's *actual* outrage. All the acrimony surrounding the show was dehumanizing.

I had anticipated this happening before I set foot in New York. Everywhere Mort worked, he lasted two or three years. But it never occurred to me to look for another job. I was still loyal to Mort and my friends on the production team.

Dr. Yeager at Ohio State University helped me understand how bully targets like me often respond to toxic work environments. "Andy, you were raised to do the right thing. You follow a predictable path. That's what bullies like because they know what you will do. They know how you are going to respond. You'll go right back to your desk."

Just as in Chicago, Mort could no longer be reined in. Worse, he was now surrounded by sycophants who encouraged, enabled, and even celebrated his destructive behavior. As long as our little group was delivering, nobody would step in to help or even address the workplace degradation.

I implored the executives to do more shows where Mort exhibited some heart and empathy, but they didn't want him to lose his combative edge. In my view, the uppercuts and roundhouse rights that Mort kept throwing were beginning to lose their impact.

Then, the ratings started to slip.

Mort was spending more time away from our production office. He now had his own office in Times Square.

And for Mort, the hits kept on coming.

On April 1, 1989, the *Los Angeles Times* reported:

> Incendiary talk show host Morton Downey Jr. reportedly struck a soundman in the head with a microphone Thursday when a television crew from the show "Inside Edition" confronted him for a surprise interview outside his New York office.
>
> The crew had hoped to speak to Downey about an alleged gold-mine scam, even though Downey had turned down a formal interview request.
>
> "Downey went absolutely berserk," said "Inside Edition" managing editor Charles Lachman, who was with the crew. "He began screaming, cursing, grabbed the boom mike and swung it into the soundman's head."
>
> Downey then climbed into his chauffeur-driven limousine and "drove off, giving the thumbs up sign" to the crowd, Lachman said.
>
> A spokesman for Downey said that the 56-year-old talk show host had "reacted" after the soundman struck him while thrusting the mike in his face.*

Three weeks later, Mort told me he was heading to San Francisco. I thought nothing of it.

Then, on April 25, 1989, late in the day, there was a news bulletin that Mort had been attacked by neo-Nazi skinheads in the San Francisco airport.

"Controversial TV talk show host Morton Downey claimed three skinheads attacked him in an airport restroom—chopping his hair and smearing him with swastikas—but authorities disputed the report," *United Press International* reported. "'Our preliminary investigation shows that this was self-inflicted

---

* "Morton Downey Jr. Scuffles with Television Crew Seeking Interview," *Los Angeles Times*, April 1, 1989, https://www.latimes.com/archives/la-xpm-1989-04-01-ca-951-story.html.

for whatever reason we don't know,' Ron Wilson, spokesman at San Francisco International Airport, said Tuesday. 'We can only assume it was for publicity.'"*

One of Mort's lifelong best friends said years later Mort didn't do it to gain publicity for the show, as many speculated, but to make his wife Lori feel bad for him and "love him even more."

I never spoke to Mort about the incident. Even though I still cared deeply for him, there was nothing to be said. It was just too pitiful.

Mort had lost all credibility, and the executives overseeing the program had had enough.

The show was canceled in July 1989.

The *New York Times* reported, "*The Morton Downey Jr. Show*, the embodiment of a boisterous, confrontational television talk show, was canceled yesterday, fifteen months after it went into national syndication. The show's cancellation was the result, executives said, of falling ratings and—more critically—erosion of advertiser support because of Mr. Downey's erratic behavior on and off camera."†

After spending years with Mort, I never truly understood him. After a while, I stopped trying. I just took Mort for who he was. I was grateful for his impact on my life, and accepted that he was the most unique, dynamic, and deeply flawed person I ever knew.

As for me, well, I was unemployed again and looking for work.

---

* "Brash TV Host's Attack Claim Disputed," UPI Archives, April 25, 1989, https://www.upi.com/Archives/1989/04/25/Brash-TV-hosts-attack-claim-disputed/3965609480000/.

† Jeremy Gerard, "Downey Show Canceled," *New York Times*, July 20, 1989, https://www.nytimes.com/1989/07/20/arts/downey-show-canceled.html.

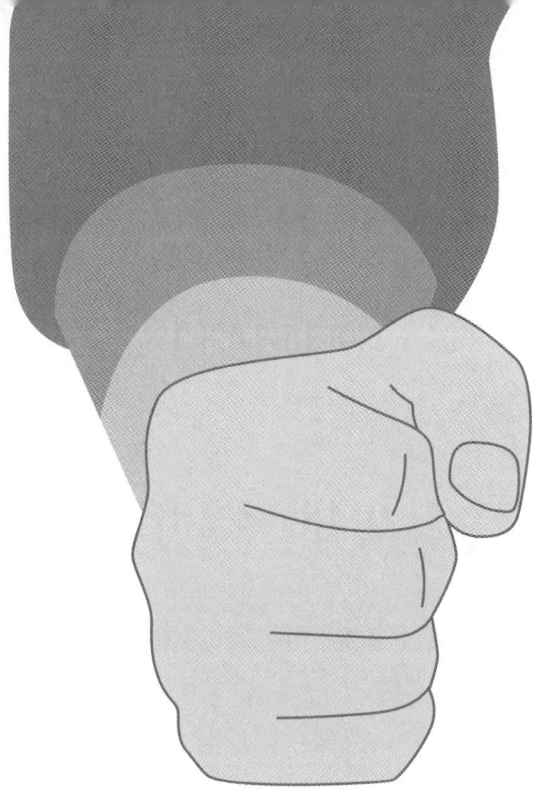

SECTION 2

LAW AND DISORDER: COURT TV

You get the best efforts from others not by lighting a fire beneath them but by building a fire within them.

—DR. BOB NELSON, LEADING AUTHORITY ON EMPLOYEE RECOGNITION, MOTIVATION, AND ENGAGEMENT

CHAPTER 10

EQUAL OPPORTUNITY BULLY

I was able to pick up some freelance work after we closed up shop on the Downey show. But I needed to find full-time employment. I had been chasing job opportunities for six months.

Bill Boggs called me about a new cable television venture called the American Trial Network. He was getting involved as executive producer and wanted to know if I might be interested in a producer role.

Umm, yes!

I wasn't familiar with the bullying term *target* yet, but with this new job I soon experienced what it feels like to have a bull's-eye on your back every day.

The bombastic CEO of *The American Lawyer* magazine, Steven Brill, was bringing his brilliant idea to life. With all the celebrity trials over the last thirty years, it is easy to forget that in the early 1990s, only a few states in this country allowed camera access to the courtroom.

Steve Brill—balding, early forties, slicked-back hair, thin lips, always in pin-striped suits with braces, and often an unlit cigar in his mouth—was out to revolutionize how the public viewed trials. Steve was a big thinker. A graduate of Yale Law School, he eschewed a life practicing law to pursue legal journalism and entrepreneurship. He was and is a highly respected writer, reporter, editor, and publisher, and he built *The American Lawyer* magazine into a significant media entity covering the legal profession.

Steve was also renowned for being one of the toughest bosses in New York media—and that's saying something. He always pointed out, "I'm tough but fair."

I call Steve Brill the "equal-opportunity bully." I observed that he was as mean, nasty, and disrespectful to CEOs and media moguls as he was to unpaid interns.

Dr. Namie of the Workplace Bullying Institute (WBI) investigated this in his 2024 survey of bully targets. In the poll, 54 percent of targets were toiling in nonmanagement roles. Of course, managers have bosses, and 38 percent of targets are in managerial roles.*

The power imbalance between employees continues to be the overwhelming factor in allowing workplace degradation to fester.

Steve was a "print guy" through and through. It was my clear impression that he didn't like or trust "TV people." He relished making us feel as though we had no journalistic integrity. Only seasoned print journalists had the proper training.

In my view, Steve never quite came to grips with the notion that he was starting a *television* cable network covering courts and the law. He resisted the idea that television had to be engaging. He thought high-minded analysis and the minutiae of court proceedings were enough to captivate a vast audience for significant periods of time, and make him a lot of money.

I was hired as a producer to launch what became Court TV with about forty other colleagues. We were tasked with finding fascinating trials nationwide where cameras would be allowed in the courtroom so America could witness jurisprudence at work.

This was revolutionary for journalism, courts, the law, and the public's right to know. Steve said, "I want to replace *L.A. Law* (the NBC hit show) with real law."

Our production office was in the basement of a building at Thirty-Ninth Street and Third Avenue in New York City. It was cramped. We may have had more mice than staff.

Our first big test—and it was just a test, months before we ever went to

---

* *2024 WBI US Workplace Bullying Survey: The National Study*, Workplace Bullying Institute, October 22, 2024, https://workplacebullying.org/2024-wbi-us-survey/.

air—was to simulate a day of live court coverage using several previously recorded trials. Anchors would do daypart shifts from 10:00 a.m. to 6:00 p.m.

Time Warner was a significant investor in Court TV and owned HBO, so we got access to its studio for our dress rehearsal. This practice day took place during my first week on the job. About half the staff had already worked at Court TV for a few months, and Steve Brill was anxious to test the live trial coverage concept for the first time.

I didn't have much to do other than observe . . . and what I observed was unmitigated mayhem.

We all arrived around 7:00 a.m., which gave us three hours to get everything together to go "live" at 10:00 a.m. Our production team didn't know where the bathrooms were, let alone where to bring the hours and hours of trial tapes. We had no idea who the director was or even which studio we were using.

Two hours went by quickly. It was already nine, and the clock was ticking faster and faster toward our drop-dead start time of ten. The crew assigned by HBO to work with us that day was in no hurry. They didn't know who Steve Brill was, nor did they care. They were up on ladders, setting up lights, moving cables, and repositioning cameras.

It was clear we would not be starting on time. *No big deal*, I thought. *This is just a rehearsal; we're still months away from going live.*

Steve Brill was turning beet red as the crew and production team tried to sort everything out. He was fuming.

"What the fuck is going on? We're going live at 10:00 a.m. How in the hell are you people not ready? Who's in charge here?"

I know it was only my first week, but I remember wondering, *Aren't you in charge, Mr. Brill?*

Dr. Namie talked with me about common behaviors he's found among bullies in his years examining toxic work environments. "Bully bosses never acknowledge responsibility, never acknowledge their damaging impact on others. They never express genuine remorse for their treatment of staff. They never look to repair or reverse the harm done to the targets . . . And they rarely, if ever, commit to changing their behavior."

Bill Boggs took the brunt of Steve Brill's vitriol, as he frantically tried to figure out how to turn this mess into a working television studio.

We finally managed to simulate a broadcast day. Anchors read scripts, tapes of trials rolled, and analysis was provided. Mr. Brill seemed pleased at the end of this ordeal.

So with our first "undressed" rehearsal out of the way, we ramped up production.

Court TV arrived in 1991. I'd been living in the Northeast for four years, making around $60,000, and I started looking for a new apartment.

Ed Glavin, my friend and former *Downey* colleague, lived in Weehawken, New Jersey, right across the river from Manhattan.

If Weehawken sounds familiar, that's because it's where the duel between Aaron Burr and Alexander Hamilton took place, forever memorialized in the musical *Hamilton*.

I saw a rental listing for the main floor of a big turn-of-the-century home. The living room looked east across the street over the cliff and the Hudson River with a full view of Midtown down to the World Trade Center towers.

Stunning. I decided this was where I wanted to live.

I took it on the spot.

There was a little slip of a park right across the street from my new home. People came from around the world to this glorious vista to take in Manhattan's power and majesty.

My upstairs neighbor was a cute little old Italian lady named Mrs. Lauricella. She didn't speak much English. She often brought me food and Italian sweets from her upstairs quarters. She was close to ninety when I moved in. Mrs. Lauricella's son, Leonard, a lawyer, handled my lease negotiation and any issues with the apartment. It was her home, but he was my landlord.

I paid $1,000 monthly for two bedrooms, a driveway to park my car, and the view. I figured this had to be one of the most incredible real estate deals in the history of the tristate area. On the Upper West Side of Manhattan, my new place would cost $4,000 a month and another $700 to park my car.

Sadly, I didn't have much time to enjoy the view from my new home. I spent twelve hours a day in the basement offices of Court TV, learning how to edit full trials, prepare notes, and get them ready to be played on the air so our anchors and reporters could dissect them.

I felt that Steve Brill treated us like the enemy despite our dedication to him and his enterprise. I never understood why. Bill Boggs recalls Steve often going "Brillistic." "It was the worst job I ever had," he told me years later.

Steve decided not to renew his contract three months into Bill's tenure.

One might wonder why Bill Boggs and the rest of us never formally addressed Mr. Brill's confrontational management style.

He wrote the checks; he owned Court TV and set the tone. Finding help or understanding from HR wasn't even a consideration. And looking for sympathetic executives was futile; they were getting bullied too.

The WBI investigated this in its 2024 study on workplace degradation and the resulting workplace culture. Dr. Namie queried the general population to explore why organizational cultures become and remain toxic.

Of those surveyed, 38 percent responded that management's lack of response or fear of retribution on those who speak up against the bully was the primary factor, 32 percent blamed the perpetrators' aggressive personality, fully 21 percent assigned responsibility to bully targets for their own fate, and 9 percent felt coworkers' reluctance to help targets was a key to the ongoing harsh work environment.*

Dr. Namie identified five key reasons companies have a bullying, toxic culture:†

1. The company encourages it and feels it is necessary in a competitive organization.
2. The company defends the behavior when an offender is a CEO,

* Workplace Bullying Institute, *2024 WBI US Workplace Bullying Survey*.

† Gary Namie, "The WBI Story: Drs. Ruth & Gary Namie—Workplace Bullying Podcast," July 14, 2022, YouTube video, 1:27:46, https://youtu.be/MSwmA-VrNIs.

executive, manager, or rainmaker.

3. The management feels it's an innocent, routine way of doing business.
4. The company considers the impact on people to be negligible.
5. The organization denies it is happening and refuses to investigate.

A new team of senior managers was brought in. Mike Archer and Steve Cohen were seasoned local TV news managers and strong broadcast journalists who would help us structure our workflow. Cohen was a genuinely kind and thoughtful news executive. Archer, his number two, proved to be a good and decent person and a fine journalist.

Steve and Mike promoted me to senior producer.

We were making inroads in getting camera access to more courtrooms, and in fact, we had an opportunity to bring a camera into a federal courtroom for the first time. It wasn't a particularly interesting case. It involved copyright fees for images of the 1950s actor and heartthrob James Dean. Allowing cameras was groundbreaking for federal courts and huge for the evolution of Court TV. Despite my promotion, I wasn't involved in preparing for this monumental event.

We all knew Brill was on edge about this first foray into the federal courts going smoothly.

Court rules specified that production teams entering the courtroom must wear a dark blazer and pants. He was adamant that our camera crew dress appropriately. On Monday, the first day of trial, the videographer arrived at the courtroom wearing light pants. Steve had gone down to the courthouse early to check on our setup. He stormed out fuming.

I got a call from a panicked Mike Archer at seven thirty in the morning. "Andy, can you get down there as quickly as possible? Brill's on a rampage."

Mike lived with his family in Philadelphia. During the week, he had an apartment in New York City but went home on Fridays and returned from Philly on Mondays. He could never make it back in time to troubleshoot the latest Brill meltdown.

"Sure. I'm already in the city. I can be downtown in thirty minutes. What's going on?"

Mike sounded as if someone had died. "Brill is furious. He's on the warpath. He was down at the courthouse and saw something he didn't like with the crew. I'm not exactly sure what happened. I'll tell him you'll handle it."

I made my way to the federal courthouse, where Brill was making a federal case out of this dress code issue.

Brill had left by the time I got there. I spoke to our camera operator. He told me he lived two stops away on the subway and could run home, change, and be back. I looked at my watch. I didn't know this early on but soon learned that trials rarely start on time. I figured our guy had forty-five minutes tops. I shuddered to think of what would happen if the courtroom was called to order without our camera guy in place, but I worried more about "the Raging Brill" coming back and seeing our guy still wearing the wrong color pants.

I didn't even want to think about what he would say or do. But I remember being slightly less anxious because I wasn't to blame for any of this. I was the problem solver. I felt bad for those back in the office who were likely experiencing Brill's wrath at that moment.

At 9:00 a.m., the court personnel, security people, court reporters, and observers started filing in. But there was no cameraperson. I just stared at the courtroom door. The bailiff came in and said, "All rise." My heart dropped.

Just as the judge arrived from the back door to his chambers, our camera operator walked through the front door. Mercifully, the trial day would begin with our camera in place and rolling. Our crew was now properly dressed.

Disaster averted.

I headed back to the office feeling good about myself. I'd swooped in like a superhero and saved the day. I returned to my desk and checked my messages. That's when the worst thing that could happen did happen. The first and only message I had was from Olga, Steve Brill's executive assistant. She was very friendly and had a beautiful English accent. "Hi, Andy," she said pleasantly. "Please come by the office." And here was the worst thing she could say: "Steve would like a word."

It was breathy and so elegantly stated and yet so ominous.

During my worst times in Steve Brill's employ, I had recurring nightmares that Brill's head—big and fleshy, black hair, greased back—was attached to a bull's body, just like that of a Minotaur, swimming around and attacking me in a boiling cauldron. It was apocalyptic. It was hellish. No joke. It was really upsetting.

You know how advice gets passed around on TikTok and other social media with the "Top 5 Indicators You Need a New Job"? I think nightmares about your boss as a monster from Greek mythology trying to eat you in a fiery pit might be one of the top indicators.

Anyway, my impression of Brill was that he was just plain mean and nasty and talked down to you like you were a complete moron and the only thing you might be capable of doing effectively was sabotaging his business.

Making the long and lonely walk toward his office following a "Steve would like a word" call was demoralizing. I wasn't quite a dead man walking, but more of an "about to get emotionally emasculated" man walking.

There was one and only one way to come out of Brill's office unscathed after such a directive: bring up the Yankees. Brill loved baseball and was a huge Yankees fan. If I could divert the conversation to how great the Yankees were playing just as I was about to get chewed out or threatened with being fired, I might be able to diffuse the situation.

But none of that would work on this day. Baseball season was months away.

Olga saw me coming. She had that look that said, *Gosh, I am so sorry for what you're about to go through.*

I walked to the door, and there he was. He glared at me. "This won't take long."

I sat down slowly.

"Do you have any idea what a massive fuckup that was this morning?"

I nodded.

"Okay, here's what we're going to do. You know what you were before?"

For a split second, I thought to myself, *A man that once had a shred of dignity?*

Brill looked at me with pure scorn. He was referring to my recent promotion to senior producer. But he couldn't quite remember what the specific title was.

"Well, you aren't that anymore," he added, taking his cigar out of his mouth and pointing it at me. He then put his unlit cigar back in his mouth.

"Now get out."

I'd just been demoted for fixing a problem. I was devastated. I had worked for years to become a senior producer.

Fred Kiel, cofounder of leadership consulting firm KRW International, conducted a seven-year landmark study included in his book *Return on Character,* published by Harvard Business Review Press. The study revealed a unique, measurable, and consistent relationship between the executive team's character and an organization's culture and ability to execute business strategy.*

When I spoke with Dr. Kiel, he told me, "As for forgiveness, we looked at how often bosses respond in a curious, forgiving way rather than a shaming and blaming way. We looked at compassion and how often they show an interest in people and their personal goals and how often they treat people as people versus objects. The differences were striking. And it showed up in every aspect of productivity and work culture."

I went back to Mike Archer and Steve Cohen, my bosses, and they said, "Forget Brill. Don't worry about it."

But I did worry about Brill. Incessantly. How could I not? And it was affecting my physical and psychological health.

I asked Dr. Namie why these bullying episodes stayed with me then and remain with me to this day, in ruminative thoughts and recurring dreams. I replay them over and over. He said, "Andy, you and the millions of bully targets like you will be traumatized when someone in authority shatters your belief system. The memories will not be erased. They go into long-term storage. It is part of the residual nature of trauma."

On the flip side, I loved working for Steve Cohen. We became confidants. He was twenty years my senior, yet he asked me how I thought he should deal

---

* Fred Kiel, "Measuring the Return on Character," *Harvard Business Review*, April 2015, https://hbr.org/2015/04/measuring-the-return-on-character.

with Brill. He was already experiencing extreme workplace stress from Brill's abusive behavior.

"Hey, Andy, would you mind taking a walk with me? I'm getting *Brilled* again," he would say with a chuckle.

The "victim walk" would become a common occurrence in my career.

Steve and I would walk across Forty-Second Street, down Fifth Avenue, and back to Thirty-Ninth and Third.

"I don't know how much more of this I can take. I've been in news my entire career and worked for some real schmucks. But I've never experienced anything like this guy."

In a 2003 *New York Magazine* feature on Brill and a book Brill had just written, acclaimed writer Michael Wolff states, "There are many reasons—not least of all the bullying—that have made media people, and especially other journalists, not love Steve Brill. But the main reason there is no love lost, I think, is that, finally, he is just too exhausting. Always in your face. Always the presumptive boss. The preternatural big man. The consummate know-it-all. The total prick."*

I implored Steve Cohen to stay—even though I knew it was a selfish request.

He didn't.

He couldn't.

Steve Cohen was gone a few months after our outdoor mental health breaks had commenced.

* Michael Wolff, "Brill-iant," *New York Magazine*, March 20, 2003, https://nymag.com/nymetro/news/media/columns/medialife/n_8517/.

CHAPTER 11

DRIVING UNDER THE INFLUENCE OF EMMA

An early case I covered was a landmark murder trial taking place just north of Los Angeles.

The defendant was a mess—a middle-aged guy with seven DUI convictions. In this, his eighth violation, his luck had run out: He'd hit another car about a mile and a half from the bar where he'd been downing shots of vodka with beer chasers and killed the other driver.

There was no good outcome for anyone in the case, but it was intriguing because it had such high stakes. Even though the accused never *intended* to hurt anyone, he was charged with murder based on his foreknowledge of what could happen if he got behind the wheel drunk once again. As I recall, this was the first time in United States jurisprudence that a drunk driver was charged with murder.

The trial was sparsely attended, but I noticed one woman who had been sitting in the courtroom every day during the pretrial hearings. She didn't seem to be a family member of either the deceased or the defendant. I soon learned that she was a staff member of the local chapter of Mothers Against Drunk Driving (MADD).

She was monitoring the trial for the organization. I introduced myself. She told me her name was Emma. I told her why I was there.

Emma told me she had never heard of Court TV, but now that she understood what we did, she was pleased we would provide national coverage of the case and the controversial new law.

"I'm glad we'll be giving this trial the attention it deserves," I said. "But, Emma, I hope you know we won't be taking a stand on the merits of the law or the guilt or innocence of the defendant. We have to be objective."

"I guess I understand that, Andy, but you have to know this is personal for me."

"I get that, Emma. You work at MADD. You have a stake in the outcome."

"You don't know the whole story. I have to go back to our headquarters, but maybe we could talk further about why this case and cases like it mean so much."

"I'm producing the trial, so I don't have much time during the day. Maybe we could meet after the trial day concludes. I'm interested in this issue, and I'm sure talking to you would help me understand the new law better. Would you be willing to do an interview with me?"

She smiled for the first time.

Later that day, after a long day of trial, I heard the courtroom door swing open.

"They told me you were in here."

It was Emma. She looked like a young movie star backlit in one of those cheesy rom-coms. Her blond hair shone in the end-of-the-day sun that was still streaming through the windows of the courtroom.

Given her role at MADD, I hesitated to suggest we grab a drink.

"Do you drink?" I asked.

"I'm with Mothers Against Drunk Driving," she said with a smirk, "not Mothers Against Drinking."

We went to a local pub with good bar food. We sat in a back corner booth, and the world became very small. I didn't have to fight for this woman's attention. I told Emma all about my day. She listened intently, with wide eyes and a caring expression. I tried not to monopolize the conversation and appear entirely self-absorbed.

"How did you get involved with MADD?" I finally asked.

"That's what I wanted to tell you, Andy."

I liked it when she spoke my name.

"I don't talk about this to many people," she started. She looked into my eyes. I looked directly into hers. "But given you are covering this case, and I know you and your network care about the issue of drunk driving, I trust I can tell you what happened to me." Emma took a breath. Her eyes welled up as she continued.

"I got engaged a year and a half ago to my police-officer boyfriend. Ron was the love of my life. We did everything together. We had a future. We were so happy. We were planning our wedding. We hadn't set a date but were having fun thinking about it."

She stopped and looked away, staring into the distance—to the other end of the bar—as if this scene she was describing was playing on the large TV screen instead of the Dodgers game.

"A little over a year ago, we were driving to see a group of friends. Mostly Ron's cop buddies and their wives and girlfriends. They had all become friends of mine," she said somewhat blankly. I noticed I was losing Emma to her grief. She wasn't so much telling me this story as telling it to herself in a therapeutic way to help reinforce that it actually happened. I wasn't sure how much the shock had worn off.

"Ron was driving. I remember him telling me some story and looking over at me with his incredible smile. We were stopped at an intersection. He's laughing about something. I loved his laugh. The light turns green, and we head into the intersection. And that's all I remember. They told me Ron was dead two months later after I came out of my coma. A drunk driver had slammed into us."

I had no idea how to react. Do I extend my hand across the table? Get up and walk over and give her a perfunctory hug? Say something lame, like, "I am so sorry"?

"I am so sorry," I said.

Emma looked at me as if she hadn't heard me. I felt this dread wash over me. I worried she hadn't told this story often and was beginning to wonder whether I was ready to be the guy with whom she finally shared this tragedy.

Emma described how she was in and out of the hospital recovering for six months. And after all this time, here's something I'll never forget. She reached up and pointed to her left eye.

"This is the only thing you can see from all my time in the hospital." She had the tiniest little scar, not more than a quarter of an inch below the brow. Out of everything she told me, I found that the most striking. I knew the emotional scarring I couldn't see was more severe.

She smiled sweetly. Our dinner was served. As we ate, my attraction to Emma grew in that clichéd, chivalrous way. *I can save you from your trauma*, I thought. *I'll be your protector*. And, of course, I couldn't be. I wouldn't be. Emma took a cab home, telling me she hadn't driven a car since the accident.

The trial moved ahead.

It didn't appear that we would hear from the victim's family members, and I doubted the defendant would testify on his own behalf. So the first week of the trial was a parade of law enforcement officials and lab technicians discussing the perp's history of drunk driving and the alcohol level the accused murderer had at the time of the crash.

One day, Emma showed up just before the mid-afternoon recess. She sat down with me in the back of the courtroom. We agreed to get together that night. She would come by my motel, and we'd figure out a spot for dinner.

As soon as our trial coverage concluded for the day, I headed back to my room to get ready for dinner. I showered and changed. Forty-five minutes later, there was a knock at my door. I took a deep breath, looked in the mirror, and opened the door. But instead of the twenty-five-year-old Emma I was expecting, I was greeted with *two* Emmas—the one I was expecting and a separate version who looked similar but maybe twenty years older.

My surprise overpowered my manners. I should've invited them in, but I stood in the doorway instead.

"Hi, I've heard quite a bit about you," the older woman said. "I'm Emma's mother, Anne."

I looked over Anne's shoulder to see Emma smiling, not looking at all embarrassed or uncomfortable.

I never could have anticipated what happened next.

"I'm so pleased you are here to cover the trial. I think it's great that you're getting to know one another. Emma told me she had confided in you about what happened. She came within a breath of losing her life. I still don't quite understand how my baby got through it," Anne said, looking down and then looking back up at me. She wiped her eyes. "And I have no idea how I've gotten through it either."

I glanced over at Emma. She was looking at me with hopeful eyes and a dose of melancholy.

"I have to work tonight, so I can't pick Emma up. I'll come by in the morning. I hope you both have a wonderful evening."

She quickly turned and headed for her car, parked just a few feet away from my door. Emma's mom opened the car door, reached inside, and softly tossed a light overnight bag to Emma. She clumsily caught it, looked at me, smiled, and shrugged. Her mother blew Emma a kiss and drove off.

I think Emma's mother wanted her daughter to move on with her life, and I was the relatively safe vehicle by which to do so.

Emma stayed with me that night. I held her tight.

I hoped that's what she needed. But I was unsure of myself. And she was unsure of me.

"Do you really care about the issue of drunk driving?" Emma asked me as we were heading to the courthouse.

"Well, of course."

"No, I mean, do you understand its impact on a victim's life?"

"No, I guess not, but hearing your story has deeply affected me."

At that moment, I was thinking about my trip with my best friend Bob right after we graduated from college. We flew to San Francisco and planned to drive down the coast. One night, we found ourselves in Carmel, California, a gorgeous upscale town overlooking the Pacific. There was nothing open other than a bar, so that's where we headed. We drank for a couple hours, and at 11:00 p.m., we headed for our nearby motel. We were pretty hammered. Bob jumped into the driver's seat.

We were aware that California had begun a nationwide effort to crack down on the epidemic of drunk driving, but at that moment, we didn't care. Our motel was just a couple miles down the road anyway.

We were about halfway to the motel when we got to a point in the road where two lanes merged into one, and another car was traveling alongside us. Bob could have slowed down to let the other car merge ahead of us, or he could have sped up to pass the other car.

He gunned it.

He got just in front of the other car, swerved to his right, and then *boom!* We hit the curb. It felt like we flew into the air with a thud before landing. We started laughing and high-fiving each other, celebrating Bob's auto-racing daring.

Then, the flashing lights pierced the darkness behind us.

"Pull over!" we heard over a loudspeaker. "Pull over to the side of the road."

I have suffered from severe anxiety my entire life. This time, though, I remember being oddly calm and not freaking out at all, even though my friend and I had just gotten pulled over for drunk driving and were likely heading to jail. Perhaps that's the best indication of how drunk I was.

I vividly remember sitting in the passenger seat watching Bob get out of the car. I have no idea how long he was out of the vehicle, and to this day, I have no idea what he said to the cop. Neither does Bob.

After some time, he returned, calmly opened the car door, and got back in.

"What happened?"

"I'm not sure why, but he didn't even give me a warning."

"Let's get out of here. Drive slowly."

We didn't talk as Bob crept along the one-mile stretch back to our motel. We got in the room, closed the door, and simultaneously and uproariously jumped up and down on the bed, laughing harder, longer, and louder at our good fortune than I can ever remember doing before or since.

I was neither smiling nor laughing at that memory now in Emma's presence.

"There is an annual candlelight vigil in Sacramento to memorialize drunk driving victims. It's happening this weekend. Will you go with me? I think it would help your understanding and reporting of this case."

"You know, I think that really would. Maybe I can get some extra interviews."

I also wondered to myself if it was cause for termination if Brill found out I was spending the weekend with Emma. But going to the vigil was appropriate given the case I was covering, and besides, the weekends were mine to do what I wanted.

Then again, journalists shouldn't be sharing a room with one of the lead advocates in an ongoing case.

Yup. I'd be fired if Brill found out.

I wasn't thinking enough about journalistic ethics, the severity of the drunk driving problem in California, my previous poor judgment, or my own unprofessional behavior.

I was thinking of a weekend away with Emma!

We drove up to Sacramento. It was about a five-hour drive. I was so happy to be with her, away from the court case, her mother, and the sorrow she wore like a blanket. It was colorful, to be sure, and it kept her warm to a degree, but it also closed her off from me and, I suspected, from the rest of the world.

We arrived at the state capitol shortly before the evening candlelight vigil began. I envisioned a couple of state legislators making boring speeches followed by a moment of silence, and then I hoped we could quickly exit and find a nice, quiet restaurant.

I don't recall if state legislators started the proceedings or if perhaps a local minister provided the invocation. But I do remember the candles. All the lit candles, hundreds of them, representing all those who had died on California roads at the hands of drunk drivers.

I'm not sure I quite understood what I was witnessing until a few people came to the podium.

"I'm Naomi Mills, and this is Steve Mills. We're here on behalf of our daughter Sylvia. She was fourteen."

"I'm Sandy Reynolds. I'm here to remember my husband, Charlie. He was thirty-seven."

"I'm José Ramirez." He was standing with his arms around his two little girls. "My wife was killed six months ago by a drunk driver while she was heading home from work."

"I'm Sue Houston, and this is Dick Houston." They paused. Dick Houston turned his back to the crowd. His wife hugged him. "Our two children, ages ten and eight, and our babysitter were killed as they drove home from school a year ago."

The enormity of these tragic, senseless deaths washed over me. I looked around. Tears were falling. Anguish had brought all these people out of their seats as they walked solemnly up to the podium.

I looked over my shoulder. The long line of people queuing up to testify, to drag their heavy hearts up those stairs and back down again, made my eyes ache.

It reminded me of the people I'd observed in images from the Holocaust. No hope, no life. These people were putting one foot in front of the other. I had no idea how they were doing it.

The candles, which had looked romantic and heartwarming when we arrived, now looked angry as the flames flickered, and darkness seemed to overtake the light. I couldn't look at Emma. I was too ashamed of my callousness. I hoped she couldn't see me. Then, it occurred to me that she had seen right through me all along.

I suppose some in attendance found warmth and comfort in honoring the victims. I was shocked and saddened by the sheer numbers and the randomness of the carnage.

We walked back to the car as the candles were extinguished. On the ten-minute drive back to the hotel, we didn't talk much.

I had clarity about a few things as I spent a sleepless night lying beside Emma, who slept soundly. I'd never drink and drive again—and I never have. Also, I knew whatever naive illusion I had of healing Emma had to end.

I returned to covering the murder trial. The contrite defendant was convicted. I was glad he was going away, albeit too late to stop the misery he caused.

I liked cases with winners and losers. But everybody lost in this case. There weren't even family members on either side in the courtroom at the reading of the verdict. There were no hugs, no tears of relief or joy, and no fist pumps of justice rendered and justice received.

After the trial concluded, I lost touch with Emma. I returned to New York. I quickly moved on with my life.

I fear Emma had a much more difficult task doing the same.

CHAPTER 12

GUILTY OR NOT GUILTY, SOMEBODY'S GOT TO BE LYING

Verdicts always got my heart pounding. That's why I loved this work. It wasn't just the captivating moments in the courtroom. This was great journalism *and* great storytelling. And I learned that if you were going to opine about the guilt or innocence of a headline-making defendant, you'd best watch the entire trial. Otherwise, your opinion can only be flawed.

We were making the legal system accessible to people who cared about and were interested in our court system, and we were doing it uniquely and innovatively. There were already reporters covering the courts in cities across the country, but they could never take you inside the courtroom the way we were doing it.

I'll never forget the case in which a female high school teacher in her thirties was accused of having sex with one of her underage male students. Her defense? She was being set up. It was all lies to get back at her for giving the student a bad grade. I remember watching the trial, and I just couldn't figure out if she was guilty or innocent. I didn't envy the jurors who had that responsibility—or who at least had to determine if there was enough reasonable doubt to acquit.

I also noticed something odd about this case: Not a single person in the courtroom (from what we observed) supported the defendant. Not even a husband, partner, mother, father, or friend.

When the jurors filed in to announce the verdict, something happened to me that had never happened in covering previous cases. Watching made me feel like a voyeur, getting prurient satisfaction and even a bit of entertainment value out of this.

The defendant and her attorneys stood, and the foreperson read the verdict. "We the jury find the defendant . . . guilty on the first count of statutory rape." After that, the woman let out a primal, guttural screech. It was like no other human sound I'd ever heard. In the throes of grief, she fell to the ground crying and clawing at herself while our cameras captured this former high school teacher losing her humanity.

She became a shell of herself. Like a feral child, falling and writhing on the floor of the courtroom, shrieking, devoid of self-worth and self-respect, crying hysterically, her life stripped away. She had no future. She was now and forevermore a convicted sex offender.

I couldn't help but wonder whether a genuinely guilty person would respond this way.

If you had watched the trial and supported the jury's verdict, you likely felt she had it coming. If you thought this woman innocent, then you had to wonder about our system of justice and the absolute torture she was going through with no recourse and nobody there to comfort her.

She continued rocking back and forth on the ground until the bailiffs handcuffed her, propped her up—still screaming—and dragged her out of the courtroom and back to jail.

I can still hear those screams.

Court TV and television coverage of actual trials were becoming part of the culture. However, at least in the first year or two, when someone heard I worked at Court TV, they often said, "Oh, I love that show. What's Judge Judy really like?"

The common misconception is that the 1995 O. J. Simpson case put Court TV on the cable-television map. Nope. It was the 1991 William Kennedy Smith rape trial in Palm Beach, Florida, that grabbed the country's attention like no courtroom trial before it, because we made rape and murder trials a spectator sport.

Smith's mother was the youngest daughter of Joseph P. Kennedy and Rose Fitzgerald Kennedy, which made him the nephew of President John F. Kennedy, Senator Robert Kennedy, and Senator Ted Kennedy.

William Kennedy Smith was accused of rape after an incident at the Kennedy compound in Palm Beach on Good Friday, March 29, 1991. Smith, then thirty years old, was at a popular watering hole called Au Bar in Palm Beach with Senator Ted Kennedy and his cousin Patrick J. Kennedy. While at Au Bar, Smith met Patricia Bowman, twenty-nine, and a friend. Late in the evening, all five returned to the Kennedy estate. Smith and the alleged victim decided to walk along the beach alone. Bowman later claimed that Kennedy Smith raped her on the beach; he contended the sex was consensual.

In the early 1990s, Florida had the most liberal camera-in-the-courtroom laws of any state in the union. Even so, in most cases only one camera was allowed—as is still true today. It was determined that, in this case, it would be Court TV's one camera and our one camera operator capturing the drama. This was an honor, but it was perilous. If it was deemed that our presence disrupted the trial, or worse, caused a mistrial, we would be kicked out.

I was assigned to coordinate our gavel-to-gavel coverage from Palm Beach. I was also assigned to be the "personal producer" for famed defense attorney F. Lee Bailey, who had signed on to serve as our daily expert analyst from the courthouse. Bailey was the most famous lawyer in the country at the time and had been for decades given the many high-profile people he defended.

Anything involving the Kennedy family made news, much like today's media fascination with the Kardashians or the British royal family. But a rape case involving a Kennedy that allegedly occurred on the grounds of the Kennedy estate in Palm Beach, Florida? Well, that was *huge* news.

The Kennedy family had been rocked by scandal for years with rumors of President John F. Kennedy's philandering with the likes of Marilyn Monroe and the Chappaquiddick tragedy in which Senator Ted Kennedy drove his car off a bridge on Chappaquiddick Island, Massachusetts, resulting in the drowning death of twenty-eight-year-old Mary Jo Kopechne, a campaign worker. The scandal arose because Kennedy delayed reporting the accident for nearly ten hours, raising questions about his actions, judgment, and accountability, and it severely damaged his political career and presidential prospects.

I remember Mr. Bailey telling me over drinks one night, early in the trial, "The Kennedy men have hated women for generations. It runs in their blood. I've spent a lot of time with the Kennedys. I'm not saying Kennedy Smith is guilty. Far from it. But I know the Kennedy men."

For those who don't remember this rape trial or weren't alive at the time, every news show and syndicated television program sent a reporter. It seemed like one hundred satellite trucks were parked, row after row, transmitting images throughout the country and many parts of the world.

There were limits to the coverage. As a possible victim of sexual assault, Patricia Bowman was permitted to keep her image hidden. She became as well known for the blue dot covering her face to hide her identity in the courtroom coverage as she was for what she was accusing this member of the Kennedy clan of doing (Her name was not a well-kept secret, and later, Ms. Bowman was open to disclosing her identity).

If the Court TV camera showed her or any of the jurors, a mistrial could be called, which would likely result in the end of camera access for this case. Also, it could have stalled all momentum of growing camera access in courts across the country and almost certainly would lead to the demise of Court TV.

There was so much at stake for us.

It was a "he said, she said" celebrity trial. The tabloids ate it up.

I couldn't think of a better place to spend a month in the dead of winter than Palm Beach.

The Kennedy family made the shrewd move to hire Palm Beach attorney Roy Black. He was known as "the Professor." He put together the most comprehensive, detailed, brilliantly conceived and executed defense of a client I've ever seen. His seeming photographic memory of every aspect of the case and every minute piece of evidence was mind-boggling. He put on a master class every day in how to introduce reasonable doubt into a white-hot case.

Before the days of digitization, the lawyers would bring boxes and boxes of trial documents to court every day. Black's paralegals looked like today's Amazon Prime delivery people, hauling boxes in and out every day. There's a common term—now overused—about getting "too granular." From everything I observed, Black had a masterful handle on every piece of paper in those boxes, all the way to the sand particles collected from the beach where the crime allegedly occurred. He had an astounding ability to be that granular.

Despite the witnesses at the Kennedy estate that night, including Senator Kennedy and all the witnesses who provided medical and crime scene evidence, this case came down to whether you believed Patricia Bowman or William Kennedy Smith.

Bowman had made no public statement before taking her oath in open court to "tell the whole truth and nothing but the truth." When she took the stand, it was a moment of high drama that had been anticipated for months.

Black had been harsh in his withering cross-examination of Bowman's friend, Anne Mercer. He couldn't take the same tack with Ms. Bowman and create the perception that she was being attacked and victimized once again.

The defense put a dent in the prosecution's case when it kept hammering on one specific point while questioning both Anne Mercer and Ms. Bowman.

Patricia Bowman never called 911. She testified that not only had Kennedy Smith raped her, but he'd knocked her down, and she feared for her life. She called Anne Mercer to come get her at the Kennedy estate, and Mercer arrived sometime after four in the morning and went through parts of the house with Kennedy Smith. Bowman herself had difficulty explaining why they stayed in the house with "a rapist" long after the alleged attack had occurred.

Mr. Black made the point, exclaiming for the jurors and a transfixed nationwide audience, "You mean to tell me that you stayed in the house with a rapist? If he was truly a rapist, wouldn't you have run over hot coals to get away from him?"

I still hear his raised and incredulous voice as he lectured the witnesses.

Black also asked time and time again whether it was believable that Smith would rape Bowman within easy earshot of the house, with its windows open taking in the ocean breezes, where his own family members were residing.

Bowman had a difficult time explaining her actions following the alleged attack, but she was highly credible and emotional throughout her time on the stand, often sobbing. In my view, Black and his defense team could never undermine Bowman's stark version of events. But it seemed to me that reasonable doubt may have snuck into that jury box during Black's piercing cross.

When William Kennedy Smith took the stand in his own defense, he said Black's advice was, "If I tell the truth, I will be fine." He acknowledged having what he described as consensual sex with Bowman on the beach after they'd met earlier that night.

Moira Lasch, the prosecutor, never connected with the jury like Roy Black did. She could not knock Kennedy Smith off his version of events, nor did she seem to be able to damage his credibility.

Earlier, Lasch had lost on a critical pretrial motion. She wouldn't be permitted to question other women in open court who had come forward with similar claims against Smith. This notion of bringing in testimony of "prior bad acts" was never heard by the jury, despite three other women claiming they, too, had been sexually assaulted by Smith and that, in many ways, their experiences mirrored Bowman's allegations. If a clear pattern of behavior or conduct had been established, the judge might have allowed the testimony. But generally, courts follow rules that restrict the introduction of prior bad acts to ensure a defendant is not judged based on past behavior rather than the specific charges at trial.

It hurt the prosecution's argument that none of the women had gone to the police following the alleged attack. The judge ultimately ruled against allowing the women to testify. It was a huge strategic win for the defense team before the trial had even begun.

The defense suggested Ms. Bowman was mentally unbalanced. On the stand, Smith speculated that she perhaps became angry when, while having sex, he mistakenly called her Cathy, the name of a former girlfriend.

Smith went into graphic detail regarding their sexual activity. They helped each other strip off their clothes and underwear, and Bowman acknowledged that she did not have birth control. Then, according to Kennedy Smith, she said, "We better be careful." He claimed she massaged his penis until he ejaculated. Then, moments later, flaccid, he had intercourse with Bowman. He testified that after the sex acts, he took a few laps in his family's pool.

Before leaving the stand, a defiant Kennedy Smith said, "I've searched myself every night since March 29 why [the woman] would make an allegation against me that's not true, make an allegation that would destroy my family, destroy my career, possibly send me to jail for fifteen years."

The defense rested after Kennedy Smith's testimony.

The trial established Court TV as a major media player. The network still wasn't available in many homes across America. The number of people watching the trial on Court TV was insignificant. Still, the fact that it was our camera and our blue dot used by every other network gave us millions and millions of dollars in publicity. Despite the small numbers, our anchors—Fred Graham, who'd been a legal expert at CBS before joining Court TV, Cynthia McFadden, who later starred at ABC and NBC News, and Gregg Jarrett, who went on to anchor at Fox News years later—were all being recognized as journalists with integrity who had a deep respect for and understanding of the law. We were covering the trial all day and into the night. And we knew we were doing something new, something vital and special.

We were not just reporting on the lurid aspects of this latest "trial of the century" but also explaining the nuances of the law—why specific rulings were made from the bench, and what both sides were trying to prove or disprove with their particular legal strategies.

I was in our production truck at the courthouse when the announcement came through that the trial participants should return to the courtroom immediately. After just seventy-seven minutes of deliberations, the jurors had reached a verdict.

If a great drama requires real suspense, then this trial was indeed a great drama.

The *Washington Post* reported:

> William Kennedy Smith was acquitted of rape today by a jury that deliberated for seventy-seven minutes after hearing an impassioned closing argument by his attorney who said the sexual encounter that prompted the allegation was "right out of a romance novel."
>
> As the verdict was announced in a tense, hushed courtroom after ten days of testimony, Smith leapt from his chair and embraced Roy Black, his lead attorney.
>
> Four of the six jurors, including the foreman, wept openly as they glanced across the courtroom at Smith, smiling broadly at relatives and friends seated behind him.*

It was also reported that Patricia Bowman awaited the decision in the prosecutor's office and, upon hearing the verdict, fell to the floor in anguish and had to be helped up to her feet.†

At Court TV, just like everyone else, we had our opinions on the outcome after watching all the testimony. But we were objective in our journalism. And we'd learned that guilt or innocence didn't matter. What matters is reasonable doubt. Steve Brill would have it no other way, and neither would we.

What is incontrovertible and remains vexing to this day is that one of the parties—Bowman or Smith—was lying about what happened at the Kennedy estate that night. And until their deathbeds, and likely not even then, will we ever know the truth.

With the conclusion of the trial coverage and the rave reviews Court TV received for both its keen analysis and camera work, we were all proud.

It was time to move on to the next courtroom drama.

---

* Paul W. Valentine, "Jury Finds Smith Not Guilty of Rape," *Washington Post*, December 12, 1991, https://www.washingtonpost.com/archive/politics/1991/12/12/jury-finds-smith-not-guilty-of-rape/5852c7a5-f583-468b-b806-c76a640ebdc6/.

† "Willie Smith's Accuser Fainted Upon Hearing Verdict," *United Press International*, December 19, 1991, https://www.upi.com/Archives/1991/12/19/Willie-Smiths-accuser-fainted-upon-hearing-verdict/8439693118800/.

CHAPTER 13

IT'S REALLY HARD TO GET AWAY WITH MURDER

One of the most valuable lessons I learned while at Court TV—with apologies to Jennifer, my wife, a lawyer who represents domestic violence victims pro bono—is if you want to kill someone, especially your wife or husband, you need to do it yourself. There's just no way around it. And even when you take matters into your own hands, it's tough to get away with murder.

In Hollywood, hit men tend to be ruthless, handsome, and cunning. Yet, in real life and death, we were forever covering cases of people who hired incompetent contract killers, who botched things and then, once caught, couldn't wait to take a plea deal to testify against the husband or wife who'd hired them.

That said, killer spouses themselves often fared no better.

For example, there was a guy whose wife died of rat poison. Investigators found rather easily and quickly that just weeks before, the man had bought rat poison in broad daylight at a local hardware store.

And there were just some great defenses. One of the most memorable was the "I killed my wife while sleepwalking" defense. A defendant's wife was found drowned in their pool. His defense was essentially, "I had no idea or awareness or memory of what I did, and therefore, I can't be found guilty of murder."

Yes, you can, and yes, you were.

Once cameras became a fixture in the courtroom after the William Kennedy Smith trial, the country experienced a raft of sensational trials.

I had always been intrigued by crime and punishment. Prisons and prisoners are guaranteed ratings if you can get access. I was introduced to a contact at the Louisiana State Prison, a maximum-security facility infamously known as Angola—after the former plantation—and nicknamed the "Alcatraz of the South."

I spent a day traveling to Louisiana and talking to prison administrators about video access. When I arrived back at Newark Airport the next day, I went straight to baggage claim. While waiting for my bags, I heard over the airport public address system, "Andy Regal, please go to an airport courtesy phone. Andy Regal to an airport courtesy phone, please." I couldn't imagine why they paged me, but I knew it couldn't be good.

I found a phone and picked up the receiver.

"Is this Mr. Regal?"

"Yes."

"Hold, please."

The next thing I heard was Olga, Steven Brill's assistant, saying the seven worst words imaginable: "Hi, Andy, Steve would like a word."

Oh no. What have I done?

"Regal. Where the hell are you, and what the hell are you doing?"

"Remember, Steve," I answered, "I went to Angola Prison to follow up on some story opportunities."

"I don't give a shit about that. Get your ass back to the office now!"

No matter where I was or what I was doing, the possibility of Brill bullying me was ever-present.

"I will, Steve. As soon as I get my—"

I was going to say bags, but he'd already hung up.

CHAPTER 14

SHE'S THE ONE

In my entire life, I have never dated someone I met in a bar or at a party. I didn't have a girlfriend until my junior year of college, and I didn't lose my virginity until I was twenty-one. I had no game, and working twelve-hour days didn't do much for my social life.

But somehow I was able to find romance in the office.

At Court TV, I found I had a true love of the law, and then I found a true love for one of its lawyers. Her name was Kristin Jeannette-Meyers.

Kristin was a lawyer-reporter with Court TV. Blonde, five foot three, in her midtwenties—I could sense she had that specific something to make it big on television.

To be a successful reporter or anchor, especially in New York, you must be unusually self-absorbed and believe you are the most competent and important person in the room (if not the world). Even if these traits are the result of great insecurity, controlling your psyche and allowing the outsized ego to thrive will serve you in this most competitive media market.

Kristin had it. She had ambition, but more importantly, she had intelligence and talent. She was comfortable in front of the camera, and even in those early days as a novice reporter, she could explain complex legal matters simply and accurately. She was a clear, concise, authoritative thinker and communicator—and she looked great doing it. She was a dynamo. I wasn't Kristin's boss, but as a senior producer, I started working with her closely as I did with all the reporters and producers. It was thrilling to collaborate with her.

And yes, I was becoming attracted to her.

It was the summer of 1991, and somehow—I'm not sure why—Kristin and I decided to go to Action Park in New Jersey. Did she ask me? Yes, I'm pretty sure she did. I couldn't wait to spend the day with her outside the office.

We'd already established a rapport—a fun, flirty banter over the few months working together. Kristin was on her way; I was convinced. I wanted to go wherever she went. So, we went to a water park. It was one of those magical dates you remember for the rest of your life. It was a gorgeous day. There was so much anticipation.

We slid, we swam, we laughed, we splashed. We had fun. I was falling in love with her. We stayed and played all day. I drove Kristin back to the city. It was early evening, and the sun was setting over the Hudson River as I looked west from Kristin's apartment on Fourteenth Street. She invited me up when we got to her apartment.

I accepted the invitation.

Our clandestine and often stormy relationship began that night.

CHAPTER 15

SCOOPED

My courtship with Kristin overwhelmed my emotions, as did my work covering the courts.

The Jeffrey Dahmer case may have impacted me the most of all the cases I covered.

As a top producer at Court TV, I coordinated our highest-profile cases. As a bonus, this meant getting out of the office for weeks at a time, providing brief respites from Steve Brill's bullying.

I didn't relish being in the bitter Milwaukee cold and snow. However, the Dahmer case shocked and intrigued me. I'd always had an interest, if not an obsession, with serial killers.

By the time I was assigned to cover his sanity hearing in 1992, Dahmer had already confessed and pleaded guilty. I was tasked with coordinating coverage of his sentencing, which would determine his mental state at the time of the crimes and whether he'd spend his life in state prison or a mental hospital. It promised to be a fascinating examination of not just a sexually depraved killer but a modern-day cannibal.

After the hearing, victim impact statements would be permitted. Family members of his victims would speak directly to Dahmer in the courtroom about the incalculable pain and suffering he caused them and those he'd tortured and killed.

The media covering the case came from all over the world. The courthouse set up a media room where we could all watch a trial feed from Court TV's camera in the back of the courtroom.

On one of the first days of the hearing, a *Washington Post* reporter assigned to cover the case leaned over to me.

"You're from Court TV, right?"

I nodded.

"Can you explain why the judge overruled that objection?"

I was so flattered that the reporter from the *Post* was asking me about points of law. He might have assumed I was an attorney. But more than that, I realized it reflected the credibility and respect that Court TV had garnered in a short amount of time. Thankfully, I'd been paying attention, and I knew the answer.

It wasn't difficult to be rapt by the testimony, not just for the sensational nature of the proceeding but for the folksy brilliance of Dahmer's Milwaukee-based criminal defense attorney.

Gerald (Gerry) Boyle, a proud Irish Catholic originally from the South Side of Chicago, was a recovering alcoholic. When I met him, he hadn't had a drop of alcohol in twenty years. Twenty pounds overweight, balding with silver hair, and fifty-five years old, Gerry Boyle could tell a story better than anyone, inside or outside the courtroom. Ribald or otherwise. Nobody ever enjoyed a good hearty laugh more than Gerry.

And no defendant ever had a better advocate.

Gerry Boyle related to the jurors with integrity, intelligence, humility, and genuine warmth more effectively than any lawyer I've ever observed. He even found a way to throw in just the slightest bit of much-needed humanity while defending, as best he could, one of the most heinous murderers in American history.

Jeffrey Dahmer's father, Lionel, hired Mr. Boyle. An interview before, during, or after the trial with Jeffrey Dahmer himself would never happen. So I set my sights on getting Lionel to talk to me. Neither he nor his wife, Shari, Jeffrey's stepmother, had spoken to the media since Jeffrey had been arrested and the grim evidence discovered.

Before being introduced to Gerry Boyle, I became friendly with his daughter. Bridget was an attorney assisting her father in Dahmer's defense. She was smart and Midwestern-friendly. A few days away from the start of the competency hearing, I approached Bridget about a potential interview with Lionel.

"I know the Dahmers are off-limits, and the chances of doing an interview are slim to none, but would you be willing to just give Mr. Dahmer a note from me requesting a meeting? It would be off camera so I can introduce myself and see where it goes from there."

"For some reason, Andy, I trust you and Court TV. They haven't done any interviews and, as far as I know, have no intention of doing so, but let me see what I can do."

I thanked Bridget profusely and told her I would also like to meet her father and get an interview with him at some point.

"That's much more likely. My dad loves to talk! And he's never met a camera he didn't like."

In my note to the Dahmers, I simply stated who I was, that Court TV was responsible for the camera in the courtroom, and that we were serious journalists with the highest level of professionalism and would never sensationalize or exploit their story in any way. And then, I requested a sit-down, again without cameras, just for them to "get to know me."

Besides getting a jailhouse interview with Jeffrey himself, this was the biggest "get."

And I was with an upstart cable network, while every major news magazine and tabloid syndicated show was there vying for any exclusive they could find. Two days later, I was sitting at our table in the media room when Bridget came by. I was eager to speak with her, but she kept walking. As she passed, she slid an envelope across my space. She didn't look back.

I turned the envelope over. There wasn't much in it. I looked around to see if anyone had seen the clandestine transfer. All the journalists around me seemed to be busy with their work, and even my colleagues sitting next to me were oblivious to the intrigue.

I tore open the envelope voraciously. There was a simple handwritten note: "While we're not doing interviews, we'd be willing to meet with you. We can meet for breakfast tomorrow at our hotel at 7:30. Lionel and Shari Dahmer."

I wasn't sure why I was being given this sit-down. Maybe the Boyles had paved the way, or perhaps the Dahmers appreciated the tenor of our coverage on Court TV amid the tabloid hysteria, if they were watching at all.

We were to meet at their hotel, which was well outside of town, away from the courthouse and, most importantly, away from the many hotels accommodating media members worldwide. It was an economy hotel. I walked into the room where cold cereal, room temperature eggs, and dry French toast were being served. I saw the Dahmers, seemingly fitting right in with the peripatetic salespeople—men and women, sullen faces all, trudging through life and an unforgiving Milwaukee winter.

The Dahmers went unnoticed. I approached their table. I remember Shari Dahmer meeting my eyes and extending a hand. She was fully made up, her hair styled high, and she had on a smart pantsuit. Lionel Dahmer was the epitome of unremarkable. He blended in with the coffee-colored chairs and light brown walls in his brown tweed jacket, baggy and ill-fitting brown pants, and brown shoes. He barely looked up as I introduced myself and asked if I might sit down.

I'd been rehearsing my introductory lines. It sounds flippant, but what do you say to a father and stepmother whose son has brutally abused and killed multiple boys and men and turned into a cannibal in the process?

"Thank you for agreeing to meet with me, and I'm sorry for all you're going through," I said.

I hoped to spend some time with the Dahmers and perhaps gain their trust just enough to get them to agree to an exclusive blockbuster interview.

Shari Dahmer opened the conversation. Mr. Dahmer continued staring into his plastic coffee cup. She'd married Lionel Dahmer after he divorced his first wife, Joyce Flint, in 1978. Jeffrey was eighteen at the time.

"We know it's your camera in the courtroom, and we would like you to respect our privacy."

"Of course, Mrs. Dahmer."

I promised without knowing if we would or what the parameters of her request might be.

"When you're ready to tell your side of the story from your perspective, without editing, we'll give you that opportunity."

I was starting a negotiation, or at least trying to.

"We're just regular people and have no idea how this happened. They say Jeffrey did these things, but we don't read about them much or talk about them. We're here to support him in any way we can. All of this they say about him with different men: None of us gave that much thought at all. Jeff didn't show any tendencies one way or the other, and as far as we knew, he didn't date. We did think joining the Army might help him. But that didn't work out. And we never really understood why. After his discharge from the Army, we sensed something was wrong, and we tried to get him help, but nothing like this ever came to our minds."

Suddenly, Mr. Dahmer looked at me. "My wife and I just wanted to live a quiet life together. Everyone wants to know what kind of parent I was. I can tell they're asking whether I ever abused Jeffrey. The answer is no. Never."

Shari Dahmer took her husband's hand under the table.

"I was busy. I worked hard. Yes, I had a bad marriage and wasn't always around." And then, for the first time, Mr. Dahmer raised his head to look directly at me. "Lots of families are like that, right? And they don't end up here talking to you."

I was starting to wish they had agreed to an on-camera interview. It appeared they were warming to me, or more accurately, warming to the idea of finally letting the public in, even if just a bit, to their private horror.

"I do, of course, blame myself and wonder what I could have done for Jeffrey," Mr. Dahmer added.

"It seems the best you can do now is tell your story and perhaps his, because people are only getting the sensational side of it right now," I said, playing the caring and empathetic producer role.

Shari Dahmer jumped in. "We want the world to know that we love Jeffrey and will be there for him."

"If I can help you get that message out, I'd like to do so."

"Well, we should be getting to court. I assume you need to do the same," said Lionel.

He started to get up.

The meeting was over.

I stood and thanked them for their time. As I left the hotel into the bright sun of another bitterly cold Milwaukee winter day, I tried to imagine what it must be like to be the Dahmers. I also imagined what it would be like if they gave me the exclusive interview. Suddenly, I wasn't so cold. It would be the scoop of a career. Steve Brill would see me as the star of Court TV. He'd have to acknowledge me with gratitude, a raise, and a promotion. I'd be his go-to guy. The workplace aggression would stop. The accolades would stream in, maybe the awards too.

I made a mental note to get a message back to the Dahmers thanking them once again for their time and to make a request to have a similar conversation, this time on camera. I thought I had a pretty good shot because nobody that I was aware of had even spoken to the Dahmers. I felt I was establishing a relationship with them and even a level of trust.

A couple of days later, I was in the media room as the hearing continued. The media organizations all had video monitors on their desks to watch the video feed from the courtroom. I was walking to our Court TV designated area when a promo caught my eye. I stopped and sat down. My heart was racing, and my legs became weak from what I was seeing.

It was a brash *Inside Edition* promo for that evening's show. "The Dahmers speak out for the very first time as their son's grisly sentencing hearing begins," the carnival barker of a voice-over talent exclaimed proudly. I watched in complete dismay as the promo showed the Dahmers on camera. They appeared to be in the same breakfast room at the hotel where I spoke to them. "We love Jeffrey and will be here every day in the courtroom," Lionel Dahmer said, quietly but emphatically.

"Don't miss this explosive and exclusive interview tonight and all this week on *Inside Edition*," the voice-over guy said, almost mocking me. Not only did *Inside Edition* beat me on the story, but the show had a week's worth of material with the Dahmers.

My head dropped to my desk. *How could the Dahmers have betrayed me?* I thought selfishly, as if they didn't have much more on their minds than my ambition and my career.

Well, I learned later that day—and I can't prove this, but I believe it to be accurate—that *Inside Edition* paid the Dahmers for the interview. Call it professional envy, but all of us in the media room were jealous that the tabloid show had gotten the scoop of the trial to that point. The dollar figure floating around was $150,000.

It made me feel slightly better to believe *Inside Edition* had paid for its exclusive. Steve Brill and Court TV would never embrace "pay for play." Serious journalistic enterprises never paid for stories. Those that did lost all credibility but gained all kinds of ratings and revenues.

With my journalistic integrity solidly intact but my ego in tatters and my almost award-laden career careening back to earth, I did the only thing I could: I went back to work.

It was a three-week sanity hearing, and in unusual fashion, only ten of twelve jurors had to agree that Dahmer was sane and understood the criminality of his conduct or that he wasn't in his right mind and therefore incapable of understanding right and wrong when he committed his crimes.* In the guilt phase to determine the verdict, the pain and suffering of the victims' family members isn't relevant.

In this sentencing hearing to determine punishment, the victims' family members are permitted to speak on behalf of the departed and themselves.

Nine relatives of Dahmer's victims spoke to the court about the agony they'd suffered, knowing a serial killer had brutally murdered their loved ones.

Rita Isbell spoke on behalf of her family and her deceased brother, Errol.

* COURT TV, "WI v. Jeffrey Dahmer (1992)," YouTube, https://www.youtube.com/playlist?list=PLMD8umRLJkKwl6m5RZbGklOkudKOu_sHh.

Her grief came in an outburst that was unprecedented in my experience in courtrooms, where proper decorum is paramount.

"Whatever your name is, Satan . . . I don't ever want my mother to go through this again. Never, Jeffrey. Never! Jeffrey, I hate you, motherfucker!" she shrieked and waved her hands wildly. I still get shivers today at the utter anguish and despair of all the victims' relatives, and Rita Isbell's specifically. She then started walking right toward Dahmer at the defense table. "Don't fuck with me, Jeffrey, I will kill you, goddamnit."

She had to be restrained before reaching Dahmer, who sat stoically and without expression as the bailiffs removed Ms. Isbell and a recess was called.

"You took his life like a thief in the night," said Stanley Miller, uncle of Ernest Miller, whom Dahmer killed.

"You took my son away from me. You took my daughter's only brother away from her," said Dorothy Straughter, mother of Curtis Straughter.

"I hope you go to hell," said Donald Bradehoft, brother of Joseph Bradehoft, Dahmer's last known victim and a father of three.

Dahmer never took the stand during the hearing, but he had confessed to Milwaukee police, and his confession was read into the record by the police officers who took it.

In his statement, Dahmer did express remorse for his victims and their families. He also expressed regret over two police officers who had lost their jobs after they were called to Dahmer's residence and allowed a fourteen-year-old boy who'd been drugged and tortured by Dahmer back into the serial killer's home. Dahmer convinced the officers that the boy, who did not speak English well, was ill and that Dahmer was "taking care of him."

Once the officers departed, Dahmer killed the teen.

"I just plain fooled them," Dahmer admitted.

Dahmer described in gruesome detail that it took about an hour to boil a head. He explained how he dismembered and filleted the bodies, bought a fifty-seven-gallon industrial drum, and placed body parts in it.

"I should have stayed with God. I tried and failed and created a holocaust."

Ten of Dahmer's seventeen victims were African American, and there was a thought he might have killed out of racial animus.

"I hated no one," Dahmer confessed. "These were not hate crimes."

Dahmer did speak for the first time in court just prior to the announcement of sentencing. He said, "I deserve whatever I get because of what I have done."

Dahmer wished for death for his crimes. He found value in the proceeding, hearing from the experts in the hope of better understanding his morbid cravings.

"I knew I was sick or evil or both. Now I believe I was sick," he said, referring to the diagnosis offered by three mental health experts called by Gerry Boyle in Dahmer's defense.

"I hope God has forgiven me. I know society will never be able to forgive me. I know the families of the victims will never be able to forgive me. If I could give my life right now to bring their loved ones back, I would do it. I am so very sorry. I deserve whatever I get because of what I have done. I'm prepared for your sentence."

Gerry Boyle was masterful in his defense of Dahmer. He was driving home the point that considering the totality of what Dahmer admitted to doing, how could he be found sane and responsible for his conduct? It seemed to me, however, the prosecution won the argument by stressing that Dahmer had lied to the police during an initial investigation. This clearly demonstrated he knew what he was doing was wrong, which is the legal standard that had to be proven. Dahmer was sane enough to know his actions constituted a crime, and he was trying to evade suspicion.

In February 1992, Jeffrey Dahmer was sentenced to fifteen consecutive life sentences. Nearly three years later, he was beaten to death by a fellow inmate.

Watching Dahmer in the courtroom as I did for weeks, it was impossible for me to connect the person I saw to the acts he had engaged in. I'd try to envision him in his house of horrors, and my brain would just stop short. He seemed so human. I didn't know what pure evil was supposed to look like, but I didn't imagine it looked like Jeffrey Dahmer. He didn't sound evil. I spent a lot of time with hardened criminals at Court TV, many of whom seemed like nice people. The common thread among them was that they were very sad and made the wrong decision at every turn.

"Jeffrey Dahmer was the easiest client I ever had," Gerry Boyle told me years later. "He did everything I asked of him. He was just a lost soul. People always would ask me: How could you defend such a person? And I would say, how could I not? He deserved representation as much as anyone."

In the years following the Dahmer hearing, Gerry Boyle became my confidant and friend. He has also become my life coach and mentor. He counseled me on everything from marriage to having children to raising daughters. He cared about me. He treated me like a son.

I treasured his place in my life.

Gerry Boyle died on November 17, 2024.

Rest in peace, Counselor.

CHAPTER 16

A WINDOW INTO COURT TV

In the fall of 1991, I was assigned to oversee our coverage of the Clarence Thomas Supreme Court confirmation hearings from DC.

We'd never broadcast from Washington, a big deal for our fledgling network. Unlike the major networks, we had no facilities in DC, so we rented a production studio with that quintessential and clichéd view of Washington behind the on-air anchorperson.

Fred Graham, our senior anchor, was tapped to host our coverage of this headline-making event and to christen our newfound base on the eve of these historic hearings.

Steve Brill insisted that we demonstrate our credibility among the major news networks, including CNN.

Fred was out of central casting: a silver-haired gentleman in his sixties and a lawyer. He was a pleasure to work with. Plus, when my father heard I was working side by side with the famed legal reporter, well, I'd finally made it, at least in my dad's eyes.

For many years, Fred had provided legal commentary for CBS News. My father listened religiously to Fred on WBBM-AM in Chicago from our kitchen radio before he headed to the downtown train at 6:08 a.m. every weekday.

Fred looked so right as he took his chair that morning at the anchor desk, the US Capitol standing tall over his shoulder.

This was going to be a grand and proud moment for Court TV.

I felt the specter of Brill's rage, but the scripts had been written and approved days earlier, the prompter was loaded, and the crew we'd hired was well rehearsed, clearly competent, and ready to handle this morning's launch coverage.

Around 8:45 a.m., I was in our makeshift DC control room as we made our final preparations to go live at 9:00 a.m. We had all kinds of taped packages produced to provide further analysis of our coverage, and they were approved, stacked, and ready to roll. Fred was getting his final touches of makeup. We all knew Steve Brill was watching, and we were like soldiers on parade. Our shoes were shined. Our uniforms were pressed. We were in lockstep and knew exactly what to do and how to do it. We were as prepared as possible to deliver a network-quality broadcast from Washington.

At 08:59:30, the director counted us down: "Thirty seconds to air, fifteen seconds to air, three, two, one . . . go, Fred!"

"Good morning, and welcome to a historic day for the country as we prepare for Clarence Thomas's Supreme Court confirmation hearings," Fred Graham said in his genteel and scholarly Southern twang. "It is also a historic day for us here at Court TV as we launch our inaugural broadcast from our nation's capital."

You could hear clapping over our headsets from our central control room in New York. Those of us in our control room in DC looked at each other with knowing nods. We were underway and contributing to the evolution of the Courtroom Television Network (Court TV) and the public discourse on the crucial issues related to courts, the law, and justice in America.

I looked back at the monitor as Fred continued to read the introductory script with the dignity he brought to his work and, thus, to the proceedings. I took a breath because everything was going fine.

Until . . .

Fred was not more than a minute into the broadcast when, to my absolute horror, a window washer appeared behind him. He had his full array of tools, including scaffolding, safety ropes, and suction cups, which he began to place onto our window as he cleaned. He was peering through the window into our studio to see what was happening.

In a different life or a different job, with a different boss, this would've been a laugh riot—an excellent scene for a sitcom centered in a newsroom. Fred had no idea what was happening behind him, so like the best straight man in the world, he just kept reading.

We couldn't get in his ear and explain what was happening, and even if we tried, what could he have done? We couldn't just throw to commercial during this solemn moment, so Fred just kept reading, and the window washer kept washing.

I don't remember if Brill's seething anger was on display that day. We all lived with the fact that he looked for every opportunity to accuse his staff of lacking journalistic integrity and outright incompetence, but he couldn't blame us for this.

I do remember thinking that nothing ever really went right for me. I took this as a personal affront—that Mother Nature, luck, or the gods were against me. I was crushed that a crowning moment became just another fire drill, another disappointment, and another dispiriting, if memorable, moment.

Dr. Lissette Leon, a psychiatrist in the New York area, defined this feeling to me as "the heaven's reward fallacy": "This fallacy involves the irrational expectation that you will be rewarded for all your hard work, dedication, and sacrifice. This delusion, especially concerning the workplace, leads to disappointment when the rewards don't come. Supervisor dissatisfaction or a violation of expectations can lead to anger, frustration, shame, bitterness, and depression."

Thinking the workplace should be a just place caused me decades of heartache and self-blame.

CHAPTER 17

MAYBE SHE'S NOT THE ONE

Kristin Jeannette-Meyers and I were continuing our office romance. We'd hang around in the West Village near her apartment in the West Village. We'd go to Cafe Wha?, a New York University live-music hangout, or the Chat n' Chew, where you did just what the name implied.

Kristin would never eat much when we went out. Steamed broccoli (yuck!) was it. The second course after the broccoli was cigarettes. Even though I detested smoking, it was very sexy and exhilarating hanging out in downtown New York with a beautiful, intelligent woman whose career was about to take off. We'd wake late on Sunday mornings and do what all unmarried couples do in the city—head out for brunch.

I was experiencing the quintessential New York City adventure.

When things were right with Kristin, my life was spectacular.

But it wasn't all pancakes, French toast, and warm maple syrup. There was quite a bit of steamed broccoli in our relationship.

Kristin was becoming a much-talked-about talent. She was terrific on the air, commenting on this case or that legal point and providing crucial details on the law.

She exuded incisiveness and self-assurance on camera.

As Court TV became more established, tabloid and network news outlets were calling. They wanted to feature Kristin's insights whenever a headline-making case or legal issue arose.

As Kristin's on-camera profile was rising, it seemed to me, so was her narcissism.

The American Bar Association had reached out and was planning a moot court competition in which the participants—high-profile, high-powered San Francisco lawyers—would argue whether Lee Harvey Oswald was guilty beyond a reasonable doubt of assassinating President Kennedy.

Fearing an unwanted HR situation at work, Kristin and I were keeping our relationship private. That meant she and I tried never to travel simultaneously or take a day off on the same day for fear of raising suspicions and fueling gossip.

However, we were both assigned to cover this moot court competition. Kristin would be the "outside the courtroom" reporter for this fictional trial. I was assigned to coordinate Court TV's coverage of this "made-for-TV" event and serve as Kristin's on-site executive producer.

We reserved different flights and booked two rooms in the same hotel.

Kristin and I had been fighting more often about how I wasn't supportive enough of her career and didn't understand the pressures she was under. She would frequently interrogate me, and I was, admittedly, not her intellectual equal, nor did I have her cross-examination skills. She was a trained attorney, after all.

During every argument, she'd corner me and pepper me with questions using her law degree, reasoning power, and prosecutorial skills to wear me down. Kristen would finish self-satisfied despite her anger and bitterness. Her nastiness left me wholly flummoxed and bewildered.

With things a bit bumpy for us, we were both looking forward to this San Francisco trip as an exciting and unusual assignment and a paid romantic getaway. We were understandably frustrated and disappointed when we showed up at the hotel and learned they had no record of our reservations.

This was well before confirmations were sent via email, text message, and app notification.

The gentleman at the front desk told us they were completely booked for an American Bar Association event. We explained to him we were there for that very event, and while he feigned sympathy for our predicament, we were told there wasn't much he could do.

Kristin was getting more frustrated by the moment. "Let me handle this," she said to me. "Might we speak to the manager?"

Enter the general manager, a well-dressed middle-aged guy. I noticed his attention was solely focused on Kristin. "My sincerest apologies. I just don't know what happened here," he exclaimed, staring at Kristin. I'd become accustomed to this reaction from other men. Kristin was striking, but this seemed excessive.

"Aren't you on TV?" he asked.

"Yes." Kristin giggled a bit. "I'm a reporter for Court TV, and this is my producer."

I'd just received a significant demotion from Kristin. I was surprised she didn't say "my production assistant."

Kristin looked up at me with a sinister smirk.

"Oh yes, I knew it. You're absolutely brilliant! I watch you on there all the time. I love the trials," the manager gushed. "Well, I must do something for you, but I just can't squeeze you in here as much as I'd like to. I'll make this right. I promise. Let me make a call for you, Ms. Meyers."

He was looking at Kristin, and I wondered if she'd get a room. *If I'm lucky*, I thought, *maybe I'll get a bench and a blanket in a park across the street*.

Kristin's mood improved.

Five minutes later . . .

"Ms. Meyers, I've secured two rooms for you at The Mark Hotel."

Kristin and I didn't know then that the InterContinental Mark Hopkins Hotel was one of the swankiest hotels in San Francisco.

"It's very lovely," the hotel manager promised. "We will handle the cost of the rooms, of course. My sincerest apologies."

This was my first trip to San Francisco. Kristin grew up in the sticks of New Hampshire and didn't even have a television in her home until she was a teen. So neither of us knew the good fortune that had befallen us.

Our frustration quickly turned to elation when our cab drove up to The Mark.

This place was a royal palace.

We checked into both rooms but then went straight to Kristin's. Dusk had now fallen on the Bay Area. As we put the key card into the door and walked into the room, San Francisco was in front of us. We were on a high floor with the most magnificent 180-degree cityscape views. The room was just beautiful. Colors were splashed here and there. It was refined and designed. We fell onto the bed like honeymooners.

The moot court event originated from a luxury hotel, so I decided we should take advantage of the refined surroundings as an outdoor backdrop instead of having Kristin standing in an unadorned back hallway.

Kristin looked great in a red-and-black pantsuit. She was diminutive but walked with a swagger. She was a powerhouse, in control of her environment. Kristin looked the part of "talent."

I instructed the crew to set up in the floral courtyard just off the main lobby. Beautiful azaleas, roses, daffodils, and a quiet spouting fountain adorned the space. This setting would establish the proper tone.

Kristin would look great for her live shots there.

Ten minutes before going live, Kristin came outside after checking her makeup and hair for the fifth time in the last half hour. She smiled at me as she quickly walked by with her confident, if not quite haughty, air.

It was a rush to see the woman I loved in action. There were times on assignments such as these in which some guy in a suit, usually a married lawyer, would come up to me somewhat conspiratorially and ask me whether Kristin was married or had a boyfriend. And then, almost on cue, the guy would say, "I bet she's great in the bedroom."

I would smile and say, "Well, I wouldn't know anything about that, but she's great in the courtroom."

We were setting Kristin up in front of the camera, now just five minutes before air. I was playing the proud "executive" producer role. She was an egotistical talent, and I was there to support her.

Suddenly, I sensed Kristin's mood changing; I could always see this coming—but it was often too late to do anything about it. I watched her looking up, back, and around the courtyard.

"Did you notice how windy it is out here?" she asked me.

The warmth and goodwill of the last twenty-four hours were now long gone. Kristin was angrily pushing the hair out of her face.

"Don't worry, this is San Francisco. It's always a little cool and windy here. It's a beautiful shot, and you look great in it."

It was the truth. But I knew how this would play out. Kristin was like an out-of-control cable car when she started heading downhill.

"One minute to air," we were instructed from the New York control room. Kristin was now feverishly spraying her hair and patting it down. This wasn't a sandstorm in the Arabian Desert; it was a typically breezy day in San Francisco, and we were in a courtyard with walls all around us blocking the wind.

To this day, I'm still a little defensive about this.

I always knew I was about to be stabbed in the heart when Kristin, with a pained smile and a nervous giggle, would call me over as if to ask me for some sage, last-minute, expert-producing advice. She covered her lapel microphone as I leaned in toward her with apprehension.

"I will never forgive you for humiliating me this way. You did this on purpose to embarrass me. This was the dumbest fucking decision you've ever made, and you've made a lot of them."

Kristin brought back that radiant smile for the crew and the people in our New York control room who could see her clearly on camera.

I smiled, too, as I turned away from her, hoping that nobody caught on to this lovers' spat or, should I say, *haters' fight*. There was a lot of bully in Kristin Jeannette-Meyers, often directed at me. Kristin blamed me for all kinds of things while we were together.

She accused me of cheating on her. I never did. She accused me of giving others on-camera opportunities over her so I wouldn't be accused of favoritism. I don't believe I ever did.

But there, on this day, she blamed me for it being *windy in San Francisco*.

Our breakup was painful. I just couldn't take the anger and the mood swings any longer. I often didn't *like* Kristin at this point, but I still *loved* her.

I drowned my sorrows once again in the work.

CHAPTER 18

TO ALL THE MOMS I'VE LOVED BEFORE

Most days, I was at Court TV from eight in the morning to ten at night, leaving me little time to do anything else, even necessary chores like laundry. One week, I managed to drop off my clothes to be cleaned and my daily work shoes to be polished. That Saturday, I woke up with a list of housekeeping errands to take care of. First on the list was picking up the clothes and shoes.

A single light bulb illuminated my closet. I grabbed a pair of jeans from the second shelf and a T-shirt from the top shelf.

I picked up my laundry, but the shoeshine guy had forgotten to clean up my shoes. He said it would take twenty minutes, so I ran home to put my clothes away, planning to come back later.

When I got home, I ran in and stacked my freshly laundered shirts on the top shelf of my tiny closet. I noted that I couldn't put all my shirts where they needed to go. I was out of closet space.

Oh well, a problem for another day.

Or so I thought.

Driving back to the shoeshine shop, I slowed down to appreciate the stunning view. I was usually in such a hurry that I didn't appreciate the ride along the cliffs from my house. The sun, high in the eastern sky by now, shone down on the entire west side of Manhattan. The Hudson River looked majestic on this fall afternoon.

I felt a bit more relaxed. I was checking items off my weekend to-do list, and I was looking forward to spending the remainder of the day unwinding on the sofa watching college football.

I picked up my shoes and considered stopping at the grocery store, but decided to head home instead. I was ready to kick back and relax.

Back at my apartment, I unlocked and opened the door and to my utter horror found the entire apartment filled with smoke. I could hardly see the far wall fifteen feet away. I didn't know whether to run in or run out. I didn't see flames, so I rushed in. The house was made chiefly of wood, so if the place hadn't caught fire entirely yet, it would at any moment. I desperately searched for the source of the smoke, terrified that I was minutes away from completely burning down poor Mrs. Lauricella's home.

Choking on the smoke and nearly blinded by it, I opened the closet door. A cloud of black smoke came billowing out. The folded shirts I had just placed there had caught fire against the exposed light bulb I'd failed to turn off.

I ran to the bathroom. I hoped the entire closet wouldn't go up in flames before I returned.

I quickly filled a bucket while thinking, *Oh my God! Oh my God! Please let me get through this without burning the house down!*

I ran back, coughing, tears rolling down my face, and threw the water into the closet. Fortunately, it was enough to douse the burning clothes.

I slumped to the floor.

Sitting there, I realized that if I'd gone to the grocery store, I likely would've come back home to screaming fire engines in front of a house engulfed in flames reaching into the sky. I easily could've been responsible for the death of Mrs. Lauricella upstairs.

I pulled myself up, unscrewed the offending light bulb, and, in an angry ceremony, took it out to the driveway and crushed it with my boot. I should've crushed my own skull for my stupidity.

The charred odor lasted for months as a constant reminder of my negligence. I never told her son and my landlord, Leonard, who lived a few blocks away, what happened. There were no apparent signs of the fire other than a substantial black burn mark on the inside of the closet. I cleaned, scrubbed, and used bottles of air freshener to eliminate the smell of fire, but nothing worked. Even a month later, I made sure to meet Leonard outside on the driveway when he asked to speak with me about my lease.

The fire had a profound effect on me. I wasn't bothered as much by Steve Brill's bullying for a while. I had a new perspective on life. Avoiding a tragedy allowed me to breathe, so to speak, to release the tension I always felt in my chest. I wasn't so caught up in my own drama. I was in the moment, not fearful of what the world might present to me. I'd been given a gift. Someone or something had looked out for me that day.

I was full of gratitude.

Frankly, this was not a sentiment I'd cultivated in my life and not one easily held on to.

In the ensuing months, the thankfulness dissipated. I returned to trying to convince Steve Brill I was worthy of his respect. Nearly burning down the house and almost being responsible for Mrs. Lauricella's death became a distant memory.

One night, a few months later, I got off the van that drove me and other Weehawken residents back from the city. I'd been away for a couple of days visiting a friend in DC. It was well after midnight as I walked the few steps from the van stop to my front door, and I noticed an envelope taped to my door. I took it down and walked in, set down my things, and turned on the lights. I sat on my couch, looked out over the Manhattan skyline, and casually ripped open the envelope as I reflexively worried about the workweek ahead.

The note was handwritten.

"Andy, my mother passed away on Thursday. The funeral is Monday at 9:30 in the morning." The address of the local church was written on the note, and it was signed Leonard Lauricella.

Mrs. Lauricella was not only my elderly upstairs neighbor but also my friend.

Occasionally, she would knock on my door and, without speaking, take me by the hand and lead me to the deck that wrapped around the house. It was the perfect spot to enjoy the Hudson River and the magnificent city views. We'd sit there quietly, taking in the view.

Mrs. Lauricella welcomed me into her home, where she'd lived for over fifty years. We never talked much, but we communicated. We had an understanding. Who would've thought a first-generation Italian immigrant woman and a still-young television producer from Chicago would share this unique space?

All those times we sat together on her porch came flooding back.

Mrs. Lauricella was ninety-five when she died. Monday morning, instead of jumping on a van and heading into New York City, I drove ten minutes to the small parish church near our home to attend the funeral.

I was going out of obligation, but I also wanted to remember what Mrs. Lauricella meant to me and honor our time together.

I walked in with some trepidation at just about nine thirty. The church was almost empty. Fifteen or twenty people were sitting in the pews. It suddenly occurred to me that at ninety-five, she likely had outlived most of her friends and close family members, or at least those who lived nearby.

I sat toward the back of the chapel, hoping to remain as anonymous as possible. I wouldn't know anyone other than Leonard, so I planned to sit quietly, pay my respects, and then slip out as soon as it felt appropriate.

I'd been sitting there for about ten minutes when Leonard arrived alone. He looked to the front. He looked to the right. I supposed he was just seeing who was in attendance and would take his seat in the front row. He then looked to his left. I offered a little wave and a nod of sympathy. I wasn't even sure he'd recognize me in this setting. We'd only interacted a few times.

He saw me and started walking toward me. I was a bit startled, so I rose to shake his hand and offer my condolences. As he reached me, he hugged me tight and started crying uncontrollably. I could feel his back heaving as I responded to his embrace. We stayed like that for a good thirty seconds.

We never made eye contact, even as we came apart. We just patted one another on the back. He straightened himself a bit as he left to take his seat.

I looked around the church to see if others were watching this display of emotion. Nobody seemed to notice, given that we were in the back and the others were already facing the altar.

I sat down, took a deep breath, and wondered, *What was that?*

I have no idea why, among all the attendees that day, Mrs. Lauricella's son had that reaction to me and me alone. In the following months, when I would occasionally talk to him about my rent going up or some plumbing that needed fixing, we never spoke of our exchange at the funeral.

Like so many personal and professional relationships in our lifetime, where the most important feelings and emotions go unexpressed and unsaid, we don't realize our effect on some people, for better or worse.

We don't let others know their impact on us.

Something very stark occurred to me at that moment. This man's mom was ninety-five years old at the time of her passing. I remember being astonished that he was so grief-stricken given his mom died at such an advanced age.

I became all too aware of my mortality on that day and much more aware that my own mother's final day would also come. I understood for the first time that we are all sons and daughters of our moms, and if we are truly blessed to have a mom who loves us unconditionally every day of her life, as I did, it is going to be gut-wrenching and profoundly heartbreaking when our mom leaves us.

My mother, Barbara Regal, didn't make it even close to ninety-five years old. Breast cancer took her decades too soon. And when she did go, I cried and cried and cried. I cry still, years later.

And I, too, like my landlord, have found solace in the embrace of anyone who knows how special my mom was.

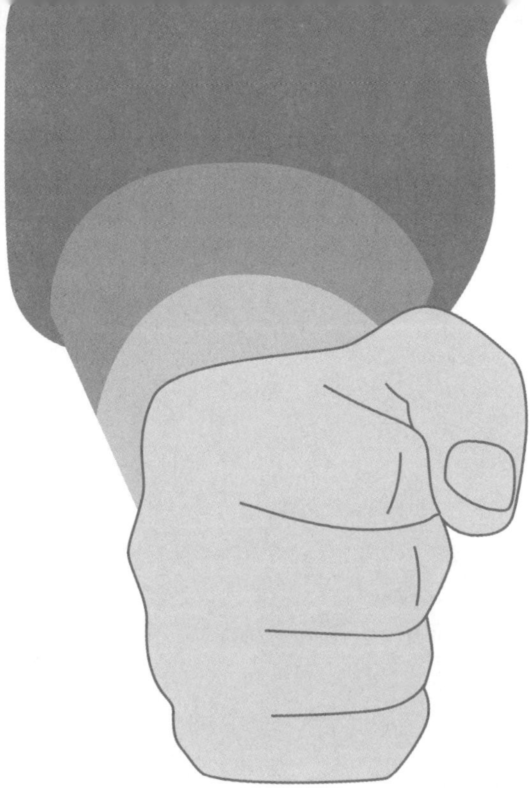

SECTION 3

I GET MY OWN SHOW . . . UNFORTUNATELY

All people feel better and do better when you give them attention, affirmation, and appreciation.

—JOHN C. MAXWELL, BESTSELLING AUTHOR AND PASTOR

CHAPTER 19

TALK ISN'T NECESSARILY CHEAP

By 1993, Court TV was becoming a cable staple, but the viewership remained relatively small. I wanted to create a court-based show like *The People's Court* but real—one that highlighted the most dramatic moments of the trials we'd covered throughout the United States. And one that could draw a larger audience than we could attract on our cable channel, which still had limited distribution across the country. I began developing plans for a syndicated half-hour news show called *Court TV: Inside America's Courts*, which became one of the highlights of my career.

Merrill Brown, Steve Brill's number two, was tasked with finding a business partner for a syndicated Court TV concept. He was bright but downtrodden by a brutal job: dealing with Steve Brill's disdain. Around forty years old then, Merrill was a good guy, quite savvy about the media landscape, and a skilled negotiator.

New Line Television, a division of the successful upstart movie studio New Line Cinema, agreed to be our partner. I wasn't a party to the initial agreement, but I knew New Line would finance the production, and we'd handle creating, developing, and producing this new show.

We had a deal!

I looked forward with great anticipation to what was ahead and my chance to create something unique, distinctive, and enduring.

Before the show could officially be green-lighted, we had to sell it to local stations at a vast Las Vegas convention called NATPE, the National Association of Television Program Executives.

The executives at New Line felt confident they could sell the show. This was the early 1990s, the heyday of daytime syndication. While in principle individual station managers had to agree to broadcast the show, the way to get a show "cleared" was to find a network or large "station group" to air it.

I'd never been to Las Vegas or such a glamorous event. The NATPE convention had it all. A mix of talk-show and game-show superstars were in attendance. Geraldo, Sally Jessy Raphael, Oprah, Maury Povich, and Phil Donahue were there. Hit game shows like *Jeopardy!*, *The Joker's Wild*, and *Wheel of Fortune* were there, as were the tabloid shows *A Current Affair*, *Inside Edition* with Bill O'Reilly, and *Entertainment Tonight* with Mary Hart. There was a mélange of musclemen, fashion models, chefs, and animal trainers, all promoting television shows for distribution both domestically and internationally.

The most significant production and syndication companies in the world were at NATPE: Telepictures, Columbia TriStar Television, King World, MGM Television, Paramount Television, Buena Vista Television (Disney), and Tribune Entertainment. On the show floor, each had massive, splashy staging area with high-tech video walls to promote its existing and new programs, and makeshift but posh office spaces where initial negotiations could take place.

Las Vegas models served as hosts at just about every booth. They handed out snacks, sweets, and drinks to those who wandered by.

Everyone was so attractive and well-dressed. They all appeared upbeat and excited to be there. In many cases, it was like a TV industry reunion, with colleagues, former colleagues, and competitors reuniting with handshakes and hugs as the festivities got underway.

And I was among them.

I was not as good-looking or nearly as well-dressed as the top sales executives and production honchos, but I was an executive producer with a show I'd developed. And it was repped by New Line Television. New Line was small but viewed as a new and vital player in the highly competitive and lucrative daytime syndication world.

Bob Friedman was holding court. He was in his early forties—youthful with thick dark hair. He held two roles at New Line, first as co-chair of Worldwide Theatrical Marketing, Licensing, and Merchandising and then as president of New Line Television, which he helped launch in 1991.

Bob was an absolute whirlwind. He presented much bigger than his diminutive size.

During a lull in the conference that first afternoon, Bob said, "Regal, let's walk the floor." I liked Bob, even if his attention span was about ten seconds. I was flattered that this top executive wanted to spend time with me. We started to walk along the main thoroughfares of the hall.

We passed the colossal musclemen, the stars of *American Gladiators*; Ricki Lake was shaking hands ahead in the distance. A long line of people waiting to meet Judge Judy snaked down the thoroughfare of the hall.

Bob would stop someone or someone would stop him every few steps.

"Hey, Bob, how's the selling going?"

"Bobby!" a woman shouted from across the way. "I'm coming by your booth later."

"See you then, Naomi," he responded.

This must've happened thirty times in ten minutes.

Bob Friedman knew everybody. And everybody knew Bob Friedman.

I didn't understand how he did it and wondered how he became so successful at such a young age. He seemed to have the business of television in his DNA. He was a true salesman, marketer, dealmaker, schmoozer. He not only *matched* the energy on the floor; he *raised* it.

The mix of big stages, big stars, and big deals was intoxicating. You could certainly see it, and, with all the food on display, you could taste it—a bounty of hors d'oeuvres, brownies, cookies, and candy, even Dove ice cream bars at one booth, which I admittedly frequented more than a few times.

The excitement pervading the event that first day was only exceeded by the anticipation of the partying that would take place that night. The biggest production companies spent millions, not just on their huge convention floor displays but also on entertaining their clients with huge, elaborate parties featuring popular artists from the '90s at Vegas's hottest venues.

That first night, I ended up staying very late at a nightclub dancing with some of New Line's sales team. I looked over and saw Geraldo right next to me. It didn't appear that he was dancing with anyone. His eyes were closed, and he was rocking back and forth. It looked like he was asleep on his feet. I was next to him for a good ten minutes. Geraldo never opened his eyes.

The second day of the convention went much the same at our booth. It was frustrating. I was waiting for acknowledgment that the show was selling and would get a green light. No such assurances were forthcoming. So, I looked forward to what the second night in Vegas might bring.

One of the real pressures of the convention had nothing to do with selling television shows. The game was not to hold out too long for someone to offer you a ticket to the best party of the night. You needed to commit to a decent invite before too long, or you'd end up with no invite and sit in your room looking out the window at the Vegas Strip, wondering what could've been. I was hoping to get an invite to the biggest bash featuring Matchbox Twenty as the headliner, or was it Third Eye Blind? Or was it the Gin Blossoms? I'm pretty sure it was one of them.

Toward the end of that second day, a male colleague from New Line asked if I wanted to join a group that was going drinking and then to a strip club. Both male and female New Line staffers were joining. With some ambivalence—and no other invitation on offer—I said yes.

It's embarrassing to talk about going to a strip club now, having been enlightened by the #MeToo movement and my own sense of right and wrong, but this was what convention attendees did after hours in Vegas at NATPE in the 1990s. I had little interest in them. I was already lonely and depressed enough; this was not my idea of fun.

I went to dinner with my colleagues but felt reticent about the strip club thing. Going to one with your best buddies for a bachelor party was awkward enough. Even on those occasions, it left me feeling uneasy, dreary, and despondent. But call it peer pressure, fear of missing out, or immaturity, I was in.

Or call it all of those.

Around ten that night, eight of us jumped into two cabs heading to the Olympic Garden Gentlemen's Club. The Strip slowly faded in the distance. After a twenty-minute drive, we reached our destination. As we pulled up, I couldn't help feeling like I'd made a mistake. I didn't want to be there. My anxiety was kicking in.

The club looked like a big box from the outside. As we turned into the circle drive, I saw the bouncers guarding the doors, flanked by two women wearing the shortest skirts I'd ever seen. I could feel my heart pounding as loudly as the bass coming through the walls from the massive speakers inside the club.

Yet again, I had to convince myself to relax and, more importantly, not to be seduced by all this club pretended to offer.

We walked in, and the place was throbbing. The music was blaring. I couldn't even talk to the people standing next to me. I hoped nobody there would recognize me, though I guess if they did, we'd be on equal footing. My colleagues didn't seem to share the same trepidation.

My goal was to find a place to sit. A table was out of the question because that would have been outrageously expensive and made me feel even worse about being there. I just wanted to find a dark place to be anonymous, if not invisible. I didn't want any of the women working there to approach me, ask me to buy them a drink, or worse, ask if I wanted a lap dance.

Benches for the wallflowers circled the entirety of the club. Perfect. I looked for a space to join the other losers and quickly sat. For the first fifteen minutes, I achieved the anonymity I so dearly craved. I was already thinking I might be able to sneak out and grab a cab back to the Strip, even if that meant going back to my room.

I'd never had a lap dance, and I promised myself I wouldn't get pressured into one on this night. I didn't like the idea of pretending I was enjoying the experience of simulated sex when I wasn't. Plus, I was mortified at the thought of a woman gyrating over me as my male and female colleagues played the voyeur. Besides, I was certain that any woman giving me a lap dance wanted to be somewhere else—anywhere else—even more than I did.

I should have known the bench strategy wouldn't work for long. The young women started working their way over. I could imagine a mean-spirited bully boss directing the women in no uncertain terms: "Get over there and squeeze them for every dollar they have, do you understand me?"

One woman after another came over and asked if I'd buy her a drink, and I'd said sheepishly, "Not right now . . . but maybe in a little while." I knew this was how the women made money, and I was starting to feel guilty for not contributing. It wasn't lost on me that this is the business model: lonely conventioneers with money and an objectifying fantasy paying for the privilege of entertaining it. It is all about our worst instincts and our worst desires.

I kept looking at the front entrance. My strongest instinct was to run for it.

And then, there she was. And yes, shake your head, scoff, laugh. But I will repeat it: There she was. She looked like a young Cher. She was maybe five foot six, had olive skin, and her hair was curled to her shoulders. I want to say I couldn't take my eyes off her. The truth is, I mostly looked down at the ground in the hopes of not appearing lascivious. I mean, where do you look when the most beautiful woman you've ever seen stands right before you . . . *topless*?

Her voice cut through the din. "Would you buy me a drink?"

"Sure, what would you like?" I yelled.

I stood and leaned way too close to her ear so she could hear me and inadvertently smelled her perfume for the first time. The fragrance went to my head. My knees went weak. She smiled. I had to settle myself and not lose sight of my intention.

She returned with our drinks.

The idea came to me in a flash.

"Would you be allowed to talk with me a bit? I'll pay you for your time."

I thought paying women for a lap dance was crude, demeaning, and unsatisfying. But paying someone to talk to me seemed novel and somehow okay, journalistic even. I would conduct a social experiment—an exclusive "gentlemen's club" interview with a professional Las Vegas dancer.

She sat down. The guys near me looked at her with utter befuddlement as they shimmied over to make room for my new best friend.

The music was blaring, but now I could try to have a conversation. I had no idea how long she'd be allowed to talk to me, but I hoped that if the twenties kept coming, her manager might be mollified, and I wouldn't have to fend off the other women who came by.

She introduced herself. "Hi, I'm Tori."

"I'm Andy," I yelled. "Thanks for talking with me . . . I'm not sure what to say to you that wouldn't be something every other guy has said to you before."

"That's one of the things most guys say to me," Tori shouted without a hint of a smile. Then she smiled. And laughed. "I'm kidding. Relax." She was even more attractive to me now.

Tori had a sense of humor.

I kept my eyes on hers, never looking down, and strangely, she seemed to be looking right at me too.

"I'm here for the TV convention," I shouted into her ear over Steven Tyler screeching "Dude (Looks Like A Lady)."

"You're a TV repairman?" she screamed back into my ear.

"No, I'm here for a TV convention," I shrieked.

I moved closer so she could hear me, and I told her about my show and that I worked at Court TV.

"So you know Judge Judy?"

Tori didn't quite discern the difference between the most celebrated real court cases of the day and those produced for television. But that didn't mean we weren't meant for each other.

Once I managed to explain what I was doing in Vegas, she seemed impressed. I was so eager to believe that most improbable of notions.

But wasn't that her job? If so, she was good at it. I was determined not to fall for the con, but now, minutes after meeting Tori, I was starting to think she was interested in me.

"Can I pay you to stay here and continue talking to me?"

I fully understand how pathetic that sounds, but she was working, and if nothing else I wanted to be a good customer. I happily handed her another twenty. But I didn't know how much talk time I was buying and how quickly she would need to return to the floor.

"This is an awkward way to start a friendship," I suggested.

"Is that what we're doing?"

"Did I just say one of those things that every guy says to you?"

"No, friendship doesn't usually come into it, to be honest."

"Okay then, what else don't you usually tell the guys that come in here?"

"I don't tell them that I hate doing lap dances, I hope to be a veterinarian someday, and I'm a quarter Jewish."

She's a quarter Jewish. I believed the first two. The last, I believe to this day, is in the stripper handbook, to be said to any and every guy who comes in and looks Jewish.

"I'd like to hear more, Tori. How long would you be allowed to stay here talking with me?"

"You'll have to get a lap dance if I stay here with you."

"I don't want you to do that."

I believed what I was saying. I also hoped she'd find my reluctance refreshing. She looked at me with an expression I couldn't quite identify. Her shoulders now held back the curls. For the first time, I could see her face. A bit of reality was creeping into this most unreal moment. Tori was starting to become a person to me—a real human being.

She got up to grab a cocktail napkin and a pen from a table nearby, then started scribbling. For the first time in quite a while, I noticed a couple of the guys I'd come to the club with staring at me. Their faces expressed a mix of astonishment, envy, and lust.

Tori returned and thrust the piece of paper somewhat surreptitiously into my hand as she leaned down to kiss me on the cheek.

"I should go."

And with that, my Cinderella disappeared into the crowd. It wasn't even midnight. I stood up as quickly as I could and exited the Olympic Gardens.

Cabs were lined up, dropping off all sorts of lecherous men. *What a sad lot we all are*, I thought to myself.

Since about third grade, I've been aware of a void in my heart and chest. That year was when Mrs. Lazar taught us cursive. My penmanship was lousy, and she was neither understanding nor forgiving. She was critical and demeaning. She made me feel bad about myself. That feeling stayed with me every time I failed to meet my own expectations.

Was this night and this beautiful woman going to change all that?

Let me call it what it felt like to me—a life-changing and life-affirming event.

Henry David Thoreau had it so right. "The mass of men lead lives of quiet desperation."

When I got in the cab, I said, "Treasure Island Hotel, please." I turned and looked back at the Olympic Gardens. Then, as we pulled away, I gently reached into my front pocket for the cocktail napkin.

I couldn't wait to see what Tori had written: "Let's talk again, TV repairman."

Then she wrote her number underneath. I smelled the napkin. It was redolent of Tori's fragrance.

I walked through the casino lobby in a daze. I kept looking at the napkin, holding it like a winning poker hand. It would be just my luck for sweat from my hands to blur the numbers. I got to the elevator and went up to my room.

I lay on my bed and took a deep breath. I could feel myself smiling. What a night! I kept staring at the napkin. Then I started writing down Tori's number on every piece of paper and pad I had so I could never lose or misplace it. I was tempted to try the number to make sure it wasn't a fake and hear Tori's voice on a recorded message. But then I thought that would seem creepy and desperate.

Before texting, you were supposed to wait a few days after a first date before calling about the possibility of a second date. I wondered what the rules were about meeting a Vegas dancer. How long should I wait to reach out? I was in Vegas for only three more days.

And then it struck me, and my heart sank: Was this simply a side hustle when she wasn't stripping? Was she looking for me to pay for her company? I wouldn't do that. I couldn't do that. I needed to know Tori *wanted* to be with me. I was trying to exorcise over thirty years of loneliness and desperation and first dates that had no second dates. Tori had just provided some electroshock therapy for all of that.

It felt like I was about to have an adventure. Oh yeah, and I had a show to sell.

CHAPTER 20

A BIG VEGAS PRODUCTION

I had a restless night replaying what had happened. This was the first time a woman—and a beautiful woman at that—had given me her number. I had a high school crush on Tori. Fireworks were going off in my head. I needed to control my emotions. I needed to get some sleep. The third full day of the convention was going to be crucial. I might be called upon to help sell the show.

The following morning, my colleagues looked bleary-eyed and tired as they drank their coffee and prepared for another day of selling. They shared stories of concerts, gaming, celebrity sightings, and drunkenness. NATPE was rife with gossip. Thankfully, word of my night or questions about it didn't come up, and I was hoping they never would.

I spent the morning standing around our booth in case someone thought I could help, leaving me with too much time to think about Tori.

What time did Tori get home after work? How late does she sleep? Will she even remember me? I had a problem finding a place where I'd have enough privacy to call her. Back then, cell phones were still enormous blocks of plastic and rubber wielded by only the fabulously wealthy or the unashamedly geeky, so I had to use the booth phone near the back of New Line's convention enclosure.

I could see it in my mind's eye. I'd be calling Tori, and Bob Friedman would come back needing to use the phone:

"Hey, can you give me a few minutes, Bob? I'm calling a stripper I met last night to see if she wants to go on a date with me tonight."

"Oh, sure, Andy. I just need to call Michael Lynne, the co-chairman and co-chief executive officer of New Line, about how sales are going for the show, but take your time."

I still didn't even know if Tori's number was legit, but I had to make a move. It was almost noon, and I had only two more nights in Vegas. I hoped she might have one or two nights off in the middle of the week.

I kept walking over to the phone, picking it up, and then setting it down.

What would I say?

What *should* I say?

When I finally got the nerve to start dialing, someone from New Line's team would come by to grab some swag from the back closet, and I'd quickly hang up, go back to the booth, and then wander back toward the phone fifteen minutes later, when the coast was clear.

I hadn't been this nervous since fifth grade when I called my classmate Teri Witt to ask her to go steady.

(Teri said yes).

I finally decided to call. It was 1:30 p.m., and most of the team had left to grab lunch before the afternoon meetings.

I had to prepare myself for the crushing disappointment that she wouldn't pick up, let alone accept an invitation to go out with me.

The phone rang. It rang again. And again.

"Hi, this is Tori." It was that raspy, sultry, a bit gravelly voice from the night before.

"Hey, Tori, it's Andy. We met last night?"

I hesitated to see if there was any recognition whatsoever. There was silence on the other end. I jumped in abruptly, wincing a bit.

"We talked for a while, and then you gave me your number."

I was again losing my resolve and devolving into Andy Regal, TV repairman.

"Oh yeah, I remember. You were sweet." Tori giggled.

It was the first time I'd heard her voice clearly. I detected a Southern accent.

"Thanks, I really enjoyed meeting you. I don't go to those clubs very often."

"That's another thing guys say to me all the time," Tori chimed in. "I, however, *do* go to those clubs all the time."

I was feeling emboldened. "Well, if you have any time off in the next couple nights, would you let me take you out to dinner? I want to get to know you better."

"I'm off tonight."

I looked around to make sure nobody was listening. I pumped my fist into the air but tried to remain composed.

"I could meet you once I'm done here at the convention floor."

"That would be nice. Okay," she said. "For some reason, I trust you, Andy."

"I won't disappoint you, Tori."

I was stuck in a not-exceptionally-well-written rom-com scene. I wasn't sure I believed a word I was saying, but I thought maybe I did.

"I'd be happy to pick you up."

Tori gave me her address. I had no idea where she lived, but nothing would stop me from finding it.

"I'll see you tonight at seven thirty. Do you like to eat? I could make a reservation."

"I love to eat," she said with a Southern drawl, a slight giggle, and an enthusiasm that almost caused me to lose my breath.

"See you tonight."

I fell back in my chair and started laughing uncontrollably. I didn't recognize who I was at that moment. I was the kid who ached for a girlfriend. I was the kid who played sports throughout high school in the hope my dream girl would notice me. I was the guy who never had a date in high school and didn't go to prom.

But somehow that was the guy who'd just made a dinner date with the most beautiful woman in Las Vegas.

This is when my trusty TV producer anxiety started to kick in. My total focus shifted to "producing" the most memorable night of my life when I was supposed to be working on the most crucial producing job of my professional life.

I needed to get a reservation at a great place, and I was fully aware that just about every good table was spoken for because NATPE was in town. I would also need to get a cab, which I knew could take up to thirty minutes if I relied on catching one in front of the hotel when the rest of the guests were heading out.

I stayed near the phone in the back of the booth, hoping no one would ask me to jump into a meeting to sell the show. My first call was to the concierge at my hotel.

"My name is Andy Regal," I said after a ten-minute hold. "I'm an executive producer with New Line Television and a guest at your hotel. I was hoping you could find me a table at any trendy restaurant in Vegas tonight. I promise I'll make it worth your while."

I was trying to sound like I'd uttered those words many times before and had the wherewithal to back them up.

"This will be very difficult, Mr. Regal, given that NATPE is in town. Every table is reserved, but let me see what I can do."

Pressing my luck, I added, "If you can get me a cab without making me wait in line forever, I'd be doubly appreciative."

I told him I'd be back in my room by six o'clock and asked him to leave me a message there, promising again to come down and show my appreciation.

At 4:45 p.m., I announced to my colleagues, "I'm going to walk the floor." I'd learned this was a typical convention maneuver when you had no meetings and nothing to do and didn't want to make that completely obvious to everyone else.

I slipped away from the booth and moved right into the stream of thousands of people "walking the floor," quickly trading the artificial light of the convention hall for the blinding Las Vegas sun.

The mix of trepidation, anxiety, vitality, and anticipation was at a level I'd never experienced. My life felt like a blank canvas that night, and for the first time in my life, I would buy a few gallons of paint and do a Jackson Pollock on that thing.

I was back at Treasure Island by about 5:30 p.m. and made a mad dash through the casino, making sure not to run full bore into a bouncer or cocktail waitress holding a tray of drinks. All I wanted was to see the light on my phone.

I burst into the room breathless. There it was, the bulb pulsating brightly in the room's dark, like a lighthouse guiding me to Tori. *Please, please, please don't be, "Mr. Regal, I am so sorry, but I couldn't help you this evening."* I cautiously pushed the message button on the phone.

"Hello, Mr. Regal. This is Steven at the concierge desk. I have secured a reservation for you this evening at 8:00 p.m. at Spago in Caesars Palace. I have also reserved a cab waiting for you at 7:15."

I had no idea what Spago was, but it sounded trendy. While I had never been to Caesars Palace, that seemed perfect too.

Oh my God. Oh my God. This is actually happening.

I fell back on my bed, nearly hyperventilating. *Okay, what's next?* I thought. My anxiety was in overdrive. *Oh yeah, I've got to run downstairs to the concierge desk. How much money do I have?*

I did some quick math to figure out how much cash I'd need for the night.

The answer: a bundle.

I wasn't good at math, and there was no way I was going to figure it out. All I knew was that money couldn't matter tonight. I wanted to look like—no, I wanted to *be*—"*that* guy."

I ran downstairs to the concierge desk, stopping to pull $500 out of the ATM. I instinctively got irked about the $4.50 service charge, which quickly made me laugh.

Man, I am so far from really being "that guy," I thought. But tonight, that's who I was determined to be—starting right then with the concierge.

"Is Steven here?"

"I'm Steven."

The concierge was a twentysomething with great teeth.

"I'm Andy Regal. You saved my life tonight with that Spago reservation."

"Hello, Mr. Regal. It's pronounced *Spah-go*, not *Spay-go*."

"Thanks, Steven. Looks like you saved me again."

I pulled a hundred out of my wallet and handed it to him. He didn't seem displeased, but his disappointment was evident. I guess saving someone's life comes at a higher price in Vegas.

Trying to cover my gaffe, I said, "That's for the dinner reservation." I reached into my wallet and took out another hundred. "And *this* is for the cab."

I thought I pulled it off. But I'm not sure it looked like I tipped people $200 all the time. Either way, Steven was all smiles.

"Enjoy your evening, sir."

I headed back to my room.

Jesus, I thought, *I just handed out $200—and my date hasn't even started yet! I might be doing that quite a bit tonight.*

And for the first time in my life, I realized how . . . *liberating* it was to spend money so cavalierly. Maybe even—dare I say it—*exhilarating*?

Huh. Maybe I *could* be "that guy."

CHAPTER 21

GUS, MY WINGMAN

Tonight, for the first time, I would be generous to myself. As I slipped back into my room, the next thought occurred: *What should I wear?*

Cue the next wave of anxiety.

I quickly showered. Fortunately, I'd brought my nicest clothes to NATPE, so I went into the closet and pulled out tan dress pants and my favorite sports coat with black, light blue, and light brown intersecting lines. I had a powder-blue shirt that matched the coat perfectly. I'd polished my shoes before I left for the convention, and they still had that shine.

Am I overdressed? I wondered as I scrutinized the man in the mirror. *No. I'm good. I'm not going to look like a TV repairman tonight.*

I doused myself with Stetson cologne and took one more look. For the first time in a while, I stared at myself. Slim, not muscular, but an athletic build. Brown hair that wasn't receding too much (yet). I kind of liked what I saw, which was unusual for me. I spit out some hotel-supplied mouthwash, checked my watch, and headed to the lobby. I had no idea if the cab would be there for me.

I hit the elevator at 7:00 p.m. to set out on my adventure. My hands cradled the slip of paper with Tori's address like a precious gem. I kept pulling it out of my wallet, looking at it, and stuffing it back into my wallet—the same ritual I do at the airport with my passport every ten minutes before an international flight.

I decided to walk through the center of the casino instead of down the much more highly trafficked corridors along the walls that lead to and from the elevators. I didn't want to run into any colleagues and engage in small talk about how things went on the floor today or, worse, where I was headed for the evening. I was supposed to be working each night, or at least networking.

Not dating.

I kept my head up in case I had to dart quickly off my path to avoid oncoming trouble, but I reached the lobby and went out the front doors. Cabs were lined up, and the queue was already fifty deep.

I went to the first bellman I saw and told him who I was and what I was looking for. He pointed to a cab parked off to the side. *Yes!* I thought as I nonchalantly handed him a twenty.

I was getting in Las Vegas shape.

The driver rolled the cab's window down as I approached.

"My name's Gus. Get in."

"Hi, I'm Andy."

I was on my way.

I read the address to him, and he seemed unsure of himself.

Oh no, I thought, looking to see if he had any communications equipment to contact a dispatcher. He had none.

"This is pretty far off the Strip," he said, suggesting wherever I was going might not be worth the effort.

He had no idea.

As we drove, I feared we'd never find the address, and I'd have no way to tell Tori I was lost.

"Are you pretty sure you know where this is?" I asked Gus.

"Well, yes and no."

Gus in no way diminished my stress.

"I'm fairly confident this address is in a massive apartment complex. I can get us there, but I can't say I know exactly where this apartment is."

I resisted looking at my watch the entire ride but could no longer stand it. It was already 7:20 p.m. We were never going to find this place.

We drove on.

"I'm pretty sure that's the complex in the distance," Gus said with some encouragement.

I could see rows and rows of low-slung buildings.

"We'll get there in about ten minutes. Don't worry, we'll find it. I promise," said my new best friend.

We rolled up to the place that matched the number Tori had given me. I hoped with all my heart that there weren't multiple apartments in this vast complex with the same number.

"Could you please wait here, Gus? If this is the right apartment, I'd like you to drive us back to the Strip."

"Sure thing, Andy."

I took a breath and headed for the ground-floor apartment. It was like a motel. No security, no doorman. I was able to walk up to the door. It was precisely 7:30 p.m. The television repairman was about to make a house call.

I paused at the door. *Here we go*, I thought, as I finally convinced my arm to knock.

When the door opened, I was surprised to see not the beautiful woman I'd met the night before but rather a kid about twelve years old. He wore gray sweatpants and a Nike T-shirt with spaghetti sauce stains. My heart sank. This had to be the wrong apartment. It was dark in the club, but I was certain Tori wasn't much older than twenty-five—too young to have a child this age.

The kid was staring up at me. I looked over his shoulder into the apartment, and there was no one else.

I collected myself enough to ask the most critical question of the night.

"Is Tori here?"

"Yeah," he said. "She's in the shower."

I heaved a massive sigh of relief. I leaned over and put my hands on my knees to catch my breath.

The boy looked at me with a distinct *What is wrong with you, old man?* glint in his eyes.

I quickly turned and raised my hand, letting Gus know we were good and pleading for him to wait for us to come back out. He waved and gave me a thumbs-up, and I thought I detected a friendly, sympathetic smile.

"You okay, dude?" the miniature doorman asked.

Did I sense a hint of sanctimony?

"May I come in? I'm Andy. I'm here to pick up Tori."

He continued looking at me. *Is this kid sizing me up?* I wondered.

"Sure, c'mon in."

I stepped inside the door into the simple apartment. It reminded me of the kind of place my friends and I shared our junior and senior years of college. The door opened into the living room, adorned with beige carpet, a bland sofa, a single chair, and a love seat. There were dirty dishes on the small, out-of-place table in front of the sofa. Spaghetti for dinner. No shock there based on the kid's shirt. Clothes were strewn across the couch and sprinkled all over the living room.

"Would it be all right if I sat down," I asked, "or should I wait outside?"

I couldn't believe I was asking him for permission, but at the same time, I didn't know who he was or what his relationship to Tori was, and the last thing I wanted to do was insult him.

"Yeah, sure, fine."

I looked around for a clean place to sit that faced the back of the apartment so I would see Tori as soon as she came out of the bedroom. I sat on the love seat.

"I'm Andy. What's your name?"

"My name's Billy."

"Hey, Billy, how do you know Tori? Do you live here?"

"Yeah, I live here."

I immediately deflated. *Tori is going to look a lot older than she did in the club*, I thought. The whole idea of her having a twelve-year-old son was ruining my fantasy.

But then, the clouds parted.

"I live a few apartments down," Billy continued. "But I stay here a lot. Tori's my neighbor."

I laughed nervously and a bit impulsively, if not uncontrollably.

"Oh," was all I could come up with, and I found myself nodding my head up and down.

At that moment, a door burst open, and Tori shot out of the bathroom. I turned quickly enough to see her mane of beautiful, dark, curly hair cascading down her shoulders and a slim woman in a towel running into what I assumed was her bedroom. It reminded me I was going on a first date with a woman I'd already seen half naked.

"Don't look. I'm so sorry I'm late," she said.

It was that same silky Southern accent from the night before. And with that, she slammed her bedroom door.

I looked over at Billy. He was tying his beat-up sneakers. He then went back to the small table to finish eating his spaghetti. I peered out the window, and mercifully, Gus was still idling outside. I started worrying about what that would cost me and then reminded myself, *I'm that guy tonight*.

Fifteen minutes passed—maybe twenty—before she finally exited her room. She was stunning in a tight black miniskirt with a beaded blue and black, low-cut, strapless top. And her shoes: four-inch stilettos that put her almost at my height, close to six feet tall. I mentioned before that she looked like a young Cher. Standing in her living room and seeing her in full light for the first time, she was a doppelgänger for Jennifer Beals in *Flashdance*.

If you don't get that reference, Google it.

Tori also looked like any number of young women walking along the Strip, turning men's heads, all thinking, *My God, who is that? And where is she going? And who is that guy?*

Tonight, I had the answer. That's Tori, we're on a date, and she's going out with me.

She walked gingerly across the room, smiling. "Hi, Andy." It was more like "HaaAnnndy." She grabbed my right arm and wrapped hers around mine. I wasn't sure if that was a show of affection or if she just needed help walking in those shoes.

She could sense my reluctance about Billy.

"He's my watchdog. He looks for a signal from me and then runs home and calls the cops. Billy, make sure to lock up before you go home."

I wondered how many times a guy was in Tori's apartment when she had to give the signal and deploy Billy into action.

We walked up to the cab, and Gus jumped out, playing the role of my chauffeur. He opened the passenger door for us. Once Tori stepped in, he quickly gave me an "attaboy" look.

It was a much quicker drive back to the Strip. We pulled up to Caesars Palace, and it was magnificent. I'd never seen anything like it. As Gus opened our doors, he presented his card.

"Andy, I'd be happy to pick you both up later, no matter the time. I'll be there in five minutes after you call. You can count on me."

I told Tori how pleased I was that she agreed to dinner. I mentioned offhandedly that I'd made a reservation at Spago. I was careful to pronounce it correctly. I couldn't tell if she knew the restaurant, but she seemed delighted. We walked through the casino.

We window-shopped, we small-talked, and we strolled. I was oddly comfortable, so much more so than countless other failed first dates I'd been on.

Spago was perfect. It was bustling. The decor was stylish but not pretentious. It was high-end without being high-drama, and the diners were relatively young and dressed for a special evening out. Tori fit right in. I gave the hostess my name.

Oh God, please don't look at me blankly and tell me you have no Regal party of two. I've already paid the concierge $200 for his efforts.

The maître d' came right over and welcomed us.

We were getting special attention, and I wasn't sure whether it was because of who I was with or because the tip was paying off.

"Right this way," he said, leading us through the dining room. "I have one of the best tables in the house waiting for you."

He led us to a booth along the right side toward the back, allowing us to witness Spago's splendor throughout our meal. It was out of the way enough that I no longer worried about being seen with Tori.

At this point, I didn't care.

I gave the maître d' forty dollars. We sat down, side by side, and it seemed we each took a deep breath.

Tori didn't take long to trust me with her life story.

She was twenty-four and grew up in Asheville, North Carolina. Her full name was Tori Grant. She had gotten married right out of high school, but that only lasted eighteen months. She was now divorced. Her ex had been in the service. She hadn't seen or heard from him in three years.

She'd been working at a clothing store outside of Asheville, but then had to escape an abusive boyfriend. So, she and a girlfriend decided to head to Vegas on a whim with no job and little money.

She turned to dancing.

"How do you feel about us meeting that way?" I asked.

"It would be silly if I judged you for going," she said. "Anyway, it's hardly a fantasy life for the girls that dance there. It becomes hard work pretty quickly. Some of the guys that come in are jerks. I can tell which ones will be that way the minute I see them come through the door. I'm a piece of meat to them. Not really a person. And that's okay, I guess. I don't view them as human beings either in some ways. They're customers. I'm a dancer. I'm a cocktail waitress. They give me money. It's a job."

The jubilant mood was fading, and I needed to change it quickly.

I wanted to ask Tori all kinds of questions to soothe or even boost my ego. I wanted to ask her, "Why me?" Why agree to go out with me out of all the guys she meets? But that seemed whiny and pointless and would reveal the real Andy Regal, not the one I wanted to portray tonight. I decided not to go there.

"Can we just celebrate?" I suggested. "I feel very fortunate to be out with you, Tori. Let's do whatever you want to do. Show me Vegas."

"This isn't exactly the Vegas I see very often," Tori said with a tinge of sadness.

We started drinking, and they were the most colorful and fanciful drinks I'd ever seen. And we started to laugh and relax. We ordered pizza and pasta and shared the most delicious fillet I'd ever eaten.

Everything tasted better on this night.

I talked about what I was doing in Vegas and the TV show I was selling with New Line. As I was talking about myself, I almost started believing the hype. I didn't mention that if it went forward, my show would be a low-budget weekly show airing in undesirable viewing periods on weekends. And that my boss, instead of appreciating what I was creating, mostly spent his time making me and the rest of his staff miserable with his bullying behavior.

On this night, I was a New York–based executive producer working for New Line which produced big-time movies. I hoped that this show, *my show*, would end up on ABC, NBC, or CBS.

I focused on enjoying the presence of this beautiful woman, who was good company. Tori was fun to talk to, and our conversation the night before made us both feel we'd already gotten over the first date jitters.

I was intrigued by her.

Spago was packed. The food came out more quickly than I expected and wanted. At the front of the restaurant, I could see a long line of folks, less fortunate than me, who hadn't secured a table in advance. I sensed the restaurant staff trying to move us through, but I wanted time to stand still. The thought of this night ending too quickly flashed in my mind. I chastised myself for allowing my ever-present anxiety to creep back in.

As we finished dinner, I could tell they were eager to get the table back. The bill was around $200. I left a fifty dollar tip.

"Let's talk about what we want to do next," I suggested.

She replied, "Why do we need a plan?"

I didn't have a good answer. It never occurred to me that we could simply . . . *be*.

I was a producer by trade and by nature. I tried to produce everything in my life, often with disappointing results. From the moment Tori had said yes, I'd driven myself crazy trying to orchestrate every detail.

She took my hand, and we headed out of the restaurant. I turned around to take it all in and remember it all. I'd never *be* this way again.

It was now sometime after midnight. I had no idea how late this night would go, but as much as I was living a fantasy, the reality was that I had to be back on the convention floor at the New Line booth first thing in the morning. And I couldn't appear half asleep.

Tori could sense that my mood had dimmed.

"What just happened?"

"This night is going way too fast," I said.

"Let's go back to my place."

Tori didn't say it seductively. It was very matter-of-fact. How many times had she uttered that line with the same lack of emotion?

"Okay," I replied. "But first, we have to get ice cream."

"Yes!" Tori exclaimed with childlike glee.

We were back on track. While walking and window-shopping through Caesars, I pulled out Gus's card and used the hotel phone.

"Hey, Gus, I'm the guy you picked up earlier and dropped off at Caesars."

"Oh sure, Andy, I remember you and your girlfriend. How's it going?"

"Uh, fine. We're still at Caesars. Could you drive us back to where we picked her up earlier in the evening?"

"Okay, I'm at our garage filling my tank. I'll be there in just a few minutes."

We got our ice cream and strolled back toward the casino's front. I was trying so hard to stay in the moment. Gus was there as we walked out into the Las Vegas night.

"Looks like you two had a good night," Gus piped in. Tori regaled Gus with all that we'd done. I shook my head and smiled. I put my arm around her, and she moved toward me.

We pulled into her subdivision. I walked Tori to her door. I wondered if her bulldog Billy might still be in the apartment.

"Andy, I had the best time," Tori said as she unlocked her door. She turned and stepped closer. "I don't want to do anything that would keep you from selling your show. And I have a double shift tomorrow. You may not know this, but quite a few of your TV show colleagues are spending more time on the floor of our club than on your convention floor!"

She looked at me with those gorgeous eyes.

We leaned in, and all I can tell you is that it was the most sensual kiss of my life. Tori's lips were supple and soft and sweet. And she smelled great.

An amazing end to the most memorable night of my life to that point.

I bounded off her doorstep. I looked over my shoulder. She was heading into her apartment.

I walked up to the taxi. Gus had his window down, and his head was leaning out.

"That's it? A kiss good night? Are you kidding me? Don't you know this is Vegas, and she's a stripper? And you get a kiss at the doorstep?"

Gus continued to rant as we headed off.

"I've been driving for twenty-five years. I've had people overdose in my cab and decide to get divorced in my cab. I had Penn in my cab. I've had countless girls give blowjobs in my back seat. But finally, I've seen it all. A good night kiss. That's a first."

Gus burst out laughing. I laughed too. I was in Vegas. The colors were dazzling. I was living. I was alive.

We drove toward the incandescent lights of the Las Vegas Strip ahead.

The canvas was covered in a wild dance of color, chaos, energy, and spontaneity. My painting was complete.

Now, I had to get back to work.

CHAPTER 22

MY HONEYMOON NIGHTMARE

Eight weeks after the NATPE convention closed, I got word from New Line execs that they'd entered into a deal with NBC to broadcast my show, *Court TV: Inside America's Courts*, on Saturdays beginning in the fall. This gave me about six months to get the weekly program up and running.

It was the thrill of my professional life—until I had to do the work. And before I became the middleman—or should I say middle punching bag—between Steve Brill and the New Line executives.

I went to New Line to meet some of the ad sales and marketing people involved in the program's overall business plan. Bob Friedman, the whirling dervish of a president at New Line Television, was showing me around the office. We ran into Michael Lynne, president and COO of New Line Cinema at the time. Bob said, "Hey, Michael, this is Andy Regal. He's the new executive producer of our show with Brill and Court TV."

Michael Lynne was a titan in the entertainment industry. Lynne and New Line were responsible over the years for such box office smashes as *The Lord of the Rings* trilogy, the *Austin Powers* movies, *Wedding Crashers*, *Straight Outta Compton*, *Dumb and Dumber*, and *The Mask*. Lynne, fiftyish, was "straight outta" central casting in a finely tailored blue suit. He had that silver-fox look. He stared right at me.

"Make it good," Michael Lynne said with a stern look. He walked away without a smile, handshake, or salutation.

I was finally an executive producer. Goal achieved. This was the honeymoon period. I could bask in the glow of creating the program and being anointed the showrunner without having to do any soul-crushing work.

Shortly after Court TV signed the coproduction deal with New Line, a group of my colleagues went to a hotel bar, and Steve Brill joined us. He always seemed much older than just the ten years that separated him from the rest of us. He told great stories, admittedly often involving some victim of his wrath or someone who'd experienced an embarrassing public or professional humiliation. Steve would let out a hearty, staccato, and what seemed to me a sadistic laugh at the punch line. In that moment, I was grateful not to be the target. Hanging out with Steve could be quite enjoyable, but it reminded me of my schoolyard days: If the bully was focused on someone other than you, it was a relief—often comic relief at someone else's expense.

When our small group had broken up, Steve motioned me over to some cushioned chairs away from my colleagues.

"Andrew, let's talk."

He pushed away a few of the glasses left on the table and scribbled on a red napkin as he started talking. "Okay, the show is sold and will be a weekly half hour on NBC stations. It'll run for fifty-two weeks on Saturdays, right?"

"Afternoons. Right." I watched and nodded, unsure what he was writing or where this was going. Steve stopped, looked up at me, and handed me the damp napkin.

"This is what I'm going to pay you."

With that, he got up and walked away. The ink from the pen was starting to run, but I could make out *$235,000* at the upper left corner of the napkin.

This was far more money than I'd ever made. I looked around and saw that nobody was watching me. I sat back in the chair and held this crumpled, moist, frail piece of napkin in my hands. This was my contract, and that had been the negotiation.

After my encounter with Tori in Las Vegas and now drinks with Brill in this hotel bar, I started to have a fondness for wet cocktail napkins. Whenever someone wrote me a note on one, it worked out well.

Inside America's Courts would be a traditional news magazine updating current high- and low-profile cases. Plus, we'd include edited highlights from the most dramatic cases Court TV had ever covered.

I wanted Kristin as one of the co-anchors of the program. Despite our tortured past, we still worked well together and still had feelings for each other. But I certainly wasn't showing her favoritism because of our relationship. At this point in her career, she was more than a rising star; she was a recognized and highly credible legal journalist.

And . . . she would've killed me if I hadn't pushed for her to be an anchor on the show.

Brill considered Kristin a real asset who could help him. He wanted her in the role, and most importantly, so did New Line.

We decided to pair her with Gregg Jarrett, an attorney and anchor at Court TV, who didn't have Kristin's profile but had the smarts. I was impressed with Gregg's work ethic and preparation. His on-air professionalism was unmatched. In his forties, Gregg had the gravitas of a network news anchor.

Gregg and Kristin looked great on camera together. Both were incisive. These two were not local news airheads. I'd brought together a formidable, driven duo for my new show.

There's quite a lot behind creating a television show. I did have the advantage of an archive of dramatic moments to choose from. Still, I needed to design and build a set, create an entire graphics package, compose show music, hire a staff, come up with a format, get approvals from Brill on every piece of journalism, and manage the relationship between Brill and New Line.

The honeymoon was over.

I was thirty-three years old and an executive producer of a national show, and I knew what I was doing. I'd been at Court TV long enough to understand how to present the law's fine points in a way that a television audience could digest and appreciate them. Most of the staffers were lawyers-turned-producers, so we were ready.

What scared me the most was that I had to deliver a show to WNBC in New York, KNBC in Los Angeles, WMAQ in Chicago, and about 220 other stations across the country. It had to be of a quality that NBC and New Line executives would find acceptable and worthy of their sizable investment and precious airtime. And I had to create a show on time every week come hell, high water, or worse—Steve Brill.

Brill's rage existed like a sniper up in the mountains. Just knowing he was there and might start firing at any moment kept me in a state of dread and digestive distress. His wrath permeated the newsroom. He nurtured a toxic work environment through intimidation, criticism, and the paucity of acknowledgment and appreciation.

It was one thing to have him crap all over a Court TV video package. He'd rant and rave, and we wouldn't run that story until he deemed it acceptable. That process was debilitating.

But now I was working without an escape hatch. If Brill didn't like how a story was written—or, more likely, if we didn't go into enough impenetrable legal minutiae for his gratification—we could miss the satellite feed of the show to the stations. Or, let me be more precise: *I'd* miss the satellite feed to the stations. They'd have no show to air. We'd be in breach of contract.

Brill would frequently call and bark out a vitriolic message, or he would put it in writing. This is an actual note Brill sent to me and my colleagues. This was not an unusual circumstance.

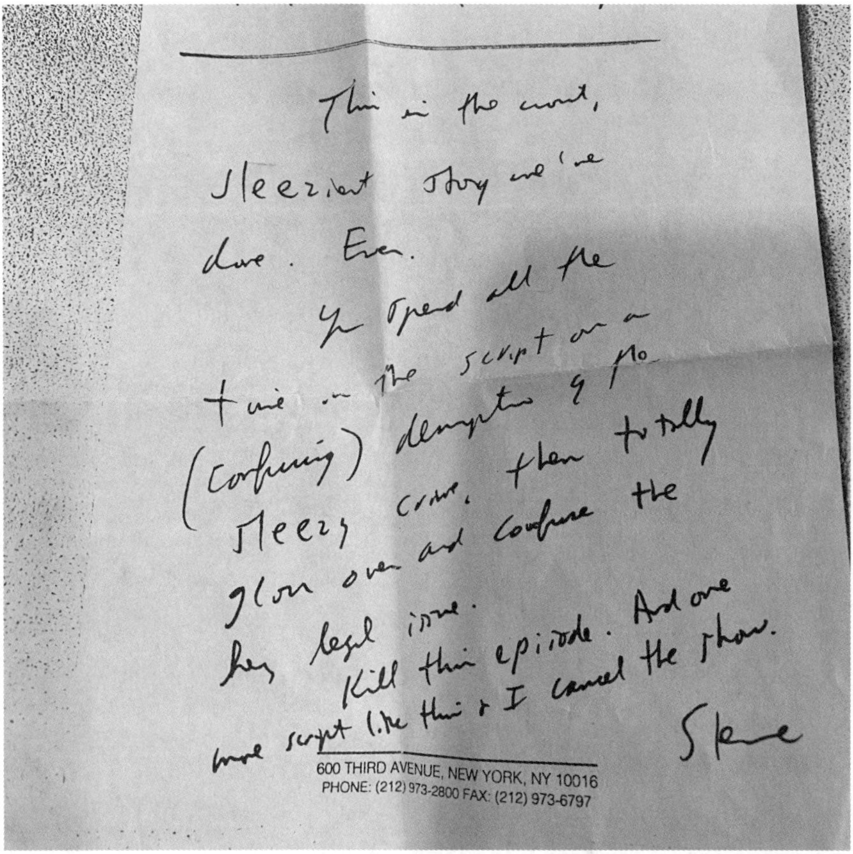
This is the worst,
sleeziest story we've
done. Ever.
You spend all the
time in the script on a
(confusing) description of the
sleezy crime, then totally
gloss over and confuse the
key legal issue.
Kill this episode. And one
more script like this & I cancel the show.
Steve
600 THIRD AVENUE, NEW YORK, NY 10016
PHONE: (212) 973-2800 FAX: (212) 973-6797

5/18/94

Steve, Andy, Allen, Sheilagh, Gregg

This is the worst, sleeziest [sic] story we've done. Ever. You spend all the time in the script on a (confusing) description of the sleezy [sic] crime, then totally gloss over and confuse the key legal issue. Kill this episode. And one more script like this, I cancel the show.

Steve

Steve Brill's vision of the show was as a further opportunity to enlighten people about our nation's jurisprudence, and he saw himself as an evangelist spreading the gospel of cameras in the courtroom.

But Bob Friedman, too, was in my ear almost from day one.

"Regal, remember this is a show for a general audience. Make the show entertaining."

"Regal, you can't let Brill take over and make it as boring as his cable network. We're doing this because we know there is enough dramatic stuff to make this work."

"Regal, this has to be the *A Current Affair* or *Inside Edition* of the courtroom. We're all dead if the show feels like a law school class. No, let me put this another way. You'll be dead. I will kill you."

Bob laughed as he said he would kill me if the show didn't just drip with lurid details of sin and violent misdeeds. But the guidance was real.

We wouldn't have hair-pulling, fists-flying spouses like Jerry Springer or the suspense of paternity tests like Maury, but we would give it our best shot. We'd unleash our serial killers, men trying to kill their wives, and millionaire-couple divorces upon America. We were gearing up to compete with those other tabloid shows.

The idea was to hook people right from the start.

We started test runs. The camera swooped in on my anchors together in the studio. The set was bright, and the news desk was glossy.

We hired a voice-over talent to set the tone: "This is Court TV's *Inside America's Courts*. Now from New York, Gregg Jarrett and Kristin Jeannette-Meyers."

I was so proud to see it all come together for the first time.

And there they were, Kristin and Gregg, ready to deliver twenty-one minutes and thirty seconds of courtroom drama and suspense.

Even though Brill demanded that we educate, he understood that courtrooms were a form of theater with strict rules that drew prying eyes by their very nature. He saw this television show as an opportunity to drive value in Court TV—and raise the value of his equity stake in his venture.

We were ready to debut *Inside America's Courts* in the fall of 1993. The main problem I was running into (and one I'd anticipated) was Brill reviewing each week's script. Even years into Court TV's existence, I'm not sure he understood or cared that television was a *visual* medium that required imagery to follow the anchors' words. The courtroom was, almost without exception, a drab and often dark place. We couldn't bring in set designers and lighting people to make the scene more pleasing to the eye.

So when Brill would get the show's script, he'd start marking it up as if it were a *New Yorker* feature magazine piece instead of a well-paced, engaging television package. He'd add verbose legal points that had no corresponding images to help viewers understand and be engaged.

So Kristin or Gregg would be on camera reading this legalese for a minute and a half to satisfy Brill. It often felt like one of those prescription drug commercials you see on TV—thirty seconds of tight, punchy ad copy and visuals followed by ninety seconds of legalese to warn you of the potential dangers and litany of side effects.

I felt the viewers turning off in droves, and I knew what would happen next.

"Regal, what the hell?"

It was Bob Friedman on the phone. He'd seen a few of the practice sessions on video.

"Regal, I hope we aren't going to see these long on-cameras with the most boring crap I've ever heard when the actual show hits air. I know this is Brill's doing. You better do something about it."

"I'm working through it, Bob."

Then, as I feared most, my phone would ring shortly thereafter.

"Hi, Andy, it's Olga. Steve would like a word."

Oh please, no. I winced.

"Andrew." Brill was seething. "I just want to remind you of one critical point that I think you may be forgetting."

You could feel the contempt coming through the phone line.

"You do *not* work for New Line Television. You work for *me.* Is there any ambiguity about that?"

"No, Steve."

"Good." He hung up.

Steve Brill was either very intuitive, or his spies were good, or both.

I had to figure out how to reconcile Brill's approach, which would weigh the show down with legal jargon, with my job to make the program a viable and entertaining half hour that could compete in the marketplace. Brill was writing all his copious script notes, which included the occasional "What the fuck does this mean?" and "How the fuck can you be so stupid to write this?" When he was done, he returned the scripts to Olga, who returned them to me.

The fact is, I wasn't scared of Bob and Brill was right; I didn't work for New Line. I liked Bob and tended to agree with him. And while I feared Brill, I knew I had to figure out a way to prevent him from sabotaging me and his show.

I decided to take a chance. I worked with Gregg and Kristin, whose opinions and expertise I valued on putting only some, not all, of Brill's esoteric pedantry into the scripts. I don't know whether he ever noticed. He never called us on it.

We were underway.

CHAPTER 23

THANK YOU, CHARLES MANSON

The show aired all over the country on Saturday afternoons at different times. Occasionally, a station would move it or even re-air it on Sunday. This occurred several times on the NBC affiliate in Denver. The station put *Inside America's Courts* on after the Denver Broncos postgame show. The Broncos have a devoted and passionate fan base, and the team was quite good in those days. The Broncos would get 50 percent of the Denver metro audience. We'd come on after, and the ratings would fall precipitously, but we'd still get double digits. That is equivalent to a massive hit show in prime time today.

When there was a game, Denver would skew the nationwide numbers and make us all look like programming geniuses. The ratings were up and down, and we could never predict. Some weeks I thought we had a strong show and we did so-so, and other times I thought the show was so-so and we'd garner a strong rating.

The year before, we had gained camera access to Manson's 1992 parole hearing. In 1969, Manson was convicted of the brutal murders of actress Sharon Tate and six others. Even a mass murderer as infamous as Charles Manson was, by law, allowed a suitability hearing to determine if he was worthy of parole. *Suitability* usually meant whether the killer still posed a threat to society.

These proceedings are set one year before an inmate's minimum eligible parole date. In most cases, the inmate is turned down after witnesses are heard from. In Charles Manson's case, family members of his victims and members of law enforcement, even after all those years, still appeared in court to argue vehemently against Manson's suitability for parole.

The California Board of Parole conducted the hearing. The issues the board was considering in Charles Manson's case were:

- The crime for which the inmate was given the life sentence
- The inmate's level of remorse
- The inmate's behavior, both good and bad, in prison
- Psychological and counseling reports
- Input from those representing the victims

Manson spoke. You couldn't help but be mesmerized by this little old man sitting at the table with the swastika tattoo just over the bridge of his nose. He is one of the most chronicled criminals of the twentieth century. He is also a raving lunatic. Manson rarely offers a cogent thought. He never argues for his release. He rants for an hour and a half in a stream of near unconsciousness that is gripping.

At the start, Ron Koenig, the parole board commissioner, reviews the details of Manson's crimes. Mr. Koenig then asks Manson if he has any corrections or additions to the record.

> MANSON: We could correct the whole thing . . . So, all that is reality to you?
>
> KOENIG: Yes . . .
>
> MANSON: Even if it never happened, it's reality to you.
>
> KOENIG: Yes, because you were found guilty by a court of law.
>
> MANSON: And all that went on in that courtroom is reality to you.

> Let me just say one thing. Nine Black Muslims and three Mexicans signed a writ that said I was Jesus Christ. Is that reality to you?*

At times Manson almost makes sense, arguing that he is not guilty of the crimes he is convicted of. That isn't the issue at this parole hearing, however. At one point, he argues:

> If you look in your own mind for every point, there's a counterpoint. For every red, there's a black. For every black, there's a red . . . I didn't tie anybody up. And I was never on the scene when anyone was killed . . . I never told anyone directly to go anywhere or do anything. I always said, and mostly it'd come from the witness stand, I said like you know what to do. You have a brain of your own . . . Everyone says that I was a leader of those people, but I was actually a follower of the children because like I never grew up. I've been in jail most of this time. So I stayed in the minds of the children.†

And then:

> Violence is no new thing to me, and people getting hurt around me is no new thing . . . They looked at me like I was a friend or a brother or a father or someone that understood because I learned in prison that you can't really tell anyone anything because everybody's got their own perspective. And all you can do is reflect people back to themselves and let them make up their own mind about things . . . But as far as lining up someone for some kind of "Helter Skelter" trip, you know, that's the district attorney's motive.‡

---

* Court TV, "CA v. Charlie Manson: 1992 Parole Hearing Part 1," California State Prison, Corcoran, California, April 21, 1992, posted February 11, 2022, YouTube video, 0:12:37, https://youtu.be/Bgyci6qXQWg.

† Court TV, "Manson: 1992 Parole Hearing," 0:13:49.

‡ Court TV, "Manson: 1992 Parole Hearing," 0:16:38.

Helter Skelter, the title of the bestselling book by the Manson family prosecutor Vincent Bugliosi, describes an apocalyptic race war that Manson was trying to ignite.

Manson argues:

> That's the only thing he could find for a motive . . . There was nothing in my mind about Helter Skelter. Helter Skelter was a song. And it was a night club . . . we opened up a little after-hours night club to make some money and play some music and do some dancing and singing and play some stuff to make enough money for dune buggies and go out into the desert . . . We would be there and when the cops would come, we would melt into other dimensions . . . It was kind of like a speakeasy in the moonshine days behind the movie set. I'm an outlaw right there and I'm a gangster and I'm bad and I'm all the things I want to be. I'm pretty free within myself. I cut people and I shoot them. I do whatever I have to do to survive in the world I live in.*

Mr. Koenig implores Manson several times to address the specific purpose of this hearing, which is to add to or amend his criminal record. These interruptions annoy Manson. He says:

> So, we're kinda like married in this thought together, like we're together whether we want to be here together or not, you know, we're stuck in this madness, you know. I don't want this job. I'm not getting paid very much, you know. And you're certainly going to get paid if you take your time . . . I have shown you some strong strength and I haven't surrendered to this by copping out to you or telling tales on someone else or by playing weak. You've medicated me, you've burnt me, you've beat me, you've stabbed me, you've

* Court TV, "Manson: 1992 Parole Hearing," 0:17:52.

> done everything you can do to me, and I'm still here. And you're still going to have to face the truth about this case sooner or later. If not here, then in the street.*

Manson is turned down for parole.

I remember hearing that Hitler was a surefire ratings grabber for the History Channel. For *Inside America's Courts,* Charles Manson was ours. I put Manson's parole hearing on air every chance I got. If there was an anniversary for the crimes he and his followers committed, if Charles Manson's birthday was coming up, if I needed a sure thing during rating periods in November, February, and May, Charlie was the headliner in the show. Charles Manson was my go-to ratings closer.

Our numbers were respectable thanks to Manson, the Denver Broncos, and a few other NFL teams, but the production schedule was brutal. Even though it was just a weekly show, this was a seven-day-a-week job. We started shooting each Thursday at about eleven in the morning, and I wouldn't be done until after three the following morning. While it looked like a standard news show, we needed quite a few takes to get each shot right. We'd make script changes on the fly, or Kristin or Gregg would notice a change that needed to be made.

After shooting, we'd edit the show until around eight o'clock Thursday night. That was when the real fun began, as Chris Strand, my creative director, and I would head to Times Square for audio editing and sweetening.

One of our biggest challenges at Court TV was capricious judges who, at the last minute, would rule that we could only have one microphone in the courtroom. Many judges thought if we were allowed to put a microphone at the lawyers' table, we'd try to eavesdrop on and maybe even broadcast confidential conversations between lawyers and clients. We never would have done that.

* Court TV, "Manson: 1992 Parole Hearing," 0:24:43.

And judges who had to allow a camera by state law but opposed it could restrict our options of where to put microphones around the courtroom making it almost impossible for the trial to be heard.

To combat the substandard audio we often had to use for the show, we traipsed over to an audio house where, from about nine at night until two or three in the morning, we worked to boost audio of the voices in a trial so our viewers weren't straining to hear the drama. This was painstaking work, trying to eliminate ambient room noise and isolate a witness's voice that might be more than ten feet away from a microphone. By one in the morning, I'd be lying on the couch trying to keep my eyes and ears open—wiped.

But that wasn't the end of it. When we were done going through the show frame by frame and putting in all the music exactly where it was meant to be, I had to walk the tape—this was before digital—over to the satellite house, which would feed the show to NBC stations across the country. This short walk through Times Square gave me a chance for some much-needed fresh air, and Times Square was an interesting place this time of the morning. It was usually me, drunk twentysomethings, prostitutes, and dealers hanging out on the corner selling a variety of drugs. I'd be home at four and back to work by ten the next morning to start working on next week's show.

I went through this grueling routine every week for two years. Such is the glamorous life of the executive producer. Yes, it was exhausting, but it was worth it. We were creating a piece of art every week.

When I played the trumpet in high school, I dreamed of becoming a conductor one day. The idea of leading an orchestra and directing the musicians to play a soaring piece of music in absolute unison to the delight of a packed house was inspiring.

I never made it to Lincoln Center, but leading my virtuosos in the newsroom and assembling this dramatic journalism into a cohesive piece of television programming viewed by millions each week was the crescendo of my professional life.

CHAPTER 24

JUDGE ITO MAKES A CRUCIAL RULING

Despite all the high-profile cases we covered in the first few years of Court TV, we had never experienced anything like the O. J. Simpson trial.

In June 1994, as the white Bronco led police on that infamous low-speed chase, I said to myself, *O. J., please turn yourself in and confess so we won't have to spend the next two years obsessed with your crimes and the ensuing trial.* I'd already convicted the guy, and no, I hadn't forgotten about that whole innocent-until-proven-guilty thing.

This would likely be a boon for the network.

And a massive pain for me.

Undoubtedly, if this (alleged) crime went to trial, it would engulf my personal and professional life. And Kristin, Court TV's star reporter, would be assigned to cover the criminal trial in Los Angeles. So, we would have to work out how to co-anchor my weekly show with Kristin as she covered O. J. in Los Angeles and Gregg held down the anchor desk in New York.

By the time the trial got underway, Kristin was getting booked on every news magazine, entertainment show, and talk show. Looking to benefit from this ratings bonanza and keep her happy, Brill allowed Kristin to appear as a paid legal analyst and contributor for CBS News.

The network had been on the air about five years when the gavel came down and the court came to order for O. J.'s murder trial. While Court TV was a recognized brand name, it still wasn't available in many cable homes across the country, and its viewership remained small. The O. J. Simpson trial was yet another opportunity for us to capture a larger audience.

The trial was well underway by May 1995. Court TV was attracting more acclaim and—now a $100 million venture—it was rapidly gaining value. So was Kristin. Her growing ego was finding ways to present itself more aggressively and egregiously. She was becoming more difficult to reason with, and impossible to deal with. She was fighting with and scoffing at colleagues, makeup artists, her co-anchor, and her ex-boyfriend.

Kristin had become a Court-TV bully.

Her vulnerability only came out on the rarest of occasions. I don't think anyone else saw it. When we were still together, on a couple of late nights, Kristin wept, with huge heaving waves of grief. But she never told me what brought on these rare exhibitions of defenselessness, and surrender.

Kristin concealed her fragile nature, and as her stock rose, she exhibited destructive, self-righteous bravado.

Camilla Dorment, a DC-based therapist who writes about her work with people who've been bullied, said in a *Washington Post* story titled, "When the 'Mean Girl' Is a Woman: How to Deal with an Adult Bully," "Oftentimes, bullies have had their own experiences of being repeatedly exploited and mistreated. The desire for dominance over another creates a temporary feeling of power and control, which acts as a defense against deep-rooted shame."*

Brill was contributing to her feeling of invincibility. He wouldn't dare disparage Kristin, at least while she was in high demand and contributing to his empire.

Lance Ito, the presiding judge over the O. J. case, likely didn't care and probably didn't know that Kristin Jeannette-Meyers was a budding network star, and seemingly untouchable.

---

* Cathy Alter, "When the 'Mean Girl' Is a Woman: How to Deal with an Adult Bully," *Washington Post*, June 7, 2021, https://www.washingtonpost.com/lifestyle/wellness/adult-bully-advice/2021/06/03/dffb8fc8-c3c5-11eb-93f5-ee9558eecf4b_story.html.

Until this happened.

The headline from the *Los Angeles Times* piece on May 19, 1995, read: "Ito Boots 2 Journalists for Talking in Court: Reporters from Court TV, USA Today Are Permanently Banned from Proceedings. Jurors Had Complained That They Were Disruptive."

The paper reported:

> Kristin Jeanette-Meyers and Gale Holland on Thursday became the latest in a long line of journalists shoved into the spotlight of the O.J. Simpson trial—this time because both were shoved out of Judge Lance A. Ito's courtroom.
>
> Jeannette-Meyers, one of the principal reporters for Court TV and a legal analyst for CBS, and Holland, a reporter for USA Today, were unceremoniously removed and permanently banned from the courtroom after jurors complained that they were talking in court.
>
> The ban came as a blow to both reporters, who declined to say much later.
>
> Appearing shaken, Jeannette-Meyers made a brief statement to reporters after her removal: "I have read the judge's order, and I am very respectful of the duty he has to keep order in his courtroom. I have apologized to him. I hope he will accept it, and I hope he will change his mind."*

Brill must have helped write Kristin's response to the judge's order. There was too much at stake. I never spoke to him about the incident, and while I heard he was incensed, I imagine he was taking great pleasure in Kristin's public censure and embarrassment. I speculated then that he would have delighted in her downfall if Court TV could come away unscathed with the camera still in place.

---

* Greg Braxton, "Ito Boots 2 Journalists for Talking in Court: Reporters from Court TV, USA Today Are Permanently Banned from Proceedings," *Los Angeles Times*, May 19, 1995, https://www.latimes.com/archives/la-xpm-1995-05-19-mn-3489-story.html.

The strategy for all of us was to avoid Brill's rage and vindictiveness, if possible. And now, Kristin had opened herself up to all of it. Her expulsion rocked our newsroom, and people were outwardly concerned about what this meant for the network—and their jobs—if Ito banned cameras from the Simpson trial.

Behind closed doors and in the far corners of Court TV, though, I know people were gleeful at this sideshow. Kristin had made quite a few enemies, and the natural envy and jealousy made for a schadenfreude bonanza.

I was in New York when the story broke. Kristin called me crying hysterically.

As much as she could be impossible and at times vengeful, I took no satisfaction from her public flogging. Although we were no longer together, I still cared about her. Kristin had this dualistic reputation. Many saw her as a dynamic, self-assured reporter starting to break big. Others viewed her as an egotistical, self-absorbed, terror of a colleague.

I couldn't understand a word she was saying as the sobbing continued, but I knew exactly what she was feeling: She had been found out. She wasn't invincible after all.

When a good friend has a deeply ingrained fatal flaw, you never call attention to it because she probably wouldn't understand—and even if she did, she couldn't do anything about it. Highlighting it would only fracture the relationship. At this time, I needed to be Kristin's trusted friend.

She cried and cried, and then she went through her specific stages of grief. First, it was the rarely seen weakness, followed by the humiliation. After she gathered herself a bit, the self-righteous indignation arose as always.

"Ito hates women. You can see how much he hates [prosecutor] Marcia Clark. He's watching me on television and hates what I'm saying. He's furious about having cameras in the courtroom. The only way he can get back at Brill is through me."

I could hear her blow her nose.

Ito ultimately reinstated Kristin, but Brill never forgave her.

She went back to covering O. J., appearing on CBS News as a legal commentator, and co-anchoring the weekly show from LA, but it was clear she was planning her escape from Court TV. She hated Brill.

I asked her not to leave before I could fulfill my dream of creating and executive producing a daily nationally syndicated court program.

Difficult as she was, if I could grow the program, I wanted her to be the star.

CHAPTER 25

"THAT'S WHY WE PAY YOU THE MEDIUM BUCKS"

About a year into the weekly show, New Line and Court TV started discussing trying to take *Inside America's Courts* daily.

Time slots would be hard to come by, but it was the natural evolution of syndication—test a weekly show to see if it performed reasonably well and then see if it could be turned into a daily asset. The big money was in grabbing advertising dollars daily.

We'd never get a prime slot in the early evening; that was *Jeopardy!*, *Wheel of Fortune*, and *Entertainment Tonight* territory. And we wouldn't get late afternoon leading into local news, but just getting into midafternoon after the soap operas, or late morning after the talk shows, could set you on your way to building a money-making machine. The key was to get on the air and stay on the air.

I was exhausted from a year of dealing with Brill's anger and the hourly, daily, and weekly deadlines, but the prospect of executive producing a weekday show that I'd created fed my ego just fine. A daily show would likely bring five times the headaches, but it was the goal we had all been working so hard to achieve.

I was ready. At least, I thought I was.

Bob Friedman indicated that NBC had a daytime slot, and while I had to continue overseeing our weekly show, it was time to begin planning for "doing a daily."

I remembered Michael Lynne's admonition to "Make it good." I guess I had. It was gratifying.

"Hello, Andy. Steve would like a word."

It was Olga again. First, my heart dropped, then it started racing. That's no way to live. Just the specter of that call from Olga was enough to ruin every moment of every day. Sometimes it was benign and not a cause for great anxiety. But I never knew that until I sat in Steve's office, heard his voice on the phone, or read the email in my inbox. By then, it would be too late.

I'd already been triggered.

This is known as *hypervigilance*, the elevated state of constantly assessing potential threats around you, fearing the next negative interaction, knowing it will come but not knowing when or in what form. Hypervigilance is often the result of trauma and is one way the body tries to protect us from threatening situations.

A psychologically safe workplace is free of fear, ridicule, and humiliation.

Court TV was not that.

Soldiers preparing for battle have every reason to live in fear. If you or a family member have a terminal illness, fear of death is justified. The rest of us should live our lives. And if someone triggers fear in us by their mere presence, we ought to either get away from them as quickly as we can or work on ourselves to put it all into perspective.

I did neither.

I just took it, never thinking about the short- and long-term effects on my physical and emotional health. Plus, if I could produce a highly rated daily show, then I would make a lot of money, win an Emmy, and possibly even earn Steve Brill's gratitude and respect.

I was staying.

Dr. Nashater Deu Solheim, a clinical and forensic psychologist, works with criminal psychopaths in prison. She is the author of *The Leadership PIN Code*, an advisor to businesses, and an executive coach on leadership.

In her TEDx talk, "What Working with Psychopaths Taught Me About Leadership," she turns her attention from the prison setting to the office.

> There are two kinds of leaders/bosses. The first creates psychological safety, bringing trust, collaboration, and sharing. The team has fun working together, even when they disagree. The other type of leader causes whispering behind closed doors, people are fearful and mistrusting of one another, unfiltered criticism, brutal honesty, and red pen all over the memo. All these behaviors are brutal towards the team. Brutal honesty kills motivation and trust. Be authentic with empathy. I encouraged the leaders to do three things. One, stay in your lane. You are not there to criticize and punish. Two, be prepared and know your team members. What motivates each person? Three, remain curious even when you feel challenged. Don't be judgmental. Be curious.*

I walked down the hall to Steve's office. I was trying to figure out what I might've done wrong or what journalistic principle we'd violated and how I would explain it, apologize for it, and fix it. I was also quickly trying to remember what the Yankees had done the night before in order to bring it up in conversation as soon as I entered his lair.

I tried to read Olga's face as I approached.

"How's he doing?" I asked tentatively.

"The usual," she said with raised eyebrows and a forced smile.

I knocked on his partially open office door.

"Come in," Steve commanded.

He was leaning back in his big, soft office chair.

"Andrew," he began.

---

* Nashater Deu Solheim, "What Working with Psychopaths Taught Me About Leadership," TEDx, November 3, 2020, YouTube video, https://www.youtube.com/watch?v=pK-MgG9xIfEg.

Using my proper first name was often a good sign. But not always.

"Hey, how about Jeter last night?" I gave it a try.

"Jeter's fucking great. And the Angels suck. They suck. Sit down. So, it looks like we're going daily. NBC has a spot for it. I'm negotiating with New Line. They're going to fund it. They'll pay us $100,000 a week for fifty-two weeks—$5.2 million as a production fee."

This wasn't a generous budget. Other shows similar to ours on the air had weekly budgets of $500,000 and more.

Then he bit down on his cigar and stared at me. It was more of a scowl.

"I know you're loyal to New Line and Bobby Friedman. Again, I strongly suggest you remember who you work for, Andrew. This is our confidential business."

I had worked tirelessly and successfully for years for Steve Brill. I'd now created and developed what essentially would be a daily thirty-minute multi-million-dollar infomercial for his brand on NBC.

My strong "heaven's reward fallacy" was deluding me again. I was expecting a ticker tape parade down Broadway, and all I got was a veiled threat and a very pointed admonition about the evanescent nature of my employment.

"You're dismissed, Andrew," Steve said, interrupting my brooding. He put his unlit cigar back in his mouth.

I was in a daze as I walked back to my desk. I was thrilled the show was moving forward in this significant way. It was no longer some weekly, weekend schedule filler. This was the world of Geraldo, Sally Jessy, Ricki Lake, *Extra*, *Inside Edition*, Montel, and Rosie O'Donnell.

This was the big time. I'd done it! Now, I had to do it all over again, but five times more often and ten times the pressure.

You know that feeling when you get a bonus at work? You feel good about it. You earned it. Great. Some extra money. When you return to your cubicle, you've already determined how much will be taken out for taxes. Then you calculate how many bills you have and what your rent and car payments are, and then you start becoming resentful that those cheap, rich, avaricious assholes you work for couldn't come up with just a few thousand more for that bonus.

After I met with Brill, I walked back to my office. I should have been celebrating a professional milestone. Instead, I was attempting to hide my despair. I had to figure out how to compete on a limited budget while dealing with Brill's seething anger and distrust.

As Mr. Brill often told me, "Andrew, that's why we pay you the medium bucks."

I had a terrific staff already in place to get the weekly show produced. Thea Trachtenberg, who went on to great success as a senior producer for *Good Morning America*, was on the team. Also Andy Hoffman, who would help launch Fox Business and become the senior executive producer for Yahoo Finance.

Given the financial limitations for the show, I hired young and highly competent attorneys, male and female, in the mold of Kristin Jeannette-Meyers, who wanted to cover the law on television as opposed to litigating it in court and who were willing to work cheap for the opportunity to be in and on television. The list included Helen Lucaitis, Frank Dehn, and Emily Mathis.

Being in television at the time was like working in Silicon Valley at its height. It held promise and status.

I hired Jon Green as my news director to help us keep track of the courtroom and justice news around the country. Jon was a jovial, small-market local news director, a good team player, and a great addition to our already stressed-out team.

I had just enough money in my budget to hire a few younger production assistants and associate producers, most but not all of whom were lawyers who could help us analyze and elucidate the law and turn it all, with the help of our senior team, into captivating television.

Even my executive assistant, Tami, an experienced attorney in her thirties, was thrilled to take the job with a salary in the $40,000 range, just for a chance to break into television. At the time, a New York attorney straight out of law school would start at $135,000 at a top law firm.

One of the lawyers I hired, Elise, was an impressive woman in her late twenties. She was smart and had an unusual enthusiasm about her. In the interview, she stated she wanted to be a journalist, and I wondered whether her true ambition, as was often the case with new hires at Court TV, was to be on-air talent.

CHAPTER 26

I AM THE CHAMPION . . . OF THE NEWSROOM

I had my team. Fifty strong.

Of course, I knew rehearsal time was crucial. I'd learned that lesson from the HBO debacle when Brill had exploded because we were unprepared at our dress rehearsal for the launch of Court TV. So, each morning for three weeks, we came to work with the mindset that we had already launched and were on the air, and by late afternoon we'd have the show produced for the following day.

Our show was to air in different "dayparts," or blocks of time, across the NBC network. We were added to the late morning or midafternoon daypart in some cities. In others, we were relegated to the wee hours of the morning, after the late-night NBC talk shows.

We had a production meeting every morning to discuss things like, What old trials with dramatic moments did we have prepared that we could slot into the show? Which current trials Court TV was covering could we feature using on-site reports and highlights? What other court and justice news was happening nationwide that Gregg and Kristin could inform the audience about?

I'd stand before my team members each morning and prepare them for the daily deadline challenge. I knew how to do this. I was in command. I'd been preparing for this since I was the captain of our kickball games back in second grade. I was ready to lead this group into day-in and day-out TV hell.

Late afternoon, I'd be in the control room preparing for our shoot, culminating the production team's work that day. Standing with my creative director, Chris Strand, and my director, Dominic Palumbo, we'd assemble the rundown for the show as the pieces came in. We needed twenty-two minutes and thirty seconds of riveting courtroom drama every day. Kristin and Gregg, to their credit, were focused on making sure the show was factual from a legal perspective. They were the last ones to review all the scripts before we rolled tape.

It was the fall of 1995, and our nationwide debut was only weeks away. We figured out how much time it took to prepare the show. We determined how many current trials we'd need and how many archival "best of" clips would be required. We created workflows to cover breaking court and crime news and get it all into the show under the deadline.

What I couldn't prepare for was Steve Brill.

There was a phone in the back of the control room. Most days during those tension-filled weeks, that phone would ring in the midafternoon once a day. Around two o'clock, I'd start staring at it, my heart pounding, not knowing if or when it might ring.

And then . . .

"Hi, Olga." I hoped my voice masked my dread.

"Hello, Andy, Steve would like a word."

And then Brill jumped on the line.

"Where did these stories I see in today's show rundown come from? Did New Line put you up to this crap? Do you think we're going to do a tawdry tabloid show? If you can't figure out how to inform the viewing audience about the law in a respectful way, I'll find someone who can. Do you understand me?"

He slammed the phone down.

Before the national premiere, I had to figure out how to change the show to appease Steve.

Remember, 95 percent of what I put in every made-for-NBC episode came from Court TV. He was furious at me for putting in trials that had already aired on the network or were currently airing on *his* cable network. Steve, in bully mode, was unreasonable. There was no reasoning with him. Trying to engage him in a discussion was futile at best. It brought out his ire even more. Debating with him was dangerous.

Mr. Brill spent a lot of time in bully mode.

I described my experience to Gary Namie from the Workplace Bullying Institute.

"I've heard your story many times before, Andy, just different versions. Brill is what I call the 'constant critic' bully. These bosses are trying to control the target's soul. They are trying to control your identity, your own self-knowledge, self-worth, and who you are. This type of bully often behaves disrespectfully and contemptuously. This is the worst kind of bully. Unconscionable."

We were now just one week away from our premiere. I was becoming increasingly unnerved. I was trying to keep morale up, and my team was working fourteen-hour days. I continued to assure the New Line execs that I was creating a viable show that could compete in the marketplace while fending off Brill's daily bullying attacks.

I was a wreck.

The all-too-frequent calls into the control room threatening to fire me, or the possibility of such, were becoming too much.

It is the Wednesday before our Monday debut—the second week of September 1995.

I am in the middle of rehearsing with Gregg and Kristin. We have only a few days left before we do this for real, and we have to get it right. Then, the Brill phone rings in the control room. I slowly pick up the receiver and take a breath.

"Andy, Steve would like a word."

Before I hear his voice, I can see him all smug, leaning back in his chair with a cigar in his mouth, enjoying every minute of the ridicule he is about to spit out at me. I always assumed I was the tenth person that day to take the brunt of his wrath. He was like a big-game hunter, and I was simply the latest quarry to enter his sights. But the fact that I was a target and Brill was aiming for another bull's-eye did not ease my anguish.

"What is this script I'm reading? This is about the worst, sophomoric writing I've ever seen. We never should've hired TV people. You know nothing about the law. This is crap, and we are never putting this on the air. Do you hear me, Andrew? Never! We're putting this show on the air to teach people about the law. Do I need to find someone else to do it my way?"

This is intended as a rhetorical question. I don't take it that way.

"Steve, go right ahead." I can't believe what is coming out of my mouth. "If you think you can find someone better than me at getting this show on the air and keeping it there, then do it. Make the change. Until then, I want the calls and the threats to stop. Just cut it out and let me get back to work."

I wait for a response. There is none. I gently hang up the phone.

I'd been looking straight down the entire conversation. Now, I look up to see everyone in the control room—Dominic, my director; Jon, my news director; and Chris, my creative director—looking at me with a mix of shock and what I'd like to remember as admiration.

"Was that really Brill?" Dominic asks, with wide-eyed astonishment and a broad grin on his face.

"Wow," is all he can add.

I can't say Steve Brill never castigated me again. He did. But he never called on that phone again and never threatened to fire me again. It was the only time in my entire career I challenged the bully. I never felt I had the requisite leverage. I was just too fearful.

We debuted with little fanfare; internally, it seemed like just another day. And that's precisely what we had set out to do.

Producing the show became routine after a few weeks. Kristin and Gregg found their rhythm. As far as we knew Brill trusted that they were communicating the finer points of the law to the audience. We also assumed he went on to his many other bullying targets. While Brill's presence was always felt, I no longer obsessed over that dreaded phone.

Each day, some disaster would befall us. A judge would decide to play golf instead of hold court, or a sensational murder trial that was supposed to get underway would be postponed for some procedural reason. But we were adept enough and had enough prerecorded material to get us to the finish line.

I never saw the sun much in my thirties while doing this show. I was at work most days by eight in the morning and was lucky to be home before nine. This went on for years. But as that first holiday season approached, there was much to celebrate. Our show was doing well enough. November sweeps had been relatively successful. We were sure to put Charles Manson in the show a couple more times, and we'd created something unique and unprecedented for a fledgling cable network.

I was exhausted but gratified. I had no social life. When I had time away from the studio, I was either working on or worrying about the next show or simply sitting exhausted, almost comatose, on my worn-out couch in Weehawken, New Jersey, eating store-bought, fat-free cookies by the box.

CHAPTER 27

I FELL IN LOVE (AGAIN)

In those days, Court TV spent freely on its Christmas party. My team and the rest of the hardworking Court TV staff deserved the celebration. It was the first time I'd had a night out since the show's debut in September.

A huge club space had been reserved on Seventy-Ninth Street on the west side of Manhattan near Broadway.

Everyone got decked out for the holiday bash, and even Steve Brill—our own Ebenezer Scrooge himself—was often in an uncharacteristically festive mood on these occasions.

I remember feeling buoyant.

Court TV had grown to a couple hundred employees, and the place was already filling up as I walked in. The club was primarily a large dance floor with bars strategically placed throughout the perimeter. Although I went alone, I was greeted immediately by my team and the Court TV staff.

I was enjoying the hors d'oeuvres and nursing my gin and tonic. I've never been a big drinker and have rarely gotten drunk, even in college. That was just fine for me tonight. If anything, I was drunk on my own self-importance, as staffer after staffer congratulated me on taking the show from a simple concept to a weekly show and now a daily show on NBC.

I was hanging out with my crew—Thea, Andy, Dominic, Mrs. T., Mr. T.,

Chris, Frank, Jon, Hannah, Tami, Grace, Michelle, Faye, Emily, Helen, and Gregg.

At some point, I started talking to Elise, the lawyer I'd recently hired. She was glowing. That smile couldn't help but spread holiday cheer. The DJ started spinning records.

"Let's dance!" she said.

"Let's go," I said without hesitation.

The music was rock, pop, and oldies that had us twist, and shout, and we did just that. After one dance, we made it two and then three. We took a break to get another drink, but we stayed by the bar talking instead of splitting off or joining the others.

I knew I was spending an inordinate amount of time with Elise at this office party instead of mingling with my staff. I selfishly felt I'd given up years of my life to Brill and Court TV, and I saw no reason why I shouldn't enjoy this party to the hilt. She could dance—I couldn't, but I let it rip as best I could. I naively told myself once or twice I was doing nothing wrong. Everyone was having such a good time. I couldn't imagine anyone would notice what I was doing.

Elise and I hit the dance floor once again. Now, the room was spinning—but not in the way you might think. It was like that playground ride that the kids sit on while the adults run around to twirl it faster and faster. You can see your playmates on the dizzying ride with you, but your parents are all a blur after a bit.

I could see Elise so clearly—her stunning smile, the long dark hair, and those big blue eyes. She was looking right at me. And in that most cliché of ways, she was the only person in the room.

Well, almost. After a few more songs and with the sweat running down my face, we exited the dance floor.

"I'll be right back," she said, excusing herself. "I need to run to the ladies' room."

If I wasn't completely mistaken, she was coming back and wanted to retake her place next to me. The moment she departed, I realized all too vividly and suddenly that Elise wasn't the only one in the room, as a pointed, blunt voice cut right through my euphoric haze.

"You can't do this. She works for you."

It was my assistant, Tami. I was abruptly and quickly sobered up from my reverie.

"I'm not doing anything, Tami. I'm enjoying the party," I said curtly (and not very convincingly). And I wasn't sure exactly who I was trying to convince.

It might seem odd that my executive assistant was involved in my personal life. Tami and I were the same age and often confided in each other.

I liked Tami. She was highly competent and a huge help in organizing my schedule and the production schedule.

We often engaged in friendly banter.

The music was loud. Something was happening. I looked around. The party was in full swing.

I'd detected no one else showing interest in my (mis?)behavior.

"You can't do this. I'm just trying to protect you. She works for you," Tami repeated.

"You're pathetic," I responded abruptly.

It was a mean-spirited retort, and I regret it to this day.

Tami stormed off, and Elise returned from the ladies' room. We danced a bit more, and while my little talk with Tami was a buzzkill, I was determined not to let her ruin the moment. I was sweating through my sports coat, so I suggested we get some air outside. It was now about eleven thirty.

Elise and I walked several blocks away from the party. We found an alley. We stopped and looked at one another. I kissed her with an intensity and passion that stunned me.

Elise said after our kiss in the alleyway, "Let's get out of here." And for the first time, we were both very much aware of what was happening, and something was *definitely* happening.

I have no idea why we headed to my place in Jersey and not hers downtown. We jumped into the first van to load up at Forty-Second and Eighth, and off we went through the Lincoln Tunnel to Weehawken. The ride would not take more than fifteen minutes. We were just staring at each other and holding hands in the back of the van.

I was intoxicated and elated.

Elise stayed with me that night; I may have even told her I loved her. I'd been suppressing feelings for her—or, perhaps more accurately, completely denying any feelings for her. It never occurred to me that something could happen between us. And then, somehow, it did.

I can't quite say what Elise was looking for. Once again, as was my psychological makeup, I was trying to compensate for all I'd missed. As misguided, selfish, and immature as this all seems, I just wanted a shot at happiness. I wanted to get rid of the longing, the depression, and the feeling that I deserved more and better. Elise was my ideal. She was the woman I'd been waiting for my entire life.

I never thought I might be doing her a terrible disservice and might be putting my career in jeopardy. I was chasing contentment—something that had eluded me. And now, my destiny was resting angelically in my bed.

We slept late, and finally, when we awoke in each other's arms, we talked about what we'd done and what we'd do next. I made it clear that I cared about her, that I wanted to see her again, and that this wasn't a one-night grave mistake.

Elise expressed similar feelings. We knew that Monday morning at work might be awkward, but we agreed not to say a word to anyone, pretend like nothing had happened, and proceed as we had the previous four months. She would do her job, and I would do mine. That seemed logical and a reasonably good plan.

And it was, except it didn't consider all the other people who weren't nearly as interested in our happiness as we were.

Driving Elise back to her apartment that Saturday, everything seemed new, fresh, and exciting. The thought of Steve Brill didn't bring fear and self-loathing. He wasn't all-important to me, and his bullying was less threatening. He no longer held my happiness and well-being in his hands.

I had something and someone more meaningful in my life. I was pretty sure this was true love.

We pulled up to her building, and there was an awkward moment where I realized I had no way of contacting her.

"Hey, could I get your number?"

Elise thought about it for a long moment. Then, in her contagious, spirited way, she laughed, reached into her purse, and tore off a piece of paper.

"Here you go. But you'll have to call it to see if I gave you my actual number."

We kissed, and she got out of the car. I watched her in amazement as she walked away, and all I could think was, *I can't believe this is happening. I think Elise is my girlfriend.*

CHAPTER 28

A COUP D'INSIDE AMERICA'S COURTS

Monday morning came. I sensed nothing different. But there were always only a few people in the office when I arrived. Every morning at nine, we had an all-staff meeting with everyone except Gregg and Kristin to go over all the assignments for that day's show. We would discuss which stories were ready to go, which had to be finished, which were happening today that needed to be covered, and which were being readied for tomorrow's show and beyond.

It was my favorite time of the day.

While leading this meeting gave me an ego boost, I must admit that doing so in front of Elise was emboldening. I was quite conscious not to act any differently than I had the last two years. I had no clue whether I had accomplished that or whether the daggers were already coming out.

We all went back to work after the morning meeting. The show got done, and we were in a familiar routine. But I had a new personal routine. Increasingly, I no longer went home alone to New Jersey, anxiety-ridden over the next day's show. I would stay at Elise's apartment in the city, or she would meet me at my place. We'd order food, talk about the day, and revel in our newfound relationship.

She was perfect. We were perfect together. She made me feel attractive, worthy, capable, and accomplished. And given that she observed me at work every day, it was like a shot of Red Bull to my self-esteem that she admired me for my leadership, creativity, and work ethic.

We were being careful and respectful of the situation.

A few weeks after Elise and I started seeing one another, I arrived at her apartment, and she was in tears.

"I haven't wanted to bring this up to you, and I was hoping it would get better, but it's just getting worse."

I didn't know exactly where this was going. I immediately felt the bliss exiting my body. "I love my job, and I love the show, but I'm getting the worst assignments, and lately, I feel like Faye talks to me like she hates me."

Faye was a strong-minded, highly competent senior producer in her late thirties or early forties. Once our morning meeting concluded, she handed out the specific assignments for that day's show.

This news put me in a quandary. I knew this situation wouldn't get better on its own. But now, if I dared to address it, I knew I'd be jeopardizing myself.

It didn't get better. And all the while, I'm thinking, *Why should Elise be punished for dating me? We're both single. And why would that make Faye angry and spiteful?*

I'd made myself vulnerable. Faye seemed to smell or taste it instinctively and realized it well before I did.

Elise and I rarely spoke at work. Before the relationship developed, we had little reason for interaction, and now we made sure to maintain the status quo. Every night when we were together, she was disconsolate. She was being assigned only the simplest production tasks when previously she'd been working on full-fledged legal stories where her law degree was advantageous. Elise would go into detail about how churlish and nasty Faye was being to her.

The most telling part of this was that there had been no issues, problems, or bullying before the holiday party.

None.

I couldn't help but wonder who else was bitter or resentful about our relationship. Every morning, I surveyed the newsroom. I'd handpicked every person there. I'd promoted them. I'd gotten them raises. I'd treated them the way I wish a boss, any boss, would've treated me. I thought I'd only been helpful, useful, and inspirational. What possible ill will could these people, *my* people, harbor against me simply because I'd met the woman of my dreams?

In the meantime, my feelings for Elise were deepening. Away from the office, we connected and communicated. I continued to believe that what we had was pure, right, and true.

Yet the situation at work was becoming untenable.

I didn't want a confrontation, but I was resolute in my assessment that this was not about protecting my girlfriend or taking her side, and it was not about favoritism. It was about Faye bullying an employee—a qualified, hardworking attorney who was, until recently, a valued contributor. As simple as that. Given my experience with workplace aggression, I couldn't overlook bullying on my team of anyone at any time. If Faye were dating someone on the team, it would never have occurred to me to try to sabotage the relationship. In my worldview, you should never intentionally hurt anyone.

I finally decided to talk to Faye about the situation. I hoped I could reason with her. I called her into my office and closed the door.

"Hey, Faye, thanks for coming in." I was trying to be warm and collegial.

"Sure, what's up?"

I could tell immediately she wasn't going to make this easy. She was stoic. And she wasn't looking me in the eye, like a juror about to convict me. So I launched into it.

"Look, I understand that a staff member feels she's not getting any assignments that take advantage of her legal background and production skills. Please make sure that she's getting an opportunity to do some of the work she was doing in the first couple months of the show and, of course, anything else you need her to do."

I tried to force a smile as if to say, *No big deal, Faye. Thanks so much for understanding. It's great that you are so open-minded and accommodating. Despite my abject fear that you're about to ruin my career and the most meaningful relationship I've ever had, it's wonderful to collaborate with you at the most important time in my career.*

I could feel the room getting smaller. She suddenly locked her eyes directly onto mine and said, "So you want me to give her preferential treatment? Is that what you're saying?"

"No, of course not, Faye. I want everyone on the staff to feel challenged, even if we all have significant aspects of our roles that are routine."

"Well, it seems obvious you're telling me to change what I'm doing. It's my job to make the assignments after you decide what stories to do. Are you now taking that role away from me?"

"No, Faye, of course not. I'm simply asking you to move the assignments around and ensure everyone feels valued."

I was doing all I could to refrain from uttering Elise's name with each point I was trying to make.

"But we're specifically talking about Elise Barrow, right?" Faye said. She crossed her arms.

"I'm simply making a point about the daily assignments, which includes her."

"But I'm still making the assignments, is that right?"

"Yes, that's still you. Absolutely. Of course."

Faye looked pleased. And even though I didn't think I'd said anything incriminating, I sensed that Faye felt she'd won. Or, perhaps more disconcerting, that she was *going* to win.

"Okay, thanks," I said to dismiss her. She stood up and didn't look at me as she exited the office.

At that moment, I knew we were in a battle against one another.

We never shared a pleasant word again.

I didn't know where to turn. Faye was the general leading an assault, and this was just the first shot fired. I didn't understand what she was fighting for, but I knew what was at stake.

I was fighting for my life.

A week or two went by. I wanted to focus solely on the show, but all I could do was wonder how much whispering, gossiping, backstabbing, and plotting was going on in the newsroom.

Being paranoid is a horrible feeling.

This was putting a terrible strain on my relationship with Elise. Our joy was tarnished; angst and strife crept in. After a long day putting the show together, I would face Elise's growing frustration.

Faye hadn't changed her tone toward Elise or the assignments she was giving her.

"She hates me—just hates me—even more now. Whatever you said to her made it worse," Elise confided to me.

It made my heart ache to see Elise suffering. I hated that I couldn't make it go away. And I also hated that I was now jeopardizing my job and my show.

"Andy, hi. This is Tara in HR. Cynthia Brill would like to talk with you. Can you come down to our offices now?"

I can't say I was shocked. It had been just too quiet for over a month or so.

"Sure, I'm coming right now."

Cynthia was Steve's wife, an accomplished lawyer in her own right.

I can't say I had any real relationship with Cynthia, but I always found her enjoyable to speak to and work with on the few occasions when a legal issue arose that required her attention.

It was another long, grim walk, like the one that usually took me to Steve Brill's office. From meetings like this one over the years, I knew that you should always avoid meetings where you don't know the agenda or who's attending.

But here I was.

This was all due to my actions. I acknowledge that. Still, I thought I was doing nothing wrong in falling in love with Elise.

"Hi, Andy, c'mon in," Cynthia said. I took the nearest chair opposite her desk. I could feel my heart pumping. It occurred to me that I might be getting fired.

"We have received a formal complaint from members of your staff related to preferential treatment of one of your employees."

I found it interesting that she didn't mention Elise's name and she used the exact phrasing that Faye had used.

"In what way have I treated this person better than others?" I asked.

"I've been told by several people that you've requested that this person receive assignments above her background and experience. I will tell you that while we have no codified rules here at Court TV related to workplace relationships, this kind of thing puts the company at risk and jeopardizes the show."

I learned quite a bit from Steve Brill while at Court TV. He taught me how to be a better journalist, and I learned from his constant bullying how not to treat your staff. He also taught me the importance of keeping my mouth shut.

"If you're in a negotiation, and the other side agrees, then shut the fuck up," Brill had instructed me. "You can only fuck it up at that point. If you don't have leverage in a negotiation, shut up and get out of there and regroup."

I didn't feel I had any leverage in this conversation.

So I shut up.

"We are monitoring this situation very carefully and won't hesitate to take action if necessary," Cynthia stated.

I stared at Cynthia.

"Do you understand the severity of the situation?"

I nodded.

"Okay, thank you for coming down."

Walking back to my office, I was trying to digest whether they had threatened to fire me. I had no idea what my rights were, and I was horrified at the thought of being escorted out of the building just as my show, the show I'd created, was about to take off. The O. J. Simpson civil trial would start in the fall, and I hoped that would guarantee ratings success.

Besides Faye, I had no idea who my actual accusers were. Cynthia Brill hadn't divulged that information. I wondered if, like in a court of law, I had a right to face my accusers. I wanted to know what they hoped to gain from all of this. If I got fired, if Elise was pulled off the show, or if both happened, how would that help our accusers? And how did my dating Elise adversely affect their lives or their jobs?

In the context of workplace bullying, **mobbing** refers to a form of collective harassment where a group of employees, often led or sanctioned by a manager or leader, target one individual with repeated hostile behaviors. Unlike one-on-one bullying, mobbing is *group bullying*, and it typically includes gossip, exclusion, undermining, and organized attempts to drive the target out of the workplace.

- **COLLECTIVE BEHAVIOR:** Multiple people participate in isolating, ridiculing, or discrediting the target.
- **POWER DYNAMICS:** It often happens when leadership either initiates or tolerates the harassment.
- **SYSTEMATIC NATURE:** It is not a single conflict but an ongoing pattern of actions intended to humiliate, ostracize, or force the employee out.
- **PSYCHOLOGICAL HARM:** Victims often report severe stress, anxiety, depression, and physical symptoms.
- **ORGANIZATIONAL DAMAGE:** Mobbing creates toxic cultures, destroys trust, and undermines collaboration.

Researchers such as Heinz Leymann, who first studied workplace mobbing in the 1980s, describe it as a form of "psychological terror" at work because it is carried out consistently, by multiple actors, over an extended period.

As soon as I sat down, my phone rang.

"What happened? What did she say?" Elise called me from an undisclosed location. She always had this breathless way of talking when looking for information that I found endlessly attractive, even at times like this. Given that she worked in a very nonprivate cubicle, she had found an empty office in another corner of the building to call me from. I was certain that everyone knew where she was going and why, but I was too busy and becoming too exhausted to lecture her on being stealthier.

"It wasn't that bad. I don't know if that was simply setting the stage for firing me."

"They can't do that. This is your show. You created it."

We were both distraught. I thought I was about to lose all that I'd worked for, and Elise felt increasingly bullied and ostracized.

When we returned to her apartment that night she said, "You know this has happened to me my entire life. Maybe I bring it on myself, but girls have always bullied me for as long as I can remember."

According to a Workplace Bullying Institute study, while female bullies comprise only 29 percent of bully bosses, they prey on other women 67 percent of the time.*

As mentioned previously, Dr. Leah Katz is a psychologist and bullying victim herself. She has written extensively on this topic and addresses it with patients in her practice. I asked Dr. Katz whether she was aware of the prevalence of women bullying other women in the workplace.

"I was bullied in graduate school by a female superior," Dr. Katz told me. "She almost ruined my career. It's shocking to me the number of people who shared that they were bullied as adults.

"Many women have told me other women bullied them. During a time when women must support other women, this reality can carry added trauma and be even more painful. The victim thinks, *There must be something wrong with me to be the target of another woman*. And often the individual doing the bullying appears to support other female colleagues, so there is doubt and fear by the target of never being listened to or validated or believed."

So was this animus directed at me or Elise? I wanted to protect her. Neither of us deserved this agony . . . did we?

We tried to enjoy the evening and watched our favorite show, *Party of Five*, but I couldn't help feeling that the bad guys were winning. I kept convincing myself that Elise and I weren't to blame; still, these conflicts at work were starting to create a wedge between us.

I needed to return my focus to the show, hoping that somehow in time this

---

* "2024 WBI US Workplace Bullying Survey: The National Study," Workplace Bullying Institute, 2024, https://workplacebullying.org/wp-content/uploads/2024/10/2024-Complete-Report.pdf.

would all be forgotten and the aggrieved parties on my staff would return to worrying about their own lives.

I started working even longer hours to prove to anyone who doubted that my priorities were in the right place. Elise couldn't wait to get away from work, even though she made it clear she wouldn't be forced to go anywhere. So now we were at odds. And the ubiquitous tension began to erode what we cherished.

I was the boss; it was my show. I was making five times what Elise made, yet she wasn't willing to bow out to save my job and our relationship. And neither was I. I couldn't blame her. Until this workplace incivility and aggression, Elise loved her role at Court TV.

Every day, I waited for another phone call asking me to come to HR. It didn't happen. I figured they were building their case. I worked late every night. Elise went out with friends. I encouraged her to do so, hoping she could find some relief and perspective away from me and Court TV.

CHAPTER 29

MY LIFE GETS CANCELED

It was October 1996, and we were preparing for the O. J. civil trial. I hoped this next salacious celebrity courtroom drama would garner strong ratings and guarantee the future of *Inside America's Courts.*

I also hoped I could finally prove to Brill that I was a loyal member of his team, someone to be valued, not scorned, and prove to our partners at New Line that I had once again "made it good."

O. J. had already been found not guilty of the murder of Nicole Brown Simpson in the criminal trial, and now, the Brown family wanted another day in court. There would be some notable differences between the two cases, even though the fact pattern presented would be much the same.

Unlike a criminal case, in which the state has the burden to prove its case beyond a reasonable doubt, the plaintiffs—the Brown family and its lawyers—had to prove that Mr. Simpson killed Nicole Brown Simpson and Ronald Goldman by a preponderance of the evidence.

In other words, nine of twelve jurors had to agree that it was more likely than not that O. J. Simpson committed the double homicide.

Opening statements in the Simpson trial didn't begin until the third week of October. This was fine with me because we were approaching the crucial November sweeps ratings period, and I was convinced the trial coverage would boost our viewership.

In the criminal case, Johnnie Cochran had made much of the allegations that the LA police detectives were racists and out to get O. J., who was a renowned sports and entertainment star. In the civil matter, very little was presented about race because the judge had ruled that such allegations were inflammatory and speculative in this case.

Each day, the O. J. case was our lead story. Having that ready-made content to start the show made things much easier. We still had to pick the best testimony and provide our incisive analysis, and we still had to fill out the day's episode with other ongoing trials and archival material.

With his Fifth Amendment right not to self-incriminate, O. J. had never testified in the criminal case. He had no such option in this case. On November 22, O. J. Simpson took the stand.

The accusations were clear, grisly, and grim.

> DANIEL M. PETROCELLI (lead lawyer for the plaintiffs): "You had gloves; you had a hat; you were wearing a dark sweat outfit, and you had a knife. And you went to Nicole Brown's condominium at 875 South Bundy, did you not, sir?
>
> O. J. SIMPSON: "That's absolutely not true."
>
> PETROCELLI: "And you confronted Nicole Brown Simpson and you killed her, didn't you?"
>
> SIMPSON: "That is absolutely not true."

A little further in the cross-examination, Petrocelli kept pressing.

> PETROCELLI: "How many times did you strike Nicole?"
>
> SIMPSON: "Never."

PETROCELLI: "How many times did you slap Nicole?"

SIMPSON: "Never."

PETROCELLI: "How many times did you kick her?"

SIMPSON: "Never."

PETROCELLI: "How many times did you beat her, sir?"

SIMPSON: "Never."

PETROCELLI: "And if Nicole said you hit her, she'd be lying, is that true?"

After an objection to this and a similar question, Petrocelli asked:

"You are aware that Nicole has told others that you hit her?"

SIMPSON: "Yes."[*]

The country was transfixed hearing O. J. speak for the first time in the courtroom.

At Simpson's criminal trial, prosecutors listed sixty-two incidents of alleged domestic abuse.[†] Not long before she died, Nicole Brown Simpson called a domestic violence shelter to express fear that Simpson was stalking her.

I hoped for a huge spike in our ratings, but the dispiriting reality was that

---

* "O.J. Simpson Civil Trial Testimony, November 22, 1996," *Jack Walraven's Simpson Trial Transcripts*, http://walraven.org/simpson/nov22-96.html.

† Robert D. McFadden, "O.J. Simpson, Athlete Whose Trial for Ex-Wife's Killing Entranced the Nation, Dies at 76," *Salt Lake Tribune*, April 11, 2024, https://www.sltrib.com/news/nation-world/2024/04/11/oj-simpson-athlete-whose-trial/.

every news and newsmagazine program in America selected the same clips of the trial, often before we aired them. So the previous day's testimony was old news by the time our show came on.

While breathlessly anticipated and the focus of conversation coast to coast, pundits felt O. J.'s performance on the stand, like many of his acting roles, was stiff and rehearsed. He denied any role in the killings but couldn't explain why much of the physical evidence seemed to point to his culpability. The trial was still going as the year was coming to an end.

Mercifully enough, the holidays were upon us. Elise and I were celebrating one year together. We had made it despite everything.

On January 16, 1997, both sides in the O. J. Simpson civil trial rested after 101 witnesses and forty-one days of testimony.

In the meantime, Elise had given up hope that Faye and the aggrieved other parties on the staff would ever show her any civility, compassion, or fairness. HR reached out to her to explore other opportunities within the network. The corporate stance was that Elise and I couldn't continue working together.

Cynthia Brill finally offered Elise a transfer.

What had begun as a romance filled with passion and promise was now mired in acrimony, mistrust, and self-interest.

It was an agonizing decision, but Elise finally accepted a transfer to another associate producer role within Court TV. I was relieved and hoped the pall hanging over our production office and our relationship would be lifted.

Nope.

Elise and I spent more time fighting, worrying, and blaming one another. Her career at Court TV was over, and we both knew it.

Instead of reminding each other about what life could be, we now reminded each other of what life had become. Elise spent more time out with her friends. I spent more time at work or in her apartment waiting for her to return.

She was now actively looking for work and couldn't wait to get away from the people who had turned on her in such an ugly and unnecessary way.

On February 4, the jury determined that Simpson was responsible for the killing of Nicole Brown Simpson and Ronald L. Goldman. He was ordered to pay $25 million in punitive damages to the families of both victims. O. J. wasn't even in court when the decision was rendered. I was hoping he would show because we were right at the start of February sweeps, and if, after hearing the jury's decision, he'd prostrated himself on the ground or attacked the jurors with a knife, that would've been good for ratings.

The very next day, another verdict was announced.

Erik Sorenson, who ran Court TV's news operation at the time and went on to run MSNBC, called a team meeting. I looked around the room at my colleagues and friends who'd helped me create this show and, over the last four years, had worked tirelessly to get it right, get it on, and "make it good." I couldn't help but eye Faye and the still unidentified group of women who'd sullied the entire experience.

Perhaps they were eyeing me with similar disdain.

Erik was six foot two, genial, almost always smiling, and had a way of making any news sound favorable. He said, "Hey, guys, you've all done such a great job with this show, but New Line has informed me that the show has been canceled."

In my line of work, the c-word is about as vulgar as it gets.

A stunned silence is all I recall, and people looking at one another in shock. I'd not been afforded the courtesy of advance notice.

"I'll be talking with Andy about further details," Erik added.

"Despite the show being canceled, it'll continue in production through May sweeps and then be in reruns through the summer to fulfill the contractual obligations. I know this is bad news, but hey, think about it this way. You aren't O. J. Simpson."

Erik was smiling as he left the room.

To this day, I don't know why the show was canceled.

"Brill is such a prick," I remember David Spiegelman, Bob Friedman's number two at New Line, repeatedly saying to me during the series. Maybe New Line didn't want to stay in partnership with Brill. Or perhaps it was a simple equation that we couldn't make a profit on the show with the ratings we were garnering.

Regardless, it was over. My dream had been realized, only to end in rejection. I commiserated with my senior team—that is, with the ones that weren't attempting to destroy my life. We went back to work. It's all we had known for such a long time. We had a show to get on the air. It's a fact of life I've seen play out quite a bit as I've gotten older: When you get tragic news, you return to the life you know.

And I went back to Elise.

"I'm glad the show got canceled." She was spiteful and resentful. "I have a second interview at *Inside Edition* tomorrow; maybe they'll offer me a job. I can't wait to get out of Court TV. The place is a horror show."

I didn't know what my future held. Brill said we'd talk in the weeks ahead. I was in a daze. I decided to do some things I hadn't had time for when the show's future was still in the balance. I scheduled knee surgery for a longstanding cartilage injury from years of playing basketball. Elise accepted that production job with *Inside Edition* one week before my surgery, but we didn't go out to raise a glass. I wasn't in a celebratory mood. Instead, Elise celebrated with her younger sister.

I loved Elise deeply despite all we had been through. My career was in shambles, but I had her, and now that we no longer worked together I looked forward to a simpler, more loving, and caring life together.

I was certain she felt the same way.

I had the knee surgery. It was outpatient, but when I got home to Weehawken, my knee hurt like hell. I'd met my closest friend Jill working during the Morton Downey years. She lived nearby and went to the pharmacy to get my pain pills. I took them and quickly fell asleep.

I woke up in pain sometime after eleven o'clock. Elise had promised to come over from the city to help me convalesce for the next couple of days, given that I wasn't ambulatory. I hadn't heard from her. I assumed she'd tried to reach me, and I was so out of it I hadn't heard the phone.

The phone rang not ten minutes after I awoke.

"Hi," she said, without her usual contagious exuberance.

"Hi, where are you?" I responded with a groan as I tried to adjust my aching leg in bed. "When are you coming by? I'm in a lot of pain."

"Andy, I'm not coming. I'm breaking up with you."

"Elise, what are you talking about? Please don't do this. Let's talk it over."

"I'm sorry, Andy. I'm done."

I'm not sure which lasted longer: Erik Sorenson's speech officially canceling my show or Elise's phone call canceling my life and our future together.

I was blindsided. Damn fool.

With my heart now aching much more than my knee, I lay on the couch crying, unable to sit up or get up. At thirty-six, for the first time in my life, I was experiencing what it is to grieve deeply. I was alone. But I had to sit up and get up, if for no other reason than to use the bathroom. So I swung my throbbing knee over the couch and put a bit of pressure on it. The pain seared to my brain. I swung my left leg over and pulled myself up using the arm of the sofa. I hobbled to the bathroom, crying in pain and sorrow.

For weeks and months afterward, I would wake from a restless sleep and feel my heart sink as reality washed over me. Sleep was the only oasis amid my all-consuming despondency.

CHAPTER 30

THERE'S FUCK YOU MONEY, AND THEN THERE'S FUCK YOU, KRISTIN, MONEY

It became increasingly clear that my career was ending at Court TV. Steve Brill's days at Court TV ended sooner than mine. Time Warner bought him out. He called me into his office to let me know he was leaving.

"Andrew, do you know what fuck-you money is? I have enough money now that I can say 'fuck you' to anybody I want."

I wasn't sure if that warranted hearty congratulations. So I decided to go with the obvious.

"Steve, from what I've seen, you've been doing that for years."

He snickered at that pleasing thought.

"Andrew, you did a great job. You'll find employment. I hope we work together again."

That was the first and only time Mr. Brill ever complimented me in all the years I worked for him.

Years later, I was told that a few months after my departure from Court TV, the HR department established what was somewhat derisively and informally known as "The Andy Regal Rules," which clearly and for the first time spelled out Court TV's protocols for dating in the workplace.

While I was accused of turning Court TV into a soap opera, Mr. Brill was pretty good at creating drama and conflict himself. Steve wasn't the only one soon heading for the door. Since the Judge Ito debacle, Kristin had been looking for and thinking about moving on. And she'd been contributing expert legal analysis on a more regular basis to CBS News, while still in Brill's employ.

Kristin had confided in me that the execs at CBS News were talking to her about joining them full-time. The deal would include legal analysis, co-anchoring the *CBS Morning News,* and frequently joining Dan Rather on the set of *CBS Evening News* to discuss headline-making courtroom stories.

It was a massive opportunity for Kristin to get to the big leagues and a huge uplift from the relative obscurity of day-to-day life at Court TV. She told me that the CBS reps would reach out to Brill any day now to ask that he simply release her a bit early from her contract so that she could join CBS News.

Kristin said the network lawyers didn't anticipate any problem getting her out of her Court TV deal.

CBS was not accustomed to dealing with Steve Brill.

"Brill is going to go absolutely nuts when he hears they've offered me a job," Kristin said gleefully. "If Brill tries to sabotage this deal for me, I'll kill him. And don't you tell anyone about this, Andy, or I'll kill you, and I mean it."

Kristin and I had been keeping confidences for years, even after our relationship ended.

"Kristin," I said, "I only want what's best for you."

While Kristin would never give me credit, I felt I'd done quite a bit in recognizing and developing her talent. I also felt this move vindicated my choice to have her anchor *Inside America's Courts*. I knew she had it, and now the top people in network news were saying the same.

All of this was happening despite her outsized ego, her outbursts, and her frequent castigation of me and everyone around her.

Kristin kept me in the loop on the conversations between Brill and CBS.

"He's apparently trying to get money out of them instead of being gracious. It's so funny, the CBS rep said to me, 'Brill is a complete asshole.'"

That was the last I heard about the negotiations until I received a company-wide email from Mr. Brill announcing Kristin's departure after her many years of service.

Steve announced to the staff that Kristin was leaving to join CBS.

His email was leaked to the *New York Post* and reported in other industry news sources:

> Kristin Jeannette-Meyers won't be the only one cashing in from this deal. I have decided to share some of the wealth with those at Court TV. CBS will pay us $25,000 to obtain Meyers' early release from her contract. I will be using these funds to compensate twenty of her former colleagues to compensate them for "pain and suffering" for having to work with the "temperamental" Meyers.*

It was cruel and vindictive. Despite Kristin's obstinate nature, she had given years to Brill and his venture.

If I'd made that list, I never would have accepted a penny.

Kristin called me from her apartment. She was bereft. It should've been one of the happiest days of her life. And once again, this was somehow my fault. As I listened to Kristin haranguing Brill, Court TV, and me, I couldn't help but wonder how this might prejudice people at CBS, who now would be wondering if they'd done the necessary due diligence.

When I saw Kristin sitting next to Dan Rather on the set of the *CBS Evening News*, I couldn't have been prouder.

One of the great loves of my life, Kristin Jeannette-Meyers, died in Los Angeles at the age of fifty-seven. The 2024 *Los Angeles Times* story, "A Rising Star at Celebrity Trials Like O. J. Simpson's. Then a Quiet, Mysterious Death," reported on her demise.

---

* John Carmody, "The TV Column," *Washington Post*, May 31, 1996, https://www.washingtonpost.com/archive/lifestyle/1996/05/31/the-tv-column/1a9978cc-6f31-4469-a89b-87f596fc4aa2/.

> "We felt like we were at the center of the universe," recalled ABC's chief legal affairs correspondent, Dan Abrams, a Court TV colleague who worked side-by-side with Jeannette-Meyers during the former NFL star's murder prosecution. By its stunning conclusion, he said, she was "a star. She was borderline a household name."
>
> Then, within a few years, Jeannette-Meyers vanished from the airwaves and the lives of broadcasting colleagues who had marveled at her work ethic and ambition.
>
> Last summer, she was found dead in Larchmont Village. A coroner's investigator who arrived in June at a dilapidated Spanish villa behind a high hedge and in view of the Hollywood sign noted the decomposed state of her remains and wrote, "It is unknown the last time the decedent was known to be alive."
>
> ". . . There appeared to be few good things in Jeannette-Meyers' life. She had a history of bipolar disorder, according to the coroner's report, and was seeking medication from multiple doctors. A Burbank osteopath who treats addicts prescribed buprenorphine, an opioid that diminishes drug cravings and withdrawal, according to an inventory of medications. Another doctor prescribed Xanax, antidepressants and a panic disorder drug. She had other pills for major depressive disorder, nausea and ADHD."*

Kristin Jeannette-Meyers's once bright light has gone dark.

---

* Harriet Ryan, "A Rising Star at Celebrity Trials Like O. J. Simpson's. Then a Quiet, Mysterious Death," *Los Angeles Times*, January 12, 2024, https://www.latimes.com/california/story/2024-01-12/for-a-journalist-who-rose-to-fame-covering-high-profile-trials-a-quiet-mysterious-death.

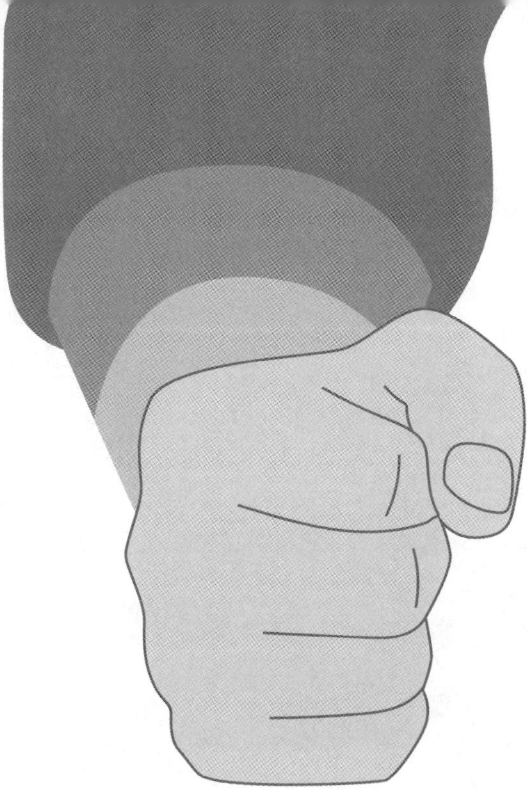

SECTION 4

BULLIES AND BOOSTERS

Your values are the soul of your leadership, and they drive your behavior.

—JOHN C. MAXWELL, PASTOR, BESTSELLING AUTHOR OF *THE 5 LEVELS OF LEADERSHIP*

CHAPTER 31

A GOODBYE, A HELLO AGAIN, AND A FAREWELL FOREVER

I often fantasized that when I finally left Court TV for a big network job, they would name a studio after me for "lifetime achievement" or some such thing.

"The Andrew Lloyd Regal Studio" sounded about right.

Instead, on a June day in 1996, a few short months after the show was canceled, around eleven thirty in the morning, I made it look like I was heading out to an early lunch, but I was quietly and forever leaving Court TV. I had no show, and they had no job for me. There was no pomp and circumstance. I wondered if Faye and her coconspirators were having a party or a hearty, vengeful laugh. They'd won. Elise and I were broken up, and I'd lost my job.

I walked briskly through the newsroom, took one look back, and that was it. For eight years, this had been my workplace and my life. Now, it was a memory. My memory. I knew I'd be pretty much forgotten by the time the elevator reached the lobby.

However, I had learned a valuable lesson that I've followed diligently in every job since I was asked politely but directly to "get out": Never, ever decorate my office with personal artifacts. Never. Ever. No artwork on the walls. No family pictures. No pithy, inspiring aphorisms. No personal coffee mugs. When they ask me to leave, I want, no, I *need*, to be ready to go. I don't want to have a walk of shame carrying boxes as everyone smirks and points at the dead man walking. Nope. I keep my head high and my arms unencumbered.

I headed onto Third Avenue and Thirty-Ninth Street, longing to hear Elise's voice. That desire only happened one hundred times a day now, down from one thousand times a day during the weeks and months after she dumped me.

The Court TV bullies were no longer in my presence, but they still leased space in my head, a miserable place to be.

When I was out walking in Manhattan, I spent most of my time scanning the stream of people coming at me like a quarterback scanning the blitzing defense. I would be mortified to see a former colleague from Court TV, and most of all, I dreaded running into Elise. If I did cross paths with her, I knew she'd be holding hands in sublime happiness with some guy who was taller, more handsome, and, unlike me, employed. A finance bro seemed about right.

And then . . .

It had to be two in the morning. I was dead asleep when my phone was ringing. At least, I thought it was. I was pretty sure it was. These things don't happen to me, and I knew this particular call could never happen. So maybe it wasn't. Regardless, I picked it up in a stupor, unaware of what I was doing or whether I was awake or still dreaming.

"Hi, Ganachey."

I hadn't heard that sweet voice or that loving nickname in a year and a half. I was certain I was having a cruel dream because only one person could be on the other end of the line.

"You have no idea how much I've missed you, Elise."

I was likely slurring my words.

"I can't talk long," she said, and now, as my head cleared a bit, I noticed she was talking in a hushed tone, almost whispering. "I just wanted to hear your voice. Are you doing okay?"

"No, not really. Can I see you?"

"No, that's not a good idea. I really can't."

"Can I call you tomorrow?" I pleaded.

I could tell I was starting to lose her already. I was afraid my dream was coming to an end.

"No, I'll call you sometime. Don't call me." She hung up. My arm, with my phone to my ear, went limp. I started to laugh hysterically, and then I started to cry uncontrollably.

Maybe it was a dream.

It wasn't unusual for me to experience heart-wrenching dreams, especially during traumatic and stressful periods in my life. Years later, after my mom passed, I'd have the most vivid dreams of being in her presence, and we'd be having a really lovely time together. As the dream progressed, it would become increasingly clear that my mom shouldn't be there. She couldn't stay. She's dead. And I would wake up weeping as if I were at her funeral.

I was so happy that at least Elise hadn't forgotten me altogether. Finally, I could wait no longer. I called her.

"I told you not to call me."

Elise wasn't angry; she was apprehensive. "I'll call you when I can, I promise."

She called me back a few days later, saying she had only a few minutes to talk. I asked her to meet me somewhere since it was so hard to talk on the phone. She hesitated, then agreed to meet at my house in Weehawken. It must've felt like a safe place for her. I wasn't awake from my dream just yet. It was going to happen. I was going to see Elise and win her back.

The anticipation of her arrival was both excruciating and thrilling.

One week later, she glided through my door like an apparition. We hugged. I'd planned a romantic picnic lunch overlooking the city at a park a few miles from my house. It was a beautiful day.

I didn't ask her about the apparent subterfuge or if she was seeing anyone. I didn't want to know. What mattered to me was that we were together again and should stay together.

We had a glorious time laughing, eating, drinking, and talking superficially about all that transpired in the last eighteen months. I kept looking at her. I couldn't believe I was sitting across from her in this idyllic environment. I didn't share that my heart had been shattered and that it still was. I didn't want to appear desperate and needy.

We returned to my house after a couple hours. The physical attraction and passion were still there.

The sun was going down.

"I have to go," she said dispassionately.

"Elise, I want us to be together. I want to get back together," I said as if repeating myself might make more sense to her and be more convincing. I hadn't broached the subject until that moment.

"Andy, I can't. I just can't."

Elise started gathering her things.

"Well, we're not becoming friends now," I said. "I won't do that."

"I know, I know," she said.

She looked at my front door and then back at me. We kissed one last time. I knew she wouldn't be back once she walked out. I watched as she pulled out of my driveway, down Boulevard East, toward the Lincoln Tunnel.

I never spoke to Elise again. But she gave me a true gift that day. I still have no idea why she chose to share one more day with me. But I was over the grieving and the heartbreak. I knew she loved me, hadn't forgotten me, and I accepted that she didn't want to share the rest of her life with me.

I was ready and able to move on.

CHAPTER 32

NOT-SO-GREAT STUFF

I subscribe to the notion that when one door closes, another one can slam in your face even harder. For months, I sent out résumés, had "informational" interviews, job interviews, coffee conversations, and worthless conversations.

Then, I heard that CNBC was beginning a new slate of prime-time shows.

I decided to pursue a job there. I liked CNBC and became interested in its daytime investing programming. Their new ideas for prime time made quite a bit of sense.

I was scheduled to meet with Bob Reichblum, the new executive producer of prime time at CNBC. Bob had an impressive résumé. He'd been an executive producer at local stations in New York and Detroit and a news director in DC and Miami, and most recently, he'd served as the executive producer for *Good Morning America* from 1993 to 1996. This was a guy I could learn from and respect.

I feared my enemies at Court TV would learn that I was pursuing this job and sabotage it. After exiting Court TV, and any time I looked for work thereafter, I'd be on job interviews, and invariably, as the interviewers inspected my résumé, they would exclaim, "Oh, you must know so-and-so." At times, it was someone who liked me and respected me—other times, not so much.

Whenever this happened, I could feel myself pale as I awaited the name.

If it was a likely detractor, I went home worried sick that my interviewer would contact that person.

And when I didn't get the job, I assumed they had.

"The bullying doesn't end when they get rid of the target. Now, the target has to worry about what the bullies are saying about the target externally," said Maureen Duffy, psychologist, and coauthor of *Overcoming Mobbing: A Recovery Guide for Workplace Aggression and Bullying*, in an interview with me.

Maureen described my exact experience. "The now-former bully boss might speak negatively to prospective employers. Even if that hasn't happened yet, when the target is looking for work again, she has to worry that the bully might do so. The bully remains omnipresent."

Bob Reichblum walked casually toward me. I braced myself for a big-city network bully of a boss. But he welcomed me with the widest, friendliest smile and an outstretched hand. Immediately, he felt like a human lifeline. He was a nonthreatening guy. Bald at the top of his head with thinning hair on the sides, Bob was trim and wore a standard blue suit and a striped shirt with no tie. That was his daily uniform.

I was put at ease immediately. I couldn't help but think how different it would be to work for Bob than it had been working for Steve Brill for six years. He felt like a big brother. The kind of guy who looked out for you when you needed it instead of threatening you and your friends with a beatdown.

I hoped this wasn't an act on Bob's part.

This reminds me of a story about a deceased person interviewing for a job in the afterlife. Champagne and caviar are flowing, and everyone is fashionably dressed, attractive, euphoric, and gushing with praise about the work environment and the opportunities for advancement. It seems like heaven, but surprisingly, it's hell.

Well, the candidate also has a chance to visit heaven. And that's pretty good too. Employees are lounging about lazily, floating on clouds while staffers sing the boss's praises and play the harp. So, now the job candidate must decide where to spend eternity. Two good choices. She decides hell was a little more enjoyable. So she asks to go back there.

The elevator heads down, and when it opens, she is surrounded by a desolate wasteland, replete with dumpster fires, garbage strewn about, and filth everywhere. Disagreeable people in rags are walking by like zombies.

The bully bosses are screaming at the employees.

"I don't understand," says the bewildered interviewee. "The other day, I was here, and there was a country club and a golf course, and we ate to our hearts' content. Everyone was joyous. The bosses were so caring. Everyone here is miserable?"

"Oh yes," says Satan's HR rep. "Yesterday, we were recruiting you. Now you're staff."

I hoped that Bob wasn't the devil.

I wanted to hug him on the way out. He'd listened to me, valued my experience, and appreciated my insights on how I would EP the show.

Three days later, Bob called to offer me the job. He seemed as eager to provide me with the role as I was to accept it.

Two weeks later, I was in Fort Lee, New Jersey, for my first day as executive producer of *Great Stuff* on CNBC prime time.

"Regs! How's your first week at the new gig? I think this is going to be a great opportunity for you."

It was my agent, Adam.

"Thanks so much for checking in, Adam. I like it here so far. Reichblum is a great guy. Everyone is friendly, and I think the show will be fun and different. It feels great to be back at it. And if they like this show, maybe they'll let me develop other prime-time programming."

Well, that door was open for just a moment before my foot got slammed as it shut.

Great Stuff, the show I created and executive produced for CNBC about people spending on lavish and outrageous items, lasted about six months. My kindhearted boss Bob Reichblum was let go shortly thereafter. It turned out that the "serious" business executives who controlled the daytime programming decided they didn't like the entertainment-style strategy that CNBC prime-time programmers had undertaken. They pretty much got rid of the entire prime-time staff they'd hired in the past year and brought in Geraldo and his team to do a nightly show on the Bill Clinton sex scandal.

It was a dreary time to be back home in Weehawken and out of work again.

The weather taunted me with its soft early-fall breeze and blue skies; with my bleak demeanor I couldn't enjoy anything.

My only respite was a little oasis across the street from my house—the little postage stamp of a park. Just a bit of grass with room for some people to sit and others to stroll along and take in the grandeur of New York City—from the World Trade Center towers up to and beyond the George Washington Bridge. All the promises that America had to offer and all the power of human imagination and execution were in one magnificent panorama of land and sea. Sitting there, I felt a hint of optimism and the hope that I might have a future here in New York. I was fortunate that life had led me to this special place. People came from around the globe for a quick day trip to Weehawken to gaze back across the Hudson River to New York City and get a grand perspective of the magnificent physical world in front of them.

I was trying to get perspective on my life and circumstances. I looked at the city, now washed in light and dark browns and shades of red as the sun set. I abruptly stood up and turned to head back to my apartment, feeling relief from the ever-present tension in my chest. It occurred to me, albeit fleetingly, that maybe I was right where I should be and I wasn't a total failure.

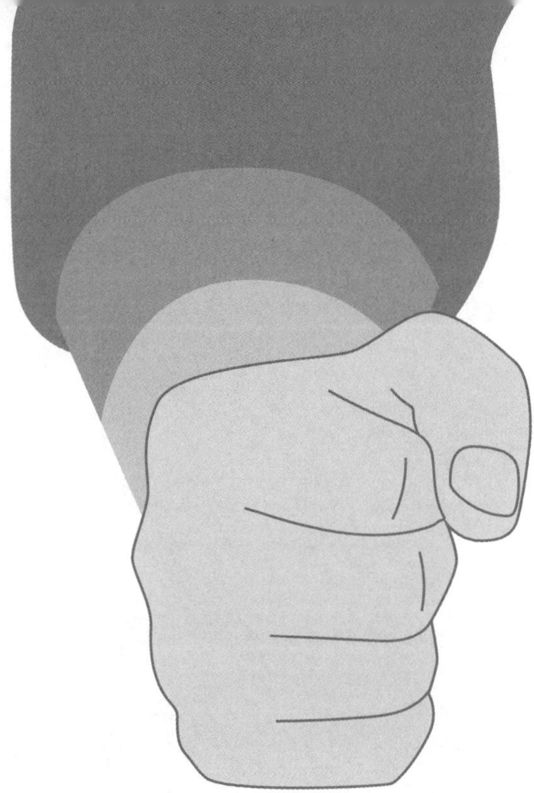

SECTION 5

YOU CAN GO HOME AGAIN . . . IF THE BULLY HAS MOVED OUT

The challenge of leadership is to be strong, but not rude; be kind, but not weak; be bold, but not bully; be thoughtful, but not lazy; be humble, but not timid; be proud, but not arrogant; have humor, but without folly.

—JIM ROHN, ENTREPRENEUR, AUTHOR, AND MOTIVATIONAL SPEAKER

CHAPTER 33

EITHER THE TOUGHEST OR SECOND-TOUGHEST SHERIFF IN AMERICA

Throughout my life, I worried about . . . everything. It's called *catastrophic thinking*, ruminating over irrational and worst-case outcomes.

"Getting attached to outcomes that we have little control over can easily set us up for a life of suffering," Dr. Leah Katz told me. "If we can recognize our urge to put too much stock in the outcome, make space for uncertainty and change, and connect to ourselves in all the moments, we set ourselves up for a lighter life."

It was now 1999. I'd been gone from Court TV for two years.

"Andy, would you consider coming back to Court TV?" I was meeting with Sheilagh McGee, who'd worked for me as a senior producer overseeing documentaries at the network and since my departure had quickly risen to a top programming role. She was one of my absolute favorite people—a terrific video journalist and storyteller. We were good friends.

"I need someone to oversee our show with Nancy Grace, and we're developing a new show with Johnnie Cochran. You'd be perfect, and I'd have you develop other programming too. Your title would be vice president of original programming."

I was going back home. Brill was gone, and I was going to work for someone

I respected and adored. Plus, I knew Nancy Grace well and was eager to work with her. The idea of developing and executive producing a nightly show with Johnnie Cochran following his brilliant defense of O. J. thrilled me. Cochran was controversial and reviled by many. I couldn't wait to get to know the brilliant attorney who wore those beautifully tailored suits.

I accepted Sheilagh's offer on the spot and hugged my new boss.

As we embraced I thought to myself, *This time will be different*.

I remember coming back into the building that first day. I stood in the lobby for a couple of minutes just taking it in. It was surreal. Not bizarre; more unreal. I was getting another chance at the place where I'd done my best work, but this time under better circumstances.

I was welcomed on my first day. It felt good. Most of the people who'd engineered my dismissal were no longer there. I quickly took responsibility for Nancy Grace's nightly show, *Closing Arguments*, looking at the day's courtroom and justice headlines. Nancy had made her name as a firebrand prosecutor and victims' rights advocate in Atlanta before becoming a commentator first at Court TV and then on CNN's sister station, Headline News.

Nancy's fiancé was murdered when she was nineteen, which motivated her to enroll in law school and to care deeply about victims of violent crime.

I loved working with Nancy. She was funny and high energy, and had a very playful, sarcastic way about her. You had to be ready for every interaction with her, whether talking about that night's show, something in the news, or someone at Court TV.

Nancy *loved* to gossip.

But when she was in the studio, and the light went on, she was keenly focused and ready to perform. And perform she did. She was terrific on the air.

Henry Schleiff replaced Brill as CEO of Court TV, and he couldn't have been more different. While Brill used intimidation to drive his success as an entrepreneur, Henry Schleiff used humor. He made people laugh. He could've made a living as a Catskills comic.

Schleiff looked the part of a programming executive—fifty years old with salt-and-pepper hair, expensive, conservative suits, and an angular face. He was fun to be around. And, of course, his business acumen in the cable television world was well-established and well-known.

Henry had been successful everywhere he'd been. Before joining Court TV, he had served as executive vice president at Studios USA, an executive at Viacom International, senior vice president at HBO, and head of HBO Enterprises.

Schleiff wanted to create an entire slate of crime and justice programming. I was in heaven.

There was just one thing: Henry didn't exactly share my appreciation for Nancy's idiosyncrasies.

"Andy, you have to fire her," Henry would say, rolling his eyes and shaking his head. "She just goes on the air and says whatever comes into her head."

"Henry, just let me work with Nancy. She comes to play every day. She's great for the network."

As was Johnnie Cochran.

Johnnie was one of the kindest, gentlest, and most understanding people I've ever worked with. While Steve Brill was an equal-opportunity bully, Johnnie Cochran was an equal-opportunity gentleman. Instead of using his power and influence to rage at people with impunity, Cochran knew that since he had power and prestige, he could be nice to people and still get what he wanted. He was cordial and pleasant to everyone who came into his sphere. From intern to mogul, Johnnie displayed warmth and interest to anyone who wanted to say hello and shake his hand. In all the time we worked together, I saw him angry only once.

I was standing in our newsroom, and Johnnie was strolling toward me. Johnnie would arrive at our office early afternoon for his evening show. I always looked forward to seeing him. We all did. On that day, he was walking with more purpose. I noticed he didn't stop to talk to team members, as was his custom.

"Andy, can I talk to you?"

We moved to a quiet corner.

"Listen, Andy, I've spoken to Henry a couple times about his idea to rename my show *The Devil's Advocate*. I keep telling him I don't represent devils. And he doesn't listen. He keeps bringing it up repeatedly, trying to sell me on the idea. It's an insult to me, my clients, and defendants. I will quit before I host a show called *The Devil's Advocate*."

Henry eventually got the message. He dropped the idea. He also never forced me to fire Nancy.

While sitting in my office watching our network one day, I saw a man in his fifties being interviewed. From his uniform and badge I knew he was a law enforcement officer. He spoke with bravura. He was cocksure. He was a TV natural. He was a lightning rod. He jumped through the screen.

"I am the toughest sheriff in America," North Carolina's Gerald Hege told me later. "In my county, the sheriffs have traditionally worn regular business clothes—no more. My deputies wear fatigues and combat boots. We're in a war down here in Davidson County, and I know what war is like. I'm a proud Vietnam veteran."

Sheriff Hege went on to describe his disciplinary initiatives.

"I took out all the televisions and the books, other than the Bible, and all the girlie magazines, and I had the inmates paint the entire jail pink with blue teary-eyed teddy bears as a constant reminder that their macho instincts have no place in my jail. Let's say I changed the look and feel of my jail and my prisoners. My misdemeanor inmates wear blue jumpsuits, the sex offenders wear green, and the felons get bright orange."

I ran down to Sheilagh's office after the program.

"I just saw this amazing sheriff on our air. I don't know what we could do with him, but I'd like to ask him if he might have some thoughts about programming we could develop together."

"I caught the last part of the interview," Sheilagh said. "Did I hear right? He calls himself the toughest sheriff in America? Sure, go ahead. Give him a call and see what he says."

I called him ten minutes later.

"May I speak to Sheriff Hege, please?"

"Let me see if he's in. May I say who's calling?"

"This is Andy Regal. I'm VP of original programming at Court TV in New York."

A few moments later, Hege came on the line.

"This is Sheriff Gerald Hege."

"Sheriff, this is Andy Regal from Court TV in New York."

"You ain't some liberal Yankee, are you, Mr. Regal? I don't like liberals."

"Well, Sheriff, I don't like bad television. I just finished watching you on Court TV, and you, Sheriff, are very good. I like people who are good on TV."

"Mighty nice of you, son. I don't know nothin' 'bout TV, but I know what this country needs, and I certainly know what my county and its prisoners need."

"Well, that's what I wanted to talk to you about, sir. About the possibility of having you on our air more often and perhaps even discussing ideas for a show featuring you."

"Well, I'm pretty busy running my jail and disciplining my inmates," he said. "You like barbecue, son? We got the best North Carolina barbecue here in Davidson County. We got the best barbecue anywhere. If you're serious, come on down from that ivory tower of yours in New York, and I'll show you around."

Two weeks later, I was landing at Charlotte Douglas International Airport. The drive to the Davidson County jail would take about an hour. I'd never been to North Carolina, and the ride was scenic and pleasant. It was primarily woodsy roads lined with middle-class and lower-middle-class homes.

This was rural North Carolina. The towns had a church every few blocks. Furniture makers and furniture stores dotted the landscape. This part of the country is known for its wood furniture, and it takes great pride in it.

I couldn't help noticing how many eateries had signs proudly proclaiming "Best Barbecue in All of North Carolina."

Sheriff Hege had offered to give me a tour of the jail and take me to lunch once I arrived. I pulled into the parking lot. The correctional facility was a typical low-slung government-style drab building. Despite the dull facade, I knew the place was filled with human drama and tragedy, missed opportunities, bad decisions, and lost souls. I wondered if I'd have a chance to hear those stories and maybe even give the inmates a voice.

I had great anticipation about going behind closed doors and behind bars.

I sat in the waiting area for about ten minutes before one of Sheriff Hege's deputies brought me back into his office.

"How ya doin', Andy?" Sheriff Hege said. "Welcome to Davidson County, North Carolina. This place used to be known first and foremost for barbecue. But now it's known for Hege."

The sheriff was handsome and slightly overweight, likely from all that delicious barbecue. He wasn't fast-moving, but he was physically imposing.

I was now about to witness the complete Hege experience.

First, I noticed all the Hege merchandise on his desk and around the office. He'd created Sheriff Hege posters. One showed the sheriff wielding a shotgun, with the text "Old habits are hard to break." Another showed him brandishing a large stick, with three shotgun-wielding deputies by his side and the text "This ain't Mayberry, and I ain't Andy!" And yet another exclaimed, "Do the crime, scumbag, and you'll do the time." Sheriff Hege was also hawking his own barbecue sauce, Sheriff Hege bobbleheads, and baseball caps.

All kinds of photos adorned his office, with what appeared to be local dignitaries and many high-profile NASCAR drivers. Former driver and now team owner Richard Childress lived nearby in a huge mansion and was a close friend and supporter of the sheriff.

Hege even had permanent TV studio lights in his office for the local and regional reporters who showed up almost daily looking for a story, a few hard-hitting quotes, and surefire ratings. I was thankful the national media hadn't yet arrived on his doorstep.

"Welcome to the Hege Show," he said.

I sat down and took it all in.

"I don't believe in rehabilitation. There's no coddling of criminals. They're mostly scumbags. But I do believe in redemption. I treat every one of my inmates as human beings. We're all flawed. The people here have made terrible mistakes and terrible choices, and they'll pay the consequences. You bet I painted my jail pink to get attention. I want as many people as possible on the outside to say to themselves, *I never want to go there.* I painted this jail pink to embarrass the people in here, so they say, *I never want to go back in there again.*"

I noticed a small model car on his desk with a spider logo. I didn't dare touch it, but I asked about it.

"You're going to get a rare treat, son. We'll take a little ride in my car in just a bit on our way to lunch."

He stood up and came around the desk, all six feet two inches of Southern sheriff. I noticed his military-style boots. They were part of the sheriff's mandatory department uniform—and a key aspect of his mystique.

"Let's take a walk."

At the end of a short hallway, we got buzzed into the secure part of the jail. My senses were immediately assaulted by body odor, ammonia, and just plain humid, stale, acrid air. It must have been eighty-five degrees. No airflow. The air was heavy, muggy, and damp, with no place to go, much like the inmates.

We walked through the all-male section and passed inmates who, at that moment, were out of their cells. They greeted the sheriff with a level of respect and, in some cases, even cordiality bordering on admiration.

"Hey, Sheriff! How ya doin'?" said one inmate who passed us.

"Make sure you get your work done, Jimmy," Sheriff Hege replied.

"Morning, Sheriff," said another while mopping the floor.

"Looks good," Hege said, casually inspecting the floor.

"Thanks, Sheriff." The inmate appeared to be gratified by the compliment.

Other inmates were in their cells, reading or writing or playing cards. I tried not to stare as they peered out. I felt guilty about being on the outside looking in. I couldn't begin to imagine how they felt watching me watching them.

I didn't detect fear or loathing in this diverse group of inmates. It was the opposite. They seemed happy to see Hege. I wondered if they were experiencing Stockholm syndrome. I even thought I detected a paternal aspect to the relationships.

"The people in here have been invisible most of their lives. Their parents, if they even had parents, ignored 'em or abused 'em," the sheriff explained. "I look each and every one of them in the eye. I talk to them. They may hate the way I run my jail, they may even hate me, but I may be one of the only people in their lives to treat them like human beings. Now, that does mean punishing them, in my case, for what they've done, but it also means giving them a sense of dignity while they're in here.

"Look, we have inmates here who've committed almost every kind of crime: bad checks, assault with a deadly weapon, crack use, selling crack, selling their bodies, all manner of sex crimes, breaking and entering, domestic violence, manslaughter, murder, drunk driving—the list goes on and on. They all come through here."

We were finally buzzed back out. I took a deep breath as the cool, fresh air from the outside world came rushing toward me. As my head cleared, I knew exactly the show I wanted to develop with Sheriff Hege. If I could just figure out how to get this done, I knew it would be unique in the marketplace.

"Let's take a drive," Sheriff Hege suggested with a wry smile. We headed out to the parking lot, and there it was, "The Spider Car."

As we walked toward the menacing black Impala SS, he ran through the firepower he had on his person and in the car. We headed out.

"I think we'll take the scenic route instead of the main roads."

We were a couple miles from the jail when he started opening up the engine. Sheriff Hege looked over and smiled. We took off with a roar. I peeked over at the odometer as I held on for dear life. We were going over one hundred miles per hour.

As previously advertised, we were going to the sheriff's favorite local barbecue joint, a spacious wood-paneled restaurant with shiny, white-and-red checkered tablecloths and hard plastic matching chairs. The place was bustling. Shouts of "Hey, Sheriff" rang out from all corners.

We sat down toward the back, and a smiling server handed us plastic menus. Sweet tea, of course, was the drink of choice. I was ready to pitch.

"Sheriff, I want to produce the first-ever ongoing series originating from a jail. I want you to be the host. And you'll interview the inmates with the most compelling and dramatic life stories. All the other inmates will make up the studio audience. You'd host your own talk show in your own jail."

I couldn't see how he could say no.

I waited for his response. Sheriff Hege looked at me for a moment. He smiled.

"I seen those other guys like Geraldo do that job. I could do better. Let me think about it."

After lunch we drove back to the jail, within the speed limit this time.

"I need to figure some things out. And talk to the boss," Sheriff Hege said.

"Sure, of course; take your time, Sheriff. I'll call you in the next few days once I'm back in New York."

I wondered what exactly he had to figure out. From what I saw, Hege had unusual authority and autonomy over his jail and how he ran things. So who was Sheriff Hege's boss? I thought it best not to question the sheriff. I just wanted to let him think about my concept, hoping it played sufficiently to his outsized ego.

This was the best concept I'd conjured up. It was so simple, raw, and real—and with Sheriff Hege hosting the show, you'd never know what would happen next. Even better, he had a great sense of humor.

But Hege wasn't the only one who had things to work out. I did too.

For instance, where specifically in the jail would we shoot the show? And would we be allowed to have the inmates serve as the audience members? Where would we find sufficient space to do all that? It just wouldn't be the same show if Sheriff Hege was talking to a couple of inmates in his office.

I wanted a spectacle.

I couldn't wait to tell Sheilagh all about my trip.

When I got back to the office, I described the environment in Davidson County and the sheriff's cult of personality.

"That's amazing," Sheilagh said. Her enthusiasm was uplifting.

I spoke with the sheriff again soon after. "I spoke to the boss about this TV show of yours," he said.

"Forgive me, Sheriff, but is the boss you've been referring to the mayor or a police commissioner in the area?"

"The mayor? Hell no, Andy. I'm talking about my wife!"

I smiled to myself and shook my head at my obvious oversight. *Of course he's talking about his wife! Who else could rein this guy in?*

He continued, "She said I can do the show as long as I come home for supper on the nights you're here."

That left the matter of how and where we'd shoot the show.

"Sheriff, I believe your inmates have stories that need to be told, and you're the man who knows these people as well as their own family members. I mean, you live with these people day to day."

Was I laying it on too thick for the sheriff? Not possible. And I also happened to believe what I was saying.

"What will make this show compelling from a visual standpoint is if we can have the inmates in their colored and striped uniforms in the audience.

"How much room do you need, Andy?"

"Well, I don't know if it's possible, but room for you to walk around a bit."

I knew he'd be more imposing on his feet with his combat boots in full view than if he sat behind a desk.

"And with as many inmates in the audience as possible."

"Well, I don't see why we can't do that except for the sex offenders and murderers. I can't let them out. But the rest could all benefit from hearing what I have to say, and I have plenty to say. And they can learn from each other's mistakes. Every person in here has made a lifetime full of mistakes.

"We'll just do it in Cell Block F. That's a big ol' space. We'll have to clear out the entire block and move all the inmates into other cells so your guys can do what y'all need to do with the lights and cameras."

"Sheriff, we'll need a full day to set up."

I wanted him to understand what this was going to take. We'd be moving all the inmates out of their cells, displacing them for two days every time we came to shoot.

I felt ambivalent about doing that and thought this must be some kind of civil rights violation, but I convinced myself that it was Hege's jail. The inmates might indeed get valuable information from this experience and a sorely needed diversion.

Was I exploiting the inmates for entertainment value? Yes. Would I go to hell for this? Maybe. But hopefully, I could win an Emmy first.

"I will need to come a couple days in advance of the taping to interview inmates. We're going to turn your jail into a working television studio."

"I like the sound of that, Andy."

It was happening. The show was coming together, and any concern regarding the well-being of the inmates was pushed into the far recesses of my mind.

I was thrilled by the prospect of shooting in this huge rectangular space, which consisted of two floors of cells, one cell essentially on top of the other, up and down the block, and a wide space in the middle where the inmates often congregated when they were permitted to be out of their cells. This space would be perfect for the audience. We could fit in more than fifty chairs.

I laughed to myself thinking how difficult it was to find audience members to fill up a studio for a live, daily talk show in New York or LA. Audience coordination is one of the most challenging jobs in television. But here we'd have a "captive" audience for our show.

With most of the details worked out, Sheilagh officially green-lighted the program. I felt more confident than ever that this show could be a hit. Sheriff Hege's "tough love"—or is it "tough hate"?—showmanship combined with a rotating cast of maladjusted characters exposing their lives of woe would create a riveting viewing experience. Plus, the set would be filled with inmates in prison garb encircled by jail cells. If you happened to see that scene while channel surfing, you'd have to stop and watch.

I enlisted my friend and colleague Jack Niesi, who'd worked with me on *Inside America's Courts*, to be our director and assemble our production team. In his fifties, Jack was a jolly, kindhearted, Staten Island–born-and-bred Italian with a graying beard and infectious laugh.

We discussed the show and what it would take to get it on the air.

The next thing we had to do was go back down to North Carolina.

I began talking to inmates and gauging their interest and willingness to appear on national television to discuss their crimes. I had to prove my hunch that the prison was full of captivating stories worth unearthing and sharing with millions of viewers.

CHAPTER 34

I'M NOT DEAD YET . . . YET

One of Sheriff Hege's strictest and most inflexible doctrines, which he talked about frequently, was his policy of "no deals." No plea deals and no special treatment for anyone. It didn't matter who you were or who you knew, or how much money you had. You do the crime; you'll pay the price and do the time.

I learned what that really meant on my next trip to Davidson County.

Jack and I flew into Charlotte. We rented a car, and I started driving toward the jail. There was never any traffic once you got out of the airport, and now that I'd made this trip before, I knew what I was doing and where I was going. Jack and I were engrossed in conversation about the show we were developing, about Sheriff Hege, and about Court TV. We'd been driving for a little less than an hour, when suddenly, I heard a brief, staccato siren. I looked into my rearview mirror, and the lights were flashing.

"Oh no," I said. I pulled over onto the gravel shoulder of the highway.

While waiting for the officer to leave his car and approach mine, I noticed it was from Davidson County. We must've crossed over the county line when one of the sheriff's deputies spied me speeding.

I was watching in my sideview mirror as the deputy approached. I'd already been introduced to a few of the deputies, all of whom had been eager to help on the show. I didn't recognize this one, as he looked like all the others in his camouflage fatigues, military-style combat boots, and dark sunglasses.

He peered into our car, looking somewhat suspiciously at Jack and me.

"Do you know you were going seventy-three in a fifty-five-mile-per-hour zone, sir?"

"No, Officer, I really had no idea."

He asked for my license.

"New York, huh?" the officer said, examining the card and nodding in what I took as explicit disapproval. "What's your hurry? Do you have business here in North Carolina?"

It was the moment of truth. I could tell him I was on my way to the sheriff's office because I was the producer of his new television show. But I was concerned that Hege would find out and be furious that I tried to curry favor with his deputy. I couldn't take the chance of angering the sheriff just when we were about to disrupt his life and that of the inmates. We needed the sheriff in the best frame of mind during this trip.

"We just flew in, Officer. We're in the TV production business."

The officer perked up.

"Oh, you oughta do a story on our sheriff. He gets lots of headlines."

"Thanks for the tip," I said, forcing a smile and hiding my face as best I could in case we met again at the jail later in the day.

He headed back to his car. I was hoping for a warning. He came back and handed me the ticket.

"Have a nice day," he said, "and obey all speed limits while in our state."

Jack and I got to the jail about twenty minutes later. We were in the little production office the sheriff provided. The space was not much bigger than a jail cell.

I was reviewing some paperwork and looking through the names of the inmates who had agreed to be interviewed. There was a B&E—breaking and entering—prisoner, a crack dealer, an arsonist, a guy who wrote bad checks (badly, as he kept getting caught), and a guy who was convicted on assault charges in a bar fight.

As I immersed myself in the rap sheets, Sheriff Hege's assistant came in and said the sheriff was available to see me now.

"Welcome back, Andy," Sheriff Hege said with his usual Southern charm. He appeared to be in an unusually festive mood. "How was your flight from up north?"

"Oh, just fine, Sheriff. Ready to go to work."

The sheriff came out from around the desk and gave me a knowing look.

"And how was that drive in?"

I knew I was busted . . . but I was also pretty sure that when Sheriff Hege was in bully mode and interrogating a suspect, he didn't have a huge grin on his face.

"So, lead foot, you crossed the county line, and you couldn't wait to start violating our laws?"

"How do you know about that?"

I hadn't admitted guilt just yet. It was more like pleading for mercy from the judge, jury, and executioner.

"I know everything that goes on in Davidson County. Don't you know that by now?" Sheriff Hege said. "Let me see the ticket."

I pulled it out of my briefcase. He looked at it and tossed it on his desk.

"I'll take care of it."

Every strict and inflexible doctrine had some flexibility, I guessed.

"Oh no, Sheriff," I quickly but politely objected.

And just as quickly, he said, "I got it. Now, get back to work on gettin' us a hit show."

I guess "no deals" looks better on a poster than "some deals."

Jack hired the crew. We were just about ready to premiere the first episode. Here's how we decided to open the show:

> VOICE-OVER: (gruff, commanding, sergeant-like voice) This is Sheriff Gerald Hege.

SHERIFF HEGE: Fifty percent hate my guts.

VOICE-OVER: A zero-tolerance crime fighter.

HEGE: I love the smell of handcuffs in the morning.

VOICE-OVER: He makes his own rules.

HEGE: My thing is simply no deals. I'm takin' on the whole world.

VOICE-OVER: He goes his own way.

HEGE: I'm going to lock you up. Put you in stripes.

VOICE-OVER: And no matter how you may feel about him.

INMATE: He's scum.

UNIDENTIFIED MIDDLE-AGED WHITE MAN: He's got a tremendous ego.

VOICE-OVER: He's the law, and you're about to enter his world. Inside Cell Block F, from the toughest jail in America, the toughest sheriff in America.*

During this show open, various images flash on the screen: Sheriff Hege holding a bat, an attack dog growling menacingly, screeching tires as Sheriff Hege's Spider Car speeds away, a blazing sheriff's badge. We see inmates in stripes behind bars looking forlorn, and then we see one inmate being handcuffed.

---

* *Live from Cell Block F*, produced by Court TV, aired July 20, 1999, The Paley Center for Media, https://www.paleycenter.org/collection/item/?q=once&p=90&item=T:65418.

As the intro fades, the camera shows the viewer's perspective from behind bars. The barred doors open, and we are brought into Cell Block F with a crane shot. We see fifty inmates assembled in the audience, surrounded by individual cells. All the prisoners in attendance volunteered to take part in the taping. They often thanked me for the opportunity to get out of their cells for a couple of hours. Sheriff Hege, in full formal police attire, sits opposite an inmate toward the front of the cellblock.

"I'd like to welcome you to *Inside Cell Block F*," Sheriff Hege says, looking around his jail. "The Pink Alcatraz, or Hege Pink as they call it down here in North Carolina."

Hege was very relaxed. He moved comfortably from sheriff to talk show host.

Anthony Coleman was one of our first so-called guests. He was an eighteen-year-old inmate whose father was shot and killed when he was four. Anthony discussed his drug charges, gun charges, and the night he led police on a high-speed, one-hundred-mile-per-hour car chase through a grocery store parking lot, putting civilians' and law enforcement officers' lives in danger.

"I'm sorry. I'm sorry for what I done," Anthony said at the conclusion of the interview.*

Another inmate who agreed to be interviewed was a thirty-six-year-old recovering crack addict convicted of assaulting a police officer. The slender woman with a pleasant face had two daughters, ages thirteen and ten. When I spoke to her about being on the show, she was eager to do it. She wanted to serve as an example of what drugs can do to a person's life.

She described her crack addiction this way: "It's a mad rush. It affects your brain. It's a good high. A really good high."

As she started to explain how it affected her family, she broke down in tears: "I took a lot away from my kids for a long time when I started using. I didn't think of my kids at that time. No, not at that time. It's like you don't think about nothing but that. It takes over your whole train of thought, and

* The Paley Center for Media, *Live from Cell Block F.*

you do stupid things. It's really tough being away from my family, being away from my children."

Sheriff Hege asked her if she could be a good mother to her daughters. "Yes, by God's power. God can do anything. I'm not a bad person. It doesn't take a bad person to get hooked on drugs. All it took was one hit. One mistake gets you put in here."

For as long as we produced this unique series in this unique environment, our goal was to provide the inmates some degree of dignity despite the harm they'd caused themselves and others and perhaps humanize the inmate population in a way no program had before.

The most unbelievable guest we ever had was a heroin addict who went by the name of Peter Mack. I have no idea where the name came from, but everyone called her Peter Mack. Peter was a woman with a ready smile and a very sweet disposition. I guessed her to be in her early fifties. I'd come to know Peter over the weeks and months, coming down to the jail and producing the show. I looked forward to seeing her. She was forever in and out of jail. She'd lost her freedom once again but said she was better off here.

One day at the jail, I was feeling down, and Peter came toward me across the cellblock, mop in hand, wearing her pinstripes and her ear-to-ear grin.

I was immediately lifted from my downcast mood.

"Welcome back, Andy," she said, embracing me with a sturdy hug. She'd never expressed interest in being on the show until I asked her this simple question:

"Peter, how do you do it? You always seem to be in such a good mood."

And then she told me this story.

"Andy, I cherish every day on this earth thanks to Jesus Christ. I've had an addiction, and it does get the best of me at times. I will admit to that. But I love life, and I will tell you why. A few years ago, I was in a very bad way. It was just too easy to get smack. It was everywhere. One day, I got a bad dose, and I OD'd. I don't remember all that much of anything about that day. So, you ask how come I love life so much 'cause of a day I don't even remember? Well, I do remember this. I woke up from overdosin'. I looked around, and I was at the morgue, and they'd put a toe tag on me and everything."

I just looked at her in amazement. I didn't know whether to laugh or cry. Peter just shook her head, chuckled at the memory, and added, "I sat up, took the toe tag off, grabbed my shoes that were on the next stretcher over, and walked right out of there. God almighty saved me that day. It wasn't my day. And in service to him, I honor each day that the sun comes up, whether I can see the sun or not. My purpose now is to bring sunshine into other people's lives."

This story had a profound effect on me. I couldn't verify it. I had so many questions for Peter. But I didn't want her to think that I doubted her veracity. I wanted to believe her.

And I do.

"Peter, would you like to tell your story to thousands of people watching our show and perhaps bring some light into their dark lives?"

"I think I would."

And she did. Peter wouldn't let anything or anyone keep her from sharing her light. A national audience witnessed Peter Mack telling her truth. I trust her story inspired thousands, if not hundreds of thousands, the way it did me.

CHAPTER 35

HIND SLEIGHT IS 20/20

Within six months *Inside Cell Block F* became a Court TV cable hit. At the beginning of 2000, ratings were climbing, and Court TV had purchased the popular program *Cops* in syndication, which served as a strong lead-in.

Our show was getting attention. One day, about eight episodes into our season, a PR person from Court TV called to tell me that the producers of *20/20*, the popular ABC News magazine show, had contacted them and wanted to do a feature piece on *Inside Cell Block F*.

I was thrilled. In the network's history, no national newsmagazine had ever done a feature on an original program produced by Court TV.

A segment on *20/20* with that kind of audience would raise public awareness of the show. This exposure could send our ratings skyrocketing. As the creator and executive producer of the show, I knew I'd be featured in the piece—which would be very good for my career. Not only would a national audience see me, but Henry, our new CEO, and his number two, Art Bell, would tap me as an essential creative mind as they crafted the present and future of Court TV.

A few days later, Court TV's PR person contacted me asking if *20/20*'s reporter and crew could spend a couple days at the jail the next time we were there shooting. Our next scheduled production date was in two weeks.

"Of course they can come," I said, trying to hide my excitement. "I'll just confirm with the sheriff, but knowing him, he'll meet the crew at the airport, even if he knows the local bank is being robbed."

"Okay, sounds good," the flack said. "And, Andy, if you can help the crew with their interviews of the sheriff and the inmates, we'd all appreciate it."

"Sure, no problem at all."

Then I hesitated. When would the PR person talk to me about my interview with the *20/20* producers? Perhaps everyone involved knew I'd be at the jail, and they could coordinate the interview directly with me in North Carolina. Right then and right there, I should've said, "Can you find out from the producers exactly what time they want to interview the creator and executive producer, because I'll be very busy down there?" But I said nothing because I didn't want to appear needy and vulnerable.

"I'll help the crew in any way I can."

The *20/20* team showed up as planned. We were beginning to turn the cellblock into a working studio. Jack and I felt guilty, wondering where the inmates were sleeping when we were taping the show and whether their new accommodations were even more crowded and stark than the tiny cells here.

The *20/20* crew headed straight to Sheriff Hege's office to prepare for the first of several interviews with him. I remember walking by his office and looking in. The ABC team had more lights, more cameras, and more people for a simple interview than we had for our entire show.

I felt more than a pang of jealousy. *Wait a minute, that's my sheriff. I discovered him*, I thought, not wanting to share him. I was going to walk in and introduce myself and find the senior producer on the shoot, but my childish ego said to play hard to get.

Don't look desperate, I said to myself. After all, they needed my perspective for their story. How did I come up with the concept of the show? How did I find Sheriff Hege? How do I choose the inmates for the show? What do I think of Sheriff Hege? What effect did a hit show like this have on Court TV? What other shows had I developed? I'd wait for them to come to me, and when they did, I'd be the cool development executive willing to talk to them but at my convenience and on my terms.

And then the first day went by. And the second. The ABC crew was all over the jail. I saw them everywhere as I sought out inmates for that week's *Inside Cell Block F* taping.

It now occurred to me that maybe my PR people had neglected to require that the *20/20* crew interview me and highlight Court TV in exchange for this unfettered and exclusive access to Sheriff Hege. It also occurred to me that I might have to swallow what little pride I had and introduce myself.

"Hey, all," I said, walking up to about eight people setting up cameras and lights in one of the now-unoccupied cells. I was trying to act as though I was the host of this party and I was coming over to greet my grateful guests. The response I got, or at least the feeling I got, was more, *Hey, we're really busy here, but if you're going to interrupt us, we're going to take a much-needed break.*

Some crew members walked out of the cell, and one middle-aged man emerged and came toward me. I don't remember his name. I only remember doing exactly what I promised myself I wouldn't do. I became the guy out of his league on the first date, trying to make a great first impression and talking way too much.

"Hey, hope you're getting everything you need. So glad you guys are here profiling our hit show." I wanted to say *my* show but thought better of it. "What do you think of Sheriff Hege? Isn't he great? Can you believe our setup here? A working jail turned into a television studio. By the way, I'm Andy Regal, the executive producer."

I stuck out my hand.

He didn't ask me one question about the show.

I never asked him if he wanted to interview me or explain the insight I could provide. I should have. At that very moment, I was back in junior high school watching Eric Parmacek making out with Jackie Morris and wondering when, if ever, my day would come. Today would not be that day. We parted ways after a few more unpleasantries.

We didn't even shake hands.

The piece aired a couple months later. I'd almost forgotten about it, but I was watching an ABC show, and a promo came on for *20/20*, highlighting the segment on Hege. The piece aired a few days later, and what should've been a triumphant night in my career was an abject disappointment. I dreaded watching it. I didn't even tell anyone I knew it was airing. I was now all too aware that the segment was about Hege, as if ABC had discovered him. They showed clips of the show. My show. They mentioned Court TV only in passing.

I wondered and still wonder to this day if the behind-the-scenes *20/20* piece on *Inside Cell Block F* was the only one in the history of television in which there was zero interest in sitting down with the person fully responsible for creating and producing the show they were profiling. I pay attention to such things. Believe me.

I shouldn't have let them treat me this way. I should have stood up for myself and my *show.* Once again, self-doubt and self-blame enveloped me.

CHAPTER 36

SHE PUT A FORK IN IT

I was sitting on a stoop next to the restaurant I'd picked for a blind date.

"She's really pretty, and she's a lawyer. Her name is Jennifer, and she went to Columbia for undergrad and law school," Bill Boggs, my former boss and dear friend, gushed excitedly over the phone. Bill was friendly with the woman's venture-capitalist father and thought we might be a match. "She's brilliant. I met her last night. She's interested in getting together with you."

I trusted his judgment on such matters.

Bill suggested I make a reservation at Chez Josephine, a restaurant on the west side of Midtown. If we didn't click, I could make a quick getaway back to the vans by Port Authority and get home to Weehawken.

I was early. She was late. I hadn't seen a picture, as is the custom with online dating today, so every few minutes, I looked east, assuming she'd be coming from that direction. Bill's description had boosted my hopes. If she was unattractive, I wanted to recover from my disappointment before we said hello.

On my sixth or seventh glance down the street, I saw a young woman walking purposefully toward me. She was petite with shoulder-length brown hair. When she was halfway down the block, I noticed she was wearing a fitted, short business skirt suit with a black and white striped T-shirt underneath.

I stood up to greet her. She was pretty and fit. She looked up at me and smiled. *Bill did a really good job on this one.*

I'd come right from work, so I was still carrying my hard, square briefcase. I'd chosen khaki pants, dress shoes, a light blue button-down, and my favorite cream-colored sports coat for the evening. I learned later that Jennifer's first impression was: He's nice-looking, but this will be a bit of a project if we like one another. That briefcase, those old shoes, and the sports coat have got to go.

We sat down. Jennifer explained that she was on the Atkins diet and was eschewing carbs, so she'd be ordering fish. I asked if she would mind if I ordered the risotto. It was one of my favorite dishes, and the server informed us it was a specialty of the house.

As we waited for our food to arrive, Jennifer told me she represented victims of domestic violence in court pro bono for Sanctuary for Families, a nonprofit agency located near the World Trade Center towers. This was just a couple of years before the terrible tragedy of 9/11. She was from Scarsdale, a New York suburb, and had an older brother, Ted, a media studies professor. Her mother, Elaine, a psychologist, and father, Joel, were in the process of getting divorced, which I could tell, even in this casual conversation, was difficult for her. But then she revealed, "My father was recently diagnosed with Parkinson's disease, and with my parents divorcing, his care is my responsibility. So, there's that."

She took a mouthful of salad and tried to remain appropriately stoic for a first date. This was a tragic circumstance for any loving daughter, especially given her father was only in his mid-fifties.

Our main courses arrived.

We changed the subject, and the conversation was now upbeat, flowing, and easy. I was trying to impress her with the cases I covered at Court TV, and she was doing much the same, describing the emotional and difficult work of representing women in awful circumstances throughout the five boroughs.

Then, as we were becoming more comfortable and bantering, she abruptly leaned over the table and planted her fork right in my plate, scooping up a significant amount of risotto and sticking it with gusto into her waiting mouth.

I was taken aback. I dislike sharing my food, especially if it's delicious. But isn't there a rule somewhere in the official *First Date Handbook* that one must never, ever place one's fork in one's date's food—at least not without first asking permission?

Aside from that unpardonable faux pas, Jennifer was a fun, engaging, intelligent, and refreshing date. I called Bill upon returning home.

"Well?" he asked.

"I can't say it's love at first sight. She's really attractive, but I have to tell you, there's something about this girl. I think it's something like admiration at first sight. She's impressive, accomplished, and fun. She's into sports and music and loves to dance. And maybe more than anything, she comes off as really driven, competent, independent, and not needy. I've never felt quite this way after a first date."

"That sounds to me like love at first date, if not love at first sight," Bill said, laughing.

When my father met Jennifer months later, he took me aside and said, "Don't blow this one. Do not let this girl get away."

We wed two and a half years after our first date.

I've had trouble finding supportive and empathetic bosses in my career. Lucky for me, in my late thirties, I found my life partner.

She's been the best thing that's ever happened to me, now going on twenty-five years.

CHAPTER 37

PREPARE FOR TAKEOFF AND A CRASH LANDING

Jack and I reached the end of our shooting schedule for the first season of *Inside Cell Block F*. Nobody at Court TV noticed or seemed to care about our accomplishment. So we decided to have our own celebratory wrap party.

We clinked beer bottles. Henry Schleiff would be paying for dinner even if we both felt he and his new team hadn't given us the recognition we deserved for creating this unique and attention-grabbing show. We never received a positive comment from Henry or the executive team on any episode we produced—no acknowledgment of the ratings and no mention of plans to continue the show. I kept waiting to be invited to a brainstorming meeting to discuss other programming ideas I might have, given that the Hege show was so successful.

As the weeks progressed, reruns of *Cops*, the syndicated smash hit, followed by *Inside Cell Block F*, continued to attract strong numbers.

I should've asked Henry or his number two, Art Bell, about it. Jack and I felt we'd done everything to make the show an asset for the network. We'd been given a million-dollar budget to produce as many shows as possible. We produced twenty-five shows with Sheriff Hege and came in $50,000 under budget.

But the better the show performed, the less I seemed to be involved in plans for the future of Court TV. My anxiety was growing. My title was VP of original programming, but Henry and Art brought new programming and production people into the network. The energy was palpable, and I wasn't a part of it.

I'm the only one here who's created a hit, I argued to Henry . . . in my head.

I felt exposed, unappreciated, vulnerable, and expendable. Was I just being paranoid?

I wasn't the only one feeling left out.

Sheilagh, our programming head, who'd brought me back to Court TV and had been so supportive of Sheriff Hege's show, started standing up at every meeting instead of sitting around the large table like the rest of us.

"How come you don't sit down?" I asked her playfully in the hallway after wondering why she stood for a full hour. She gestured for me to follow her into her office.

"My back is killing me. I can't even sit down. I've never in my life had a back problem, but this stress is killing me. Henry stopped talking to me and including me in meetings. I've been shunned and shoved aside, and I have no idea why. Nobody is talking to me. I've never been so miserable."

I'd been detained in Cell Block F for the last year and had no idea what Sheilagh was going through. I did sense that those of us from the previous management team weren't being integrated into Henry's future plans. Two weeks later, my dear friend, boss, and trusted colleague Sheilagh McGee was gone.

It was a huge loss for Court TV.

It was a huge loss for me.

I continued to be nagged by disquieting ruminations that I wasn't part of Henry's brain trust and Court TV's future. One morning, a senior colleague passed me hurriedly in the hallway and said, "Hey, Andy, see you at the off-site this weekend."

I turned and, over my shoulder, muttered, "Oh yeah, sure. Looking forward to it."

I raced back to my desk to see if I'd overlooked the email invite. It was nowhere to be found. I was too uneasy to ask any of my coworkers for details, and I figured it must've been an oversight. I decided to go directly to Henry to straighten it all out. I rarely dealt with him other than in large group situations, and I thought this was a good opportunity to get in front of him and remind him of all the positive contributions I was making to his successful programming strategy. I got on his calendar.

As I walked to our meeting, I realized I'd never been invited to Henry's office. I remember hearing that he was doing some major renovations and redecorating. It sounded like what Mr. Trump is doing to the East Wing of the White House.

I couldn't believe my eyes when I stepped through his office doorway. He must've knocked down the walls to two or three other offices to create his outsized lair. It looked as long as a football field. He welcomed me like a long-lost pal. We sat in one of several plush seating areas in the farthest recesses of his office.

"Andy, come in, come in. How ya doin'?"

"Excellent, Henry. Thanks for taking the time to see me."

"My pleasure, my pleasure. I do have another meeting in a few minutes. What's up?"

"Sure, this won't take much time. I just wanted to tell you how great *Inside Cell Block F* is going, and the ratings, as I'm sure you know, have been outstanding. *Cops* is the most amazing lead-in. It was a stroke of genius by you to acquire that show. And I have another concept I'm developing that I think could be another hit."

"Good, good," he said, not reacting to anything I said.

"Oh, and I wanted to ask you something. I heard about an off-site coming up over the weekend for the team, and I'm concerned I didn't see the invite."

I was about to discuss all I could offer at this strategy meeting in greater detail when he cut me off.

"Andy, don't worry about it. This thing is no big deal. There are lots of meetings. Nobody attends all of them." Henry stood. "Keep up the good work. I'm glad you came by."

He ushered me out of his office. It was an aerobic workout to make it all the way back to the door.

On Monday, I felt like a pariah. I was alone in my despair.

From what I could piece together, the entire programming department had been invited, except for Andy Regal, the VP of original programming. My colleagues all seemed to be talking about how fun and constructive the event had been. And I assumed when they weren't talking about how great it was to be a part of the in crowd, they were talking about my very noticeable absence.

It was torture to be left out.

Following that debacle, I calmed myself knowing I'd successfully pitched a concept called *Hollywood Justice*, where we'd profile celebrities in trouble with the law during a thirty-minute daily show. After *Inside America's Courts* and the O. J. trials, I knew there would always be well-known people in trouble with the law and a huge appetite to hear about them. While some other shows might touch on the subject, there wasn't anything on the air that was devoted to celebrities and the law or, more accurately, celebrities and lawlessness.

This wasn't my first attempt at creating such a show.

In 2000, I came up with another programming idea. We'd focus on the more offbeat, unusual, and even humorous trial moments we'd unearthed over the years. It was a tabloid court show. Brill never would have gone for it. Henry did. We'd cover the most heated moments between lawyers, the worst efforts by criminal defendants representing themselves, the craziest "night court" cases, the biggest-money, highest-profile divorce cases, and the wackiest judges.

We sold the concept to Tribune Entertainment, which at the time was one of the most prominent players in syndication. Tribune agreed to fund a pilot episode. I was thrilled. I'd done it again for Court TV. I'd developed a concept that a national syndicator was interested in developing.

Now, the two parties had to agree on talent. The Tribune team proposed Tavis Smiley. I was a big fan. Since 1996, Tavis had hosted and executive produced *BET Tonight* on Black Entertainment Television (BET). He interviewed major political figures and celebrities and discussed topics ranging from racial profiling and police brutality to R&B music and Hollywood gossip. We all felt he was a talent on the rise, with both credibility and an entertaining, conversational style.

Tavis Smiley was our top candidate.

By this time, I'd been dating Jennifer for just over a year, and we decided to go to France for our anniversary. I'd never been. After the transatlantic flight and stop-and-go traffic from the airport, we'd been recovering in the room for a few hours, shaking off the jet lag. There were clothes strewn all over the cramped three-hundred-square-foot room from our aborted attempt to unpack before fatigue had overcome us.

We had finally found the energy to stand up and address the mess and started talking about the fabulous weeklong adventure ahead when my BlackBerry went off. I couldn't imagine who'd be calling. A chill went through me, and I thought my parents or brother or sister may have been in an accident or fallen ill.

I opened the little square device.

"Hello," I said haltingly.

"Hi, Andy, I have Henry for you." At least his assistant didn't say, "Henry would like a word."

"Andy, what the fuck is this? I hear we're considering Tavis Smiley for the Tribune show?"

I remember Jennifer looking at me in horror. She could hear Henry. She could see my severe distress. She acknowledged years later that she had thought stories about my belligerent bosses and the newsroom bullying I suffered were exaggerated.

After this moment, she never doubted me again.

"Did you not notice his speech impediment? What the hell are you thinking? Whose brilliant idea is it to use Tavis Smiley?"

"Henry, he's not officially signed, but I think we have the best opportunity for Tribune to place the show on their stations if we use a talent they support. He's their first choice."

"Are you hard of hearing? Do we have a bad connection there in Europe?"

I could hear him yelling just fine.

And with that, he hung up on me.

Dr. Namie of the Workplace Bullying Institute defined different types of bullies for me: "This is the two-headed-snake bully—Jekyll and Hyde. This type of bully affects the target's reputation within the organization. It's hard to recognize this side of him because he comes off so often as friendly and charming."

I sat on the bed with my head in my hands. I thought this was the show concept that would prove my value to Henry. Jennifer tried her best to comfort me. I was inconsolable. The entire trip, I kept hearing him belittling me.

"No amount of comforting from family, friends, or colleagues addresses the problem. It envelops you and is in your head," says Dr. Namie. "Targets of bullying don't expect it. They fear it, but at the moment, they can't believe someone can be that evil and cruel. They beat themselves up over it. It surprises them. They can't believe what is happening, and that's what makes them targets. This is a form of gaslighting. The bullies get inside your head. It's intrusive and insidious. The result is constantly having terrible self-talk conversations. It's debilitating. Targets go to sleep with it and wake up to it."

My confidence was shaken. My self-worth shattered. Henry had knocked me down, and I had to struggle back to my feet. I still had my *Hollywood Justice* concept in the works and was pleased that at least Court TV was giving me a chance to shoot a pilot to get a sense of the entertainment and marketplace value.

I'd enlisted Jack, the director of *Inside Cell Block F*, to help me edit together the pilot, which was not all that complicated. We were going to assemble several stories involving celebrities in trouble that we'd already covered and have one of our Court TV anchors simply record what are known as wraparounds. These are short on-camera intros and outros leading from one story to another.

As I said, simple.

We edited the various clips together to create the fifteen-minute pilot. We'd also written the short scripts for the anchor to read in the studio. We couldn't get studio time to shoot the wraps before I was scheduled to go to Costa Rica with my now fiancée, Jennifer, to celebrate our engagement. We'd already postponed the trip twice due to work conflicts.

Brenda Caldwell was one of the programming executives Henry had enlisted. In her fifties, she had a warm, welcoming smile. She reminded me of a kind neighbor whose house I enjoyed going to for lunch when I was a kid when my mom couldn't be home. Brenda was one of Henry Schleiff's chieftains. I didn't know exactly what she did. She'd been at Court TV only a short time, while I'd been there almost eight years during two tours of duty. I wanted to ensure Brenda knew all my accomplishments because I needed her approval.

However, in speaking with some of my longtime colleagues, I was warned in hushed tones about Brenda. It was their opinion that she couldn't be trusted.

Well, my mother always said, "Make up your own mind about people." Brenda had a direct line to Henry, so I wanted her to like me. Maybe Henry would take notice if I got her involved in my projects and gained an ally.

I would tell her how well the *Hollywood Justice* pilot was coming along and solicit her help on the one significant challenge I had in getting it done by the agreed-upon deadline.

I said to Jack, "All you have to do is shoot and edit in the intros and outros with the host. That will take an hour. It doesn't require my presence. And I'll ask Brenda if she'll cover for me if anything comes up."

I wasn't about to forego this trip again out of fear of being bullied or worse.

"Andy, don't worry about a thing. I'll take care of anything that comes up," Brenda said, smiling when we sat in her office just a few days later. "Do you have studio time next week to finish the anchor wraps?"

"Yes, we're all set. It's the day my fiancée and I are set to leave; that's the absolute earliest day I could get," I added, relieved that Brenda was being so helpful, understanding, and accommodating.

"Go on your vacation. I'll oversee the shoot and the edit. Have a great time."

Jennifer and I were settling in our seats, putting our extra items in the overhead compartment. As we sat down, we looked at each other and sighed—the stress of both our jobs finally starting to leave us. We'd been dealing with her father's Parkinson's and the reality of taking care of him for the remainder of his life.

We needed this.

The plane was at the gate and scheduled to leave on time out of Newark Airport. It was early evening and, given the winter season, already dark.

The flight attendant requested that the last few stragglers please take their seats, as the cabin doors would be shutting momentarily. I've always been a nervous flier, so I cracked open a book to occupy my mind during takeoff.

Then, my cell phone rang. I assumed it was my brother or sister wishing me a last-minute farewell. I answered, unconcerned. That nonchalance changed into alarm, my heart thumping in my chest.

It was Henry Schleiff's assistant. "Andy, I'm sorry to bother you, but Henry asked me to call you. I think you might be heading out on vacation. Henry wants you back here immediately."

"I'm on the plane heading to Costa Rica, and we're taking off in a matter of minutes!" I said, absolutely panicked but also trying to keep my voice down so as not to make everyone on the plane aware of my crisis.

"Hold on," she said.

I looked over at Jennifer, who stared back at me in horror, not quite fully understanding what was happening.

Henry's assistant came back on the line. "I can't quote Henry directly, but he said get off the plane and come to work."

I looked at Jennifer again, then toward the front of the plane. I had an aisle seat, and after first class, we were about twenty rows back. I could see the cabin door was still open. I jumped up and ran to the front, where the flight attendant was holding the phone, about to announce that the cabin doors were closing.

"I have to get off the plane," I said frantically. "I have an emergency at home, and I have to get off this plane."

"Sir, we are about to back out of the gate," said the annoyed flight attendant. "Wait just a moment."

She went and spoke to the lead flight attendant.

"Gather your things and deplane as quickly as possible."

I ran back to Jennifer. "Jen, we have to get off the plane right now. Now!"

I've only seen this look of grave concern on her face two other times in all our years together. The first time, early in our relationship, after our first full night together, I was leaving her apartment in the morning, and I could tell she was wondering if I was ever coming back. The other was this past summer when we received a call informing us that her father had passed away overnight at his nursing home.

We pulled our bags from above and thrust our scattered belongings from our seat pockets and underneath the seats in front of us into our backpacks. The next thing I remember is that we were at the baggage claim area downstairs at Newark Airport. Jennifer, who is an incredible problem solver, was thinking about how we would get back our checked bags that were now flying joyously to Costa Rica, oblivious to the fact that their owners would not be joining them.

Jennifer was compassionate and consoling as we drove back to the city.

It would take ninety excruciating minutes to return to the office.

All I could think about was when and how I would be fired. I was in shock.

Back at Court TV, I found myself in Brenda's office. She smiled and said, "I'm so sorry, Andy." And then she added (a bit too eagerly), "Henry's furious."

I sat sullenly in her office. I was convinced I'd been sabotaged and bullied.

And there I sat, bloodied, beaten down, and forlorn on the Court TV playground.

She continued, "The wraps have been completed, so there isn't any work to be done tonight, as it turns out. Why don't you head home, and we'll discuss this more tomorrow?" Brenda said with a nod and a furrowed brow.

As I walked out of her office, I obsessed over the situation. Brenda had approved my vacation and had promised to cover for me and "take care of anything that comes up."

The deadline for the pilot was arbitrary.

Brenda had agreed to deliver the video to Henry after Jack finished the edit.

No problem, I'd thought.

All I could surmise was that Brenda had conveniently neglected to tell Henry about our agreement, so he was led to believe I left for vacation irresponsibly and cavalierly.

That night, and the next day, and the next . . . Henry never asked me about the work.

He never inquired whether I had put sufficient plans in place to ensure its execution.

He had no interest in me—just enmity and disregard.

I felt powerless, mortified, and certain I'd been played.

I never contacted Henry to defend myself because he trusted Brenda implicitly. If I questioned Brenda's integrity, it would have started a war I couldn't win.

Henry Schleiff never spoke another word to me during my employment at Court TV. I was an outcast. Twenty-five years later, I still don't know for sure why he pulled me off that plane.

I recounted the incident to Maureen Duffy, coauthor of *Overcoming Mobbing*. She told me, "That bully boss and his outrageous behavior, it's a sort of dictatorial, entitled behavior, and you're there with your future wife. It's outrageous to intervene in another person's life, and this was hardly a life-threatening circumstance as you describe it.

"You tell that story, and some people hearing it or reading it will say, 'What did Andy do? He must have done something. He must have messed up in some way. He's minimizing it now to make himself look good.' Do you see how messed up that way of thinking is? That's how we think today. That's the wrong level of analysis."

Psychologist Kenneth Yeager from Ohio State University told me, "I've seen managers push down and beat down their subordinates. There is no qualm in today's work world about character assassination. It's ubiquitous. It is not getting better. It is more callous and self-serving, and it is less about the truth. I work in a world where evidence and outcomes are everything. You don't do anything to another human being without good evidence."

It was late that night of my aborted vacation, close to 9:00 p.m., when I left Brenda's office. I wondered how many people already knew of my humiliation.

Bad news travels fast, especially when schadenfreude has become part of the work culture.

I was racked with tension and couldn't sleep. I decided to get to work early the next day to avoid a walk of shame through the newsroom with everyone looking at me, shaking their heads and gossiping.

At 7:00 a.m., a few people had settled into their workday, but I looked straight ahead. I quickly ducked into my corner office overlooking Third Avenue, closed the door, and collapsed into my chair.

My heart was thumping, and my head ached from lack of sleep. I didn't know what to expect. I just sat and awaited my fate. I was tormented by suicidal ideation. A gun aimed at my head. I tried logging into my computer, and to my horror, I couldn't. *They've already shut down my access*, I assumed. I took a breath. I tried again, and it logged me in. "Thank God," I whispered to myself, my heart slowing.

I leaned back in my chair. I'd only told Jack and a select few people that I was leaving for vacation, so if anyone asked, I'd say a family member got sick and we decided to delay the trip. I didn't know how I'd face people, having experienced the worst indignity of my career. I was still going over that phone call, and Henry, through his assistant, was demanding that I exit the plane.

Had I abrogated my responsibilities so egregiously that now I deserved to be tarred and feathered and run out of town?

"The target now has artificially high levels of shame, embarrassment, fear, and guilt—all stimulated by the bully, for this is how all abusers control their victims," observed Tim Field, a pioneer in the study of workplace bullying in the UK, author of *Bully in Sight,* and founder of the UK's National Bullying Helpline. "The target feels bewildered and often still cannot believe that what is happening is happening; the target feels responsible in some way, as evidenced by the nagging thoughts, 'Why me?' and 'Why did I let it happen to me?'"*

---

* "Why Don't You Stand Up for Yourself? Asserting Your Right Not to Be Bullied, Fighting Back, Taking Action," Bully Online, The Field Foundation, archived December 27, 2015, at https://web.archive.org/web/20151227005349/http://bullyonline.org/workbully/standup.htm.

Dr. Namie, who was inspired by Field's early work, adds, "The bullies have all the control. You did not want this. You didn't ask for this. They selected you. They decide the type of bullying and when to unleash it. The power of bullying is surprise and [bullying] causes severe injury and trauma because of the surprise element. It's misery at work and home. There is a lot of guilt around being bullied. It makes you feel worthless. You think you have done something to deserve it. Victim precipitation is a lot of crap."

I sat for hours staring at my monitor, waiting for something to happen.

It came at ten thirty in the form of a perfunctory email from Brenda Caldwell.

She explained that Henry had decided to hand over all responsibility for *Hollywood Justice* to another producer. She added, "We will be discontinuing *Inside Cell Block F* at the conclusion of the season. Please instruct Jack Niesi to coordinate and expedite the edits for the final episodes."

I wanted to cry.

Two of the best show ideas I'd ever had—*Inside Cell Block F* and *Hollywood Justice*—were essentially dead.

I was disgraced. Out of utter shame, I didn't leave my office all day, or the next, or the next. I didn't have the nerve to walk to the bathroom at the other end of the office.

Someone might see me. The outcast.

I found a mostly empty Gatorade bottle in my work bag. I dumped out the remaining liquid into the garbage can underneath my desk. I locked my office door and urinated into the bottle. I closed the bottle and put it back in my bag. From that day forward, I never visited the restroom. Instead, I urinated into a bottle in my office.

I admitted to no one at work or home what I was doing behind closed doors.

Shame compels silence.

My previous contributions to this enterprise meant nothing. Even more wounding, Henry saw me as worthy of disregard and punishment.

David Yamada, professor of law and director of the New Workplace Institute at Suffolk University in Boston, is a leading expert on workplace bullying and the law. In an interview he told me the following:

> The opposite of human dignity is humiliation. Humiliation is a profoundly emotional experience. We should acknowledge humiliation in the workplace. It's a word, concept, and experience we'd all like to bury. But that won't happen. It will come right back up as mental and physical illness.
>
> I have found anecdotally that men are usually less willing to admit that they have been bullied at work. It's not part of our culture. Many men still feel they should be oblivious to it all. Or "man up" and work your way through it.

My torment would continue.

I was the VP of original programming, with no original or unoriginal programming. I was no longer invited to meetings and had no reason to call any meetings.

I sat in my office with nothing to do.

A few days into my self-imposed "office arrest," I received a call from Hannah, a producer who'd worked with and for me since the early days of Court TV. Hannah was always friendly. We had a warm and trusting relationship.

"Andy, hi, it's me, Hannah." She was whispering. "I'm so sorry you're going through all of this."

"Thanks, Hannah. I'm doing just fine," I said, lying through my teeth, not whispering.

"Listen, I want to tell you something, but you can't say where this came from, and I can't tell you my source in the newsroom. Henry and Brenda are trying to find a reason to fire you for cause. Make sure you do everything by the book, and go to any meeting you're invited to so they can't accuse you of being derelict in your job."

"Thank you, Hannah. I really appreciate it. I will."

I couldn't remember feeling so beaten down. I'd given nearly a decade of my life to helping build this network, and now the top executives were conspiring against me.

And the way I figured it, I had quite a bit to lose if they fired me for cause. I had no idea what it would take to do so or what exactly they could deny me on that basis, but I had upwards of $75,000 at stake in severance and funds vested. This was money I would need if I was suddenly thrown out into the street with no job. I put my head in my hands and threw up in my garbage can.

How would I ever get through this?

What was gained by pulling me off that plane? This pilot video isn't even going to air, why are they choosing to shun me rather than talk with me?

An article titled "Adult Bullies: How to Spot Them, and How to Handle Them" from Blush.com discusses the silent treatment:

> They won't actually tell you what you've done wrong. That's way too much to ask. Instead, they will smoke you out with their lack of communication until you break. Nobody likes to be ignored, and silence is typically the best way to "beat" someone without actually having to put yourself out there. It's a cop out. Which is why it's so popular amongst adult bullies.*

I had to take my colleague Hannah's confidential advice to heart and make sure I provided them with no (alleged) cause for dismissal.

First, I had to ensure I attended meetings that requested my attendance. That was easy enough. There was only one meeting that remained on my schedule—Henry's weekly executive team get-together.

Henry's gathering took place every Monday. And it was usually an opportunity to boast about all the wonderful things you and your team were doing.

---

* "Adult Bullies: How to Spot Them, and How to Handle Them," Blush, accessed February 15, 2025, https://joinblush.com/adult-bullies/.

I'd been hiding in my office for a week, and now, for the first time since being pulled off the plane, I'd have to face Henry and all my senior colleagues around a table for an entire hour.

I was nearly catatonic thinking about this meeting. I played it out repeatedly. What could I possibly say when it came to my turn?

"Hi, everyone. Happy Monday. Hmm, let's see. Last week, in humiliating fashion, Henry ruined a long-planned and approved vacation to Costa Rica. I'm sure you all have been gossiping about my demise and getting a good laugh at my abasement. My hit show, Inside Cell Block F, *has been unceremoniously dumped, and the pilot show that I conceived and developed,* Hollywood Justice, *has been handed over to Marlene. This week, I plan to hide out in my office, piss into a bottle, and see if I can make it through the week without being unjustly fired for cause."*

I'm shaking my head as I write this. Why was Henry intent on tormenting me?

I couldn't sleep Sunday night, but still, as was now my habit, got up at 4:30 a.m. I looked like hell—bags under my eyes, I'd lost weight. Some people eat under extreme tension, but I lose my appetite. My trip into the office was interminable.

Finally, 9:58 a.m. It was time. I urinated in my bottle for the third time that day. I left my office for the first time in a week and headed to the conference room. I used a back stairwell and kept my head down as if I was deep in thought over some crucial programming notes on the pad of paper I had that I realized I was clutching much too tightly.

I walked into the conference room, making no eye contact. A few people were already seated. You could hear Henry coming. He was always talking loudly, telling a joke or some hilarious anecdote to someone down the hall.

Henry sat down at the head of the table nearest the door. I'd usually sit near the front, but now that I was exiled, I sat at the far end of the table. I feared he might ask me to leave or sit out in the hallway like a scolded schoolboy.

He did neither.

I scribbled feverishly on my pad, just trying to occupy my mind. It was primarily little squares and lines, just doodles, and I'd write down the occasional distressing thought that crossed my mind. *How did it come to this? . . . What have I done? . . . Why do these people hate me?* I'd also try to calm myself by writing, *This, too, shall pass . . . Keep breathing. It will all be okay.* I can't imagine what my colleagues must have thought while I was seeming to take copious notes on their outstanding contributions to Henry's empire.

Even with these defense mechanisms, I hadn't figured out what to say when it was my turn to talk. The meeting was methodically working its way toward me.

The most obsequious of the group tended to speak the longest. To my great relief, a few people among the dozen or so in attendance were comfortable enough in their employment that they said, "Nothing of particular note from me this week." As the person to my right concluded her remarks, I found the strength to look up, and I stared directly at Henry and nobody else. "Nothing from me this week," I said as nonchalantly as possible, and I turned to the person to my left to make sure he understood that I'd concluded my remarks.

My agony wasn't over. I knew Marlene, now the producer of *Hollywood Justice*, had yet to speak. And speak she did. She couldn't wait to tell Henry, Brenda, and the others all the innovative things she had planned for "her" new show.

I was demoralized. I wanted to run out. I sat there and took it. I didn't want to embarrass myself further, if that was even possible, or give them cause to get rid of me.

I had to endure this meeting for several weeks before they fired me.

Not for cause.

Art Bell, Henry's number two, did Henry's dirty work. I sat down. I couldn't help thinking about Paul Simon whenever I was with Art. They looked like twins. It was a brief conversation.

"Andy, this whole escapade has proven to be your Waterloo."

At first, I thought that was pretty good because Art was comparing me to Napoleon, a great leader, conqueror, and strategist. Then, I flashed back to my high school AP European History class and recalled that, in the end, Waterloo didn't work out all that well for the little French guy.

Napoleon was exiled to Elba.

I got the guillotine.

In his 2024 poll, Dr. Namie investigated what becomes of bully victims. In 62 percent of cases, the primary factor that stops the bullying is the absurd euphemism "target displacement." According to the survey responses, termination, "constructive discharge," quitting, or transferring is the result.*

In more straightforward words, the victims lose the jobs they love for no legitimate reason—which only prolongs and intensifies the trauma.

Court TV gave me severance. The money couldn't and wouldn't dull the pain of being mistreated, disregarded, and then banished from a job and a place I cared about deeply. Where was the appreciation and admiration in exchange for my work, leadership, creativity, and dedication? The work I was doing was a professional ambition. To be in the center of things. To tell important stories to millions and lead a team of devoted people who share my passion.

I loved the work. My fatal flaw? Thinking my bosses would love me back.

For years afterward, I avoided the area around Thirty-Ninth Street and Third Avenue. Anytime I was within a half mile, my heart started pounding. I would drive or walk the long way around to stay far enough away from my former workplace. Mental health professionals identify this condition as "persistent avoidance behavior" (PAB).

According to a piece from Healthline.com, titled "Breaking the Cycle of Anxiety and Avoidance," "For some people, though, excessive anxiety can lead to unnecessary and extreme avoidance. In turn, this avoidance can have a hugely negative impact on the way that they function and their overall quality of life."†

In psychology, avoidance is defined as the act of staying away from certain things, such as situations, people, or environments, in order to prevent harmful

---

* Workplace Bullying Institute, *2024 WBI US Workplace Bullying Survey: The National Study*, October 22, 2024, https://workplacebullying.org/2024-wbi-us-survey/, p. 3.

† Eleesha Lockett, MS, "Breaking the Cycle of Anxiety and Avoidance," Healthline Media, last modified March 15, 2023, https://www.healthline.com/health/anxiety/anxiety-avoidance.

or unwanted thoughts, feelings, or consequences. While avoidance is a natural human behavior, it's also a common feature of many different severe anxiety disorders.

Throughout all of this my wife Jennifer was my stalwart. She made me feel safe. True love was at home, not at work.

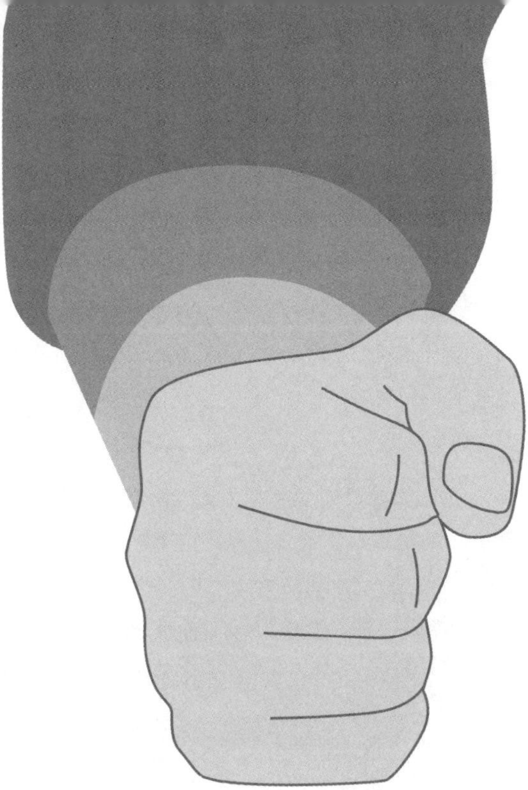

SECTION 6

LIFE AND DEATH IN THE NEWSROOM

The most basic and powerful way to connect with another person is to listen.

—RACHEL NAOMI REMEN, MEDICAL DOCTOR AND AUTHOR

CHAPTER 38

WE HIRED YOU BECAUSE WE'RE AFRAID OF HIM

It was 2003, and like most years of my career, I was looking for work because either I was scared of being out of work or I was out of work. In this case, I had been unemployed from Court TV for four months. Desperation and depression had set in. The suicidal ideation was becoming more frequent.

My agent, Adam Leibner, was on the phone.

"Regs!" Adam shouted. He was always upbeat. He'd probably just returned from a fabulous lunch with a dejected client or high-flying network executive. "MSNBC is looking for an executive producer for a new show hosted by Jerry Nachman. Do you know Nachman?" Adam inquired.

"I know that name, Ad."

"He's the former editor in chief of the *New York Post*. As I hear it, he's been advising the top brass at NBC News on news coverage at MSNBC. They've decided to launch a show around him at MS. They need an executive producer. I want to put your name in for it."

Jerry Nachman was a police reporter and political commentator before he became the editor in chief of the *Post* from 1989 to 1992. He was also a powerhouse in local news in New York City, serving as news director of WNBC-TV and vice president of CBS's flagship station in New York, WCBS. Jerry produced

Politically Incorrect, hosted by Bill Maher, during the election cycle in 2000.

MSNBC was the minor league of NBC News. However, it could be a great next move and lead to more significant opportunities with the parent network.

Sitting at home with nothing to do, watching the world go off to work and play, is a specific kind of torture. I drove the short distance to MSNBC's studio (in Secaucus, New Jersey) to meet Jerry Nachman. The studio, executive offices, and newsroom were in a vast, all-white building. Numerous satellite dishes sat impressively near the front, hailing the media's power and modern technology.

A heavy glass door invited you to walk into what felt like the future of newsgathering.

The newsroom, including sets, was lit by the many lighting grids on the ceiling, allowing the anchors and reporters to appear on camera from almost anywhere in the space.

After interviewing with Nachman, I'd meet with the two heads of MSNBC: Erik Sorenson—who I knew and respected from my days when we overlapped at Court TV and was now president and general manager of MSNBC—and his number two, Phil Griffin.

I thought my relationship with Erik might give me the edge.

Jerry Nachman's office door was open, and I knocked with confidence. He was looking down at some papers. My first impression was that he looked like one of those old men who sat too far down in the seat of his car, and all you could see was his head peering over the steering wheel.

Jerry looked old to me. He was in his mid-fifties and bald, and when he finally stood up at the end of the interview, I could see he was a good forty pounds overweight. A *New York Times* article described Jerry this way: "Mr. Nachman combined the scrappiness of city streets with the vocabulary of a professor. As a television journalist, he compared himself in interviews to Lou Grant, the gruff newsman played by Ed Asner on 'The Mary Tyler Moore Show' and the drama 'Lou Grant.'"

I could also see this guy had command from the moment I sat down. I'd spoken to people who had worked for Jerry or who knew people who'd worked for him. The story always went something like this: "He's tough, really tough, but you'll never learn more from anyone than you will from Jerry Nachman." I'd heard the same about Steve Brill. It was true; I'd learned quite a bit from Brill, but I saw the possibility that, once again, I could become a bully's target.

I steeled myself for whatever tough questions this seasoned newsman and editor had for me. The questions never came. Jerry started talking about himself, the people he knew and had worked with, and the stories he'd covered. He just kept talking. He did at one point, about fifteen minutes in, ask me where I grew up. Then he spoke for another fifteen minutes about his experiences in Chicago and the bold-faced names he knew there. He was very animated, gesticulating to amplify points of interest.

He was a captivating character.

At this point, I'd worked with enough Jerry Nachmans in my career to know I should let him talk. I assumed he was interested in how we'd work together, which meant determining if I was a good listener. He wasn't interested in what I had to say about much of anything. He either didn't care or assumed I had the skill set to do the job.

So I made sure to nod at all the right moments, laugh at just the right times, and clearly show that I understood and appreciated his cleverness, wit, and vast experience. I didn't have to put on an act.

When Jerry seemed to run out of breath after about an hour, he struggled to get out of his chair. He extended his hand and gave me a great big smile. "I like you," he said. "Let's see if we can work something out."

I was flattered and pleased.

I should've asked him to describe his management style.

Instead, I shook Jerry's hand and thanked him.

"How do you think it went, buddy?" Erik Sorenson asked me eagerly from behind his desk. I liked that Erik often called me buddy. Phil Griffin sat on the corner of Erik's desk facing me.

Erik, forever in a suit, no tie; Phil, bald, with an athletic build, youthful face, and a button-down shirt. Phil turned out to be a fun guy to be around. I should've realized that the expectant looks on each of their faces were a tell.

"I thought it went great. I got along so well with Jerry," was the most honest thing I could think of. I was excited about the role. The environment was dynamic.

In the short time it took to drive out of the parking lot, I was already thinking this time would be different.

I received an offer a few days later.

We had a lot of work to do to prepare Jerry's new show for air. The first thing we did was create a set reminiscent of an old newspaper editor's office to honor Jerry's past.

As it turned out, typewriters weren't just a set piece. Jerry never learned to use a computer. Yes, it was 2003. But one of the first things he told me was that he planned to compose his scripts on a typewriter or write them out longhand. I just looked at him and nodded.

I wasn't sure how this would work, especially if we were on deadline.

Let me say it differently: *I was sure it wouldn't work.* If Jerry wrote a script on a typewriter or—I'm wincing—longhand (it seems ludicrous now even thinking about it), we'd then have to retype it into the computer and then move it over electronically into the teleprompter. This could take ten to fifteen minutes, depending on the length of the story, and often, on deadline, you have no more than two minutes to add or change a script.

This was untenable. It was also a sensitive subject. I asked to meet with Erik and Phil. After all, they'd been working with Jerry for months before I arrived. I sensed they had a good relationship with him and might have thoughts on approaching the issue calmly, reasonably, and rationally to ensure the desired outcome. Given their senior status, I assumed one of them would offer to speak with Jerry on my behalf.

"Not a chance," Phil Griffin said, laughing, and looking at Erik. "Andy, we hired you because you can handle difficult people."

"I saw you deal with Brill. You were as good as anybody," Erik chimed in with his signature wide smile. "You can handle a bully like Nachman." Erik was trying to con me. Nobody was good at handling Mr. Brill.

"We're scared of Jerry, to be honest," Phil said, only half joking.

Almost everyone at the top levels of MSNBC felt bullied by Jerry because of his gruff manner. He got away with it because of his chummy relationship with executive management at the top of NBC News.

I walked out of the office, knowing full well that I was going to have to deal with Jerry on my own. This situation was all too familiar.

I was on the playground facing the bully again, with all the other kids gathering around and watching in amusement.

I walked back through the newsroom and went to see Jerry.

"Andy, you don't get it. I will be writing for my show, my way. I will provide it to you in plenty of time to do whatever you need to get it into the computer and then into the prompter for me to read. Capisce?"

Jerry had a tension in his voice that I anticipated but hadn't experienced yet. He glared at me with indignation tinged with what I grew to learn was abject fear.

"Okay, I'll make it work, Jerry."

"Yes, you will," Jerry said.

Over time, we established a bond. The other bullies I encountered in my career never showed any weakness. They never flinched in my presence. Jerry did. He was vulnerable.

Maybe that's why I liked him.

During rehearsals prior to our premiere, I realized Jerry was scared to death. He had to carry the show. The program would be called *Nachman*. And for the first time, Jerry would be "talent" in front of the camera and not simply the boss barking orders behind the scenes.

Our show was a news-based talk show. Without getting too technical, once one guest was on the air, our tech folks would begin working on getting the next guest set up on the satellite and making sure their audio and video were "clean." Then, the segment producer needed a few minutes to give final instructions to the guest about where to look, how long the interview was likely to last, and any late-breaking news that might impact the line of questioning.

Live television being what it is, we often had trouble getting all the guests on the air in a timely fashion. I'd be in the control room, just trying to keep it all together and hoping I could avoid an off-camera Jerry tantrum. His anger revolved around his fear of being live and not having the option of bantering with a cohost if a guest was delayed. MSNBC wouldn't give him a cohost. So, when Jerry got flustered, he'd quickly throw to a commercial break. During the break, as we desperately tried to get the next guest ready for air, he'd spend two minutes and thirty seconds spitting mad and making sure I knew it over my headset.

Some people at MSNBC described it as "television without a net."

I referred to it as "television with a novice host."

Every day would start out in a pleasant fashion. Jerry would invite me to come to his office to discuss the show while he ate. He consumed large portions of eggs, bacon, and donuts or bagels from the cafeteria for breakfast, and cheeseburgers and fries were the usual choice for lunch. He often had a cigar in his hand, and he smoked cigarettes.

Jerry was divorced, his parents had passed, he had no children, and he lived alone.

He was so astute, yet flawed and childlike. He was intractable but lovable. I felt sorry for him at times. Underneath all that bombast was a lonely man, who I also believed was a damaged man.

The show premiered with very little attention. No flowery bouquets purported to be from sitting presidents, like Morton Downey's debut. We were several months into the show, and after an entire week of Jerry being in a particularly surly and unaccommodating mood, he decided that our head writer, who'd been a news writer for MSNBC for a decade, could no longer write news for the show.

"He can't fucking write in my voice," Jerry screamed at me.

Of course, nobody could write in Jerry Nachman's voice except Jerry Nachman.

I started thinking about looking for work. It was just too much each day dealing with Jerry's increasing rage. Then I caught a break. Jerry called me and said he wasn't feeling well and wouldn't be in for a few days. I made sure to sound crestfallen.

The truth is, I was relieved knowing Jerry was sick and would be out for a bit. I'd soon come to feel awful about that initial sense of relief. It became clear that Jerry didn't just have a cold or the flu. I became worried about him. The only thing he had going in his life was his work.

Three weeks later, we were told he was being treated at Memorial Sloan Kettering Cancer Center.

A few of us from the show visited him one night after work. We knocked on his door, and there he was. I hadn't had all that much experience with hospital rooms to that point in my life, but the room was quite large and nicely appointed. It was a private room, which I thought was unusual in New York City and likely quite expensive.

The conversation was light.

He looked good and vibrant and seemed pleased to see us—much more so than he did each day at MSNBC. He was lying in bed, and for the first time since meeting Jerry, I wondered why I'd been so afraid of him. For most of my career, I've lived in fear of my bully bosses. But seeing him there, I realized Jerry was just a man who was probably more scared at that moment than I'd ever been in my entire life.

He assured us he'd be back at work soon. I was pleased to hear it.

After twenty minutes, my staff floated toward the hallway and the elevators. I held back to steal a few moments with Jerry. I couldn't help thinking how alone he was in this world.

"Regal," he said conspiratorially with a broad smile. "How do you like my room?"

"Jerry, it's the nicest hospital room I've ever seen," I said, feeling good that this had the benefit of being the truth and knowing it was important to him.

"I know a guy," he said with pride. "There are only four rooms like this in the entire place. A source tells me Cardinal O'Connor stayed in the room next door." Nachman, ever the journalist, working the story.

Jerry passed away on January 19, 2004. The *New York Times* reported on his death:

> [Jerry Nachman] was 57. Mr. Nachman, who had said [a year earlier] that he had a malignancy in his gallbladder, was found dead yesterday morning, a spokesman for MSNBC said.

Mr. Nachman cultivated an exaggerated cigar-chomping, street-smart style, bringing both acute intelligence and dogged persistence to his pursuit of the news. For almost a generation, he was a familiar figure to newspaper readers and viewers of television news in New York City, not least because he told few stories without a strong punchline.*

I miss listening to your stories, Jerry.

---

* Douglas Martin, "Jerry Nachman Dies at 57; Award-Winning Journalist," *New York Times*, January 21, 2004, https://www.nytimes.com/2004/01/21/nyregion/jerry-nachman-dies-at-57-award-winning-journalist.html.

CHAPTER 39

LATE-BREAKING OLD NEWS

I wasn't out of a job yet; I was out of work.

Erik Sorenson assured me he would find another suitable role. The first Iraq war was in its early days, and MSNBC was transforming itself from a sleepy, low-rated, little cable news network that specialized in liberal talk into a 24/7 news operation covering the post-9/11 conflict. The executives at NBC began jettisoning the talk shows during the daytime hours and strictly going with war coverage.

The dictate came down from on high to show as much American patriotism as possible in our news broadcasts. NBC couldn't lose the ratings war for the hearts and minds of viewers to Fox News.

I was asked to executive produce during the daytime. I'd be in the control room for a four-hour block of programming.

Live war coverage was a different beast than the live but slower-paced talk shows I was used to. The job of the EP, as I was quick to find out, was all about anticipation and communication. To anticipate, troubleshoot, and communicate effectively, the executive producer had better know what they were doing.

Just one problem: I had no idea what I was doing.

The vast board in front of the executive producers allowed them to communicate with correspondents standing by around the globe, the news anchor on the set, as well as staffers working on the broadcast in the control room, such as the director, assistant director, technical director, coordinating producer, and teleprompter operator.

The buttons and toggle switches that allowed me direct access to each of these people were not labeled. You just had to know somehow—intuit, I guess—which one took you to each person's headset wherever they were around the world or around the control room.

Without consultation, my bosses scheduled me to oversee my first block of war coverage one week after I was informed that the Nachman show was over and no new show or substitute host would replace it. That week, I received zero training in the control room. Not one person ever sat with me and discussed how I was to do the job—or, more specifically, the best way to do it.

I decided to sit in the control room for a few days and watch how things worked, trying to make sense of all the moving parts. But watching an airplane pilot work and then sitting in her seat with the runway straight ahead and the engines revving and expecting to fly the plane safely, are two very different experiences.

The 2:00 p.m. to 6:00 p.m. broadcast team members would line up right outside the door to the control room where the 10:00 a.m. to 2:00 p.m. team was concluding its shift. I'm not sure why it was done this way; perhaps it was a lack of available control rooms. It was nuts. I observed absolute chaos every day.

I have no idea how to orchestrate my way through this mayhem when it is my turn—and my turn is now.

Lester Holt, who is already a star at NBC News, will be anchoring much of MSNBC's coverage. He is my anchor that day. Most of NBC's heavyweights didn't want anything to do with MSNBC in its early days, but now that the war was here, all the stars of NBC News are being drafted into duty.

On a talk show, the executive producer meets with the host frequently before the broadcast. Not in news. So before our stint I worked on the scripts and Lester, sitting somewhere else in the building, made his revisions. I never met Lester Holt before serving as his executive producer that day.

We stand at the ready of the closed control room door, waiting impatiently for the "On Air" light to turn off.

At precisely 01:57:30 p.m., the 10:00 a.m. to 2:00 p.m. team stumbles out, and we race in like we are playing musical chairs. We sit down, and the ritual begins of everyone quickly aligning their headsets, twirling knobs, pushing buttons, adjusting computer screens, logging in, and starting to speak with audio-video satellite technicians, playback operators, producers, and reporters in the field.

We have two and a half minutes, the duration of one commercial break, to set up our show—to get the anchor comfortable, check in and confirm that each of the reporters is prepared to go live in Kuwait, Saudi Arabia, Jerusalem, DC, London, and the Pentagon. Two minutes and thirty seconds for the director to confirm with the executive producer which story is first, second, third, and fourth; which associated videotapes are confirmed with the team in playback; and which scripts are updated and confirmed with any late-breaking changes. And then, if you have the luxury, the director, anchor, and executive producer spend the last fifteen seconds before hitting air reconfirming the plan for the top of the broadcast, which may have changed drastically in the previous two minutes and thirty seconds.

I am frozen. It is like one of those recurring school anxiety dreams in which you can't find your uniform and the big game is moments away, or you can't find your classroom and you have a big test today, or you forgot to go to class all semester and now it's final exams day.

MSNBC is pushing all *my* buttons. But I still don't know which of MSNBC's buttons to push.

I have no idea how to talk to Lester or even what to say to him. I might've introduced myself if I'd known which button connected me to his headset. I can see him on the monitor in the studio. He is getting settled with his copy and looking up at his camera and the prompter copy he is set to read.

Everyone seems to be doing their job except me. I remember at that moment wondering and hoping that maybe I am like a gallbladder—nice to have but not necessary. We are now fifteen seconds to air. The director yells, "Quiet!" It is a command, not a request.

I am now more a viewer than the supposed leader of this team. I lift my head to watch Lester Holt on the bank of monitors in the front of the control room do what he has done as well as any other network anchor over the last twenty-five years. He starts to deliver the news with great calm, authority, and integrity.

There is always one monitor in the control room devoted to the prompter, so anyone who wants to can follow along as Lester reads the copy. This is especially helpful to the director and assistant director because the script will indicate when a photo, video, or graphic is to be brought up onto the screen.

I am not paying particular attention to what Lester is saying (or, more accurately, what he is reading), but about twenty seconds in, I notice something. This first story sounds eerily reminiscent of a story I'd heard while training a week ago. I don't mean it sounded like an update to that story; it sounded like the same story. Lester then moves on to the next story. I start looking around the control room, much like when you're on a plane and the turbulence starts to get bad and you look around to see if any of the passengers or flight crew are experiencing your abject horror.

I'd heard this second story before too. Verbatim. This goes on for about a minute, and then the director, who sits in the front row of the control room, turns and says angrily over his shoulder to me in the back row, "Is this the right copy?"

This is not a rhetorical question.

I want to say, "Well, how the fuck do I know? I have no idea what I'm doing."

Instead, I hear over my shoulder, "Oh God, I loaded the wrong copy. This is last Monday's script."

I turn around and see the teleprompter operator, who can't be over twenty-two years old, with his head down. The prompter (usually) works because the operator puts in a day, date, and time, and the computer calls up the rundown and script for that specific broadcast. Somehow, in his haste to get ready, the young prompter operator had the right day, Monday, and the right time, 2:00 p.m., but he input *last week's* date.

Lester Holt is reading last week's news on live TV.

I turn back in time to hear Lester start reading the third story from last Monday. I can tell he knows it now too. The director gets in Lester's earpiece and yells, "Go to break! Now! Script problem."

Mid-sentence and mid-story, Lester calmly says, "We're going to take a break and be back. Stay with us."

A short promo plays immediately. Every one of us in the control room hears the promo proudly declare, "For the best in late-breaking Iraq War coverage, turn to MSNBC."

Well, the news was breaking, but not late-breaking.

I had almost four hours to rehearse what I would say to Lester to explain this horrible blunder. I could detail how I was new and never properly trained, that it was completely unfair to me, him, and the entire production team that we only had a couple minutes to get set and settled for air, and that the prompter operator was just a kid. But I was the executive producer on duty, and it was my job to oversee the entire broadcast. I was responsible for ensuring that the proper copy was in the prompter for the anchor to read.

The remaining three hours and fifty-five minutes came and went. I was traumatized. Lester might berate and belittle me and refuse to ever work with me again. He could go to Erik and Phil and demand that I be fired. I had embarrassed him on the air. I had allowed week-old news to be broadcast on a national news show anchored by one of the most highly regarded journalists in all of network news.

I decided to wait outside the studio at the conclusion of our shift and apologize to Lester.

"Hi, Lester," I said. I approached him too abruptly, like an anxious fan looking for an autograph outside the stage door. "I'm Andy Regal. I was the executive producer on duty for the last four hours. I am so sorry for what occurred at the top of the broadcast."

"Hi, Andy," he said with little emotion. I stood ready for the onslaught. "Yeah, that was rough. Let's not have that happen again. It's chaotic at the start, so focus on that first block and then look ahead to the upcoming ones. You're new with us here, right?"

I nodded.

"Well, every place does things differently and has its challenges. This kind of thing happens on occasion. Rely on your director and coordinating producer. They've all been doing this here or across the river for a long time."

He was referring to 30 Rockefeller Plaza.

"I look forward to working with you again under better circumstances." He smiled and walked away.

Our exchange didn't last more than a minute, and I'm quite certain he'd never remember our conversation or any part of this entire debacle. However, I remember vividly how grateful I was that Lester didn't use his power, authority, influence, or ego to rebuke me, ignore me, bully me, demean me, insult me, call into question my loyalty, or threaten to demote or fire me.

Instead, he engaged me in conversation to understand what happened and provided me with guidance and encouragement.

We worked well together after that without incident. I made sure of it.

To this day, I feel a sense of loyalty to Lester Holt.

Dr. Fred Kiel of leadership consulting firm KRW International has over thirty years experience with Fortune 500 CEOs and senior executives in building organizational effectiveness through leadership excellence. Dr. Kiel also presented a TEDx talk titled "Psychopaths in the C-Suite."

He told me his research finds that integrity builds a better business. He explained:

> Forgiveness drives innovation, Andy. Compassion drives workforce engagement. Integrity, responsibility, forgiveness, and compassion are the four pillars for CEOs. A measure of character is how you treat other people. Habits in common among the "virtuoso CEOs" include empathy in business decisions and considering what effect decisions will have on employees. The "I screwed up habit," in which CEOs admit their mistakes, engenders trust and respect and allows others to know it's okay if they made a mistake. It says,

> "I am just like you" to the others in the room. We are all in this together; we are co-equal as people. It's very energizing to the staff.

I wasn't a war casualty after all, but I knew I had to get out of the MSNBC bunker. I hated war coverage.

I wish Lester Holt only enjoyment, satisfaction, meaning, and health in his retirement from NBC News.

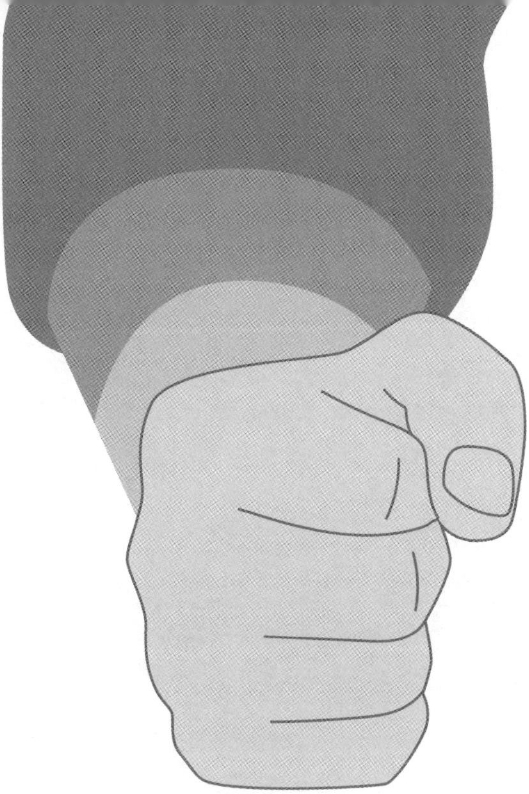

SECTION 7

GENIUSES TO THE LEFT OF ME, BULLIES TO THE RIGHT . . . HERE I AM (AGAIN)

Where there is a void in communication, negativity will fill it.

—JON GORDON, BESTSELLING AUTHOR,

THE POWER OF POSITIVE LEADERSHIP

CHAPTER 40

I WAS THE GUY UNTIL I WASN'T

I turned to Brian Bedol, a mentor from my earliest days in television. Brian's brilliant. He received his MBA from Harvard and quickly began an extraordinary career.

Brian, one of Bob Pittman's chief lieutenants, had been instrumental in developing *The Morton Downey Jr. Show*. I was amazed at his self-assuredness. He was analytical and very funny. I knew Brian would do great things, and I stayed in touch with him in the years after Downey's show was canceled.

If there's one bit of advice I'd give to any new college graduate, it is to pay attention to those you meet early in your career who you believe will achieve success. Then, make sure to stay in touch with those people.

Today was one of those days.

Brian and I had lunch once a year or so after *Downey* went off the air. He was always great about making time for me. We'd reminisce about the *Downey* days and laugh at Mort's histrionics and the wild times of getting that show off the ground. Toward the end of every lunch, I would, not subtly, plead with Brian that if he started any new venture, he should please consider me.

In May 1995, Brian had launched the Classic Sports Network. He negotiated licensing deals with the major sports leagues for their archival footage and acquired hours of historic boxing matches and other major sports events.

As much as this seemed like a dream opportunity, I didn't join Classic Sports for two primary reasons. One, I was at Court TV at the time and not ready to leave. And two, Brian never offered me a job at Classic.

Classic Sports operated as a stand-alone network for just two years before being acquired by ESPN for $175 million, and the network became part of the ESPN portfolio of networks. I remember reading about the acquisition and wondering, with a flash of envy, what the payout was for Classic's employees on a sale of $175 million. I pledged that if Brian ever started another venture in the sports space again, I'd do everything in my power to get him to hire me.

In 2002, Brian and his partner Chris Bevilacqua, a former wrestler at Penn State, announced they were launching a national college sports cable network. Chris was intelligent, thoughtful, a strong leader, and a pioneer in acquiring sports media rights. They made an impressive executive team with access to capital, which gave this first-ever network devoted to college sports a serious chance to succeed.

Long-term rights to basketball and football games among the major college conference teams had been acquired long ago by the major networks. However, a land grab was still possible in those days for the military academies, historically Black colleges and universities, and mid-major conferences. The channel would feature those smaller college football and basketball teams and grow through interest in the mostly ignored "lesser" sports at big schools such as wrestling, volleyball, softball, baseball, swimming, and soccer.

Just a few weeks after the network's official launch on February 23, 2003, I was hired as vice president of original production for College Sports Television (CSTV).

My dream of a full-time job in sports had been realized. And maybe this next time, when Brian sold CSTV I'd make millions, as I assumed the early employees of Classic Sports Network had.

When I accepted the offer and thanked Brian profusely, I assured myself that this opportunity of a lifetime would be different. It was the right job at the right time for my skill set, with management that would motivate, inspire, and appreciate my hard and good work. I was finally home.

After only a couple of weeks at CSTV, I produced my first video. It wasn't much. I don't recall the subject, but I remember that my piece was lauded in the first all-CSTV employees meeting. The entire staff was assembled in the space where all our pre- and postgame studio shows would originate. There were about fifty of us in what amounted to a construction site. There was nowhere to sit, so we all stood around where the set would ultimately be built.

Brian and Chris spoke first to the new team. The message was that we could create something special to rival ESPN in the coming years.

Rich McKenna spoke next. He was a top executive with CSTV. He stood out among the crowd. He was big, probably six feet five inches and 215 pounds, and in his early thirties, so ten years my junior. Rich looked like a football player—no surprise there. He played big-time college football. He was impressive. His larger-than-life personality fit well with his physique, big, broad smile, and perfect teeth.

McKenna spoke about the challenges of building a sports network from nothing. He detailed the limitless opportunities to partner with some of the country's top colleges and universities and highlight athletes who often received acclaim during the Olympics but received little notice during their remarkable collegiate careers. Rich said with conviction that this was all about to change. We all believed him and believed in him.

He was tasked with managing all the individual college, university, and conference relationships. He also oversaw the network's programming and ultimately was in charge of on-air talent as the network grew.

He had a big job.

Rich looked good and commanding as he spoke to the team, like a coach about to lead us all out of the locker room and onto the field.

As Rich concluded his remarks, something completely unexpected happened. He started lauding me. "I don't know if you all have had a chance to see the first video that Andy Regal produced, but it is outstanding. We are so fortunate to have someone of Andy's experience and talent with us, and he will be instrumental in shaping our video content strategy. If you haven't met Andy yet, please do so." And with that, he turned it back over to Brian.

It meant so much to have someone of Rich's authority and influence single me out in front of Brian, Chris, and the entire CSTV staff. I floated back to my office following the generous praise from the "big guy."

McKenna wasn't my boss when I started at CSTV. Long-time sports media executive Leo Sterling had been brought in to oversee all sports production, both live games and original programming, which included the short-form sports features and long-form documentaries I would produce.

We had a good time together. Leo cared deeply about the product. He had little if any ego, and he knew what he was doing. Perhaps most importantly, he appreciated me and my work. He was a good, caring, knowledgeable, and effective manager.

Early on, I was in Leo's office talking about a possible series we were developing sponsored by Nike called *Nike Training Camp*, which would profile some of the elite college athletic programs that had a Nike affiliation.

Rich noticed me in Leo's office and joined us. He liked to make the rounds. The conversation, as it often did with Rich, turned to other senior staff. Rich was clever, and he'd make a funny, derisive remark about how this one spoke or that one looked. The punchline was often that they were worthless and should be fired. Leo and I would laugh uproariously right along with Rich.

I was guilty of encouraging and enabling McKenna's denigration of our colleagues—cheering Rich on as he ridiculed my colleagues, unbeknownst to them. I was thrilled to be part of the in crowd and not one of those being belittled.

It felt good to be "Brian's and Rich's guy."

Until I wasn't. And then it didn't.

In a research study looking at male-dominated work cultures titled "Everybody but Me: Pluralistic Ignorance and the Masculinity Contest," published in the *Journal of Social Issues*, its authors describe the masculinity contest as "a set of organizational norms that fosters competition, work devotion, strength, and dominance."* In another study, described in the article "How Masculinity Contests Undermine Organizations, and What to Do About It," its authors state, "Because people *publicly* uphold the norms, it appears as though everyone endorses them . . . People in masculinity contest cultures *think* their coworkers embrace these norms when in fact they do not, breeding pervasive but silent dissatisfaction alongside active complicity as people stay quiet to prove they belong."†

Leo's team had a few technical gaffes—things that often occur in live sports production. From what I could tell, there was no conversation with Leo about how to remedy the mistakes and improve work processes. Instead, after just a year or so, one of my favorite bosses left the premises. Leo had gone from a confidant and part of the manly in-crowd to a replaceable "colleague" whose time at CSTV had come to an abrupt end.

The gabfests with Rich ended abruptly too. He called me into his office about a week after Leo's departure. "I'm running all programming now, so you'll report to me from here on out."

He was dictating to me and talking down to me. Maybe it was my ego, but I felt small looking up at my new boss, who suddenly seemed like all the old bosses.

"I need to keep up with all the programs you're developing, so from now on, cc me whenever you email anyone outside the company." I was convinced he did not want me to succeed, and spying on me was the best way to monitor my work.

I'd overseen staffs of more than fifty people with multimillion-dollar budgets, and now I would be so micromanaged, diminished, and emasculated

---

* Christin L. Munsch, Jonathan R. Weaver, Jennifer K. Bosson, and Linsey Trimble O'Connor, "Everybody but Me: Pluralistic Ignorance and the Masculinity Contest," *Journal of Social Issues*, September 2018, https://spssi.onlinelibrary.wiley.com/doi/10.1111/josi.12282.

† Jennifer L. Berdahl, Peter Glick, and Marianne Cooper, "How Masculinity Contests Undermine Organizations, and What to Do About It," SHRM, November 7, 2018, https://www.shrm.org/topics-tools/news/organizational-employee-development/how-masculinity-contests-undermine-organizations-to.

that I couldn't write a simple email without McKenna eavesdropping.

Brigette Hyacinth, a management expert and author of *Leading the Workforce of the Future*, writes:

> The corporate world is littered with such micromanagers . . . Employees want the feeling of autonomy. If employees cannot make decisions at all without their manager's input, they will feel suffocated . . . No one likes to come to work every day and feel they are walking into a penitentiary with their every movement being monitored . . . Micromanagement is a complete waste of everybody's time. It sucks the life out of employees, fosters anxiety and creates a high stress work environment . . . Select the right people . . . and then give them room to get the job done!*

Bullying is about control. McKenna had just pinned me to the ground and sat on my chest. I struggled there with my face burning like a humiliated child. He let me up long enough so I could dust myself off and quietly return to my office just down the hall.

When any significant problem occurred within the programming department, McKenna's management style was to email all involved: "How the hell did this happen?"

From my vantage point, there was no fact-finding, no listening, and certainly no problem-solving. But some form of upbraiding of the guilty (or innocent) party was likely to follow—directly or behind their back.

Dr. Yeager at Ohio State University has seen this management style in his work as the director of the Stress, Trauma and Resilience Program. He told me,

"This is the most prevalent piece that has emerged in workplace bullying. It's all about the individual and not about the collective good. Bullies are extroverts, charismatic, big personalities. They can't look dependent upon or give

---

* Brigette Hyacinth, "If You Can't Trust Your Employees to Work Flexibly, Why Hire Them in the First Place?" October 22, 2020, https://brigettehyacinth.com/if-you-cant-trust-your-employees-to-work-flexibly-why-hire-them-in-the-first-place/.

credit to anybody else for helping them. It's all about them. And in fact, they never accept responsibility for a failure. It's always on somebody else.

"Targets are rule followers. They were raised to treat people well. Andy, you were raised to do the right thing. You follow a predictable path. That's what bullies like because they know what you will do. They know how you're going to respond. They know you aren't going to attack them back because you were raised not to behave in that way. Your mother taught you better than that."

I asked Dr. Yeager if something about me and my personality provoked Rich. He replied, "Andy, bullies look for anxious people like you. They put you in situations that will make you more anxious. They enjoy watching you struggle."

I had to think about how I phrased every email I sent out. A few times, I would take a chance and not cc McKenna, and it would get back to him. He'd be furious, and I would apologize.

I thought about approaching Chris or Brian, but like so many workplace targets, I felt it was too dangerous because of my bully's stature within the organization and his proximity to power. There was no HR department to go to for guidance and support either.

I couldn't win a fight with McKenna.

He was too big.

I would end up out on the street, like Leo.

CHAPTER 41

YOU CAN STILL PULL THE RUG OUT FROM UNDER ME EVEN IF I'M STANDING ON WALL-TO-WALL CARPETING

I loved my job at CSTV and felt I was contributing significantly to its growth with the original programming I created.

Brian, the CEO, wanted a full slate of content, and I had a multimillion-dollar budget to produce programming. I turned the National Collegiate Paintball Championships into a television event. I produced a documentary film on the students fervently competing at the National Collegiate Debate Championships, and just as *Dancing with the Stars* was becoming a hit, I tried unsuccessfully to create a series *The National Collegiate Ballroom Dancing Championships*. I produced a documentary to air over Memorial Day weekend profiling collegiate athletes and coaches who had served with distinction in the military. Senator John McCain hosted the program. And I produced a collegiate solar car race across Texas.

Despite the rewarding projects I developed, the uncomfortable nature of my relationship with McKenna was affecting my emotional well-being and my future at CSTV. I had to do something. I boldly decided to see whether McKenna would have lunch with me. He was so good and comfortable in social situations; I thought if we got out of the office and had a collegial meal together, he might see me differently and start working with me instead of against me.

I spent two days trying to figure out how to approach him, which again tells you how dysfunctional it was. I was scared to ask my supervisor to have lunch with me. After much deliberation, I decided to go with the informal approach. Instead of an email, I would stop by his office, and if he was in, I'd just kind of lean in through the doorway and say, "Hey, Rich, how about lunch this week?" You know, like two guys going to grab a beer or play golf (I don't play golf). And like a golf swing, I practiced and practiced . . . in this case what I would say. I tried to relax because I knew Rich, like all bullies, could smell fear and weakness.

I walked over to his office a few times that morning, heart pounding, reciting what I'd rehearsed. All our offices were glass enclosed, so you could quickly and easily peer inside to see if someone was on the phone or in a meeting. Rich's office was empty each time I walked by. As I did a 180 to head back to my glass cell, I breathed a sigh of relief even though I wanted to get this over with. I hoped my offer would foster additional communication and improve the lack of collaboration, which I felt was cloaking outright animus.

The next time I crept toward his office, he was there.

"Hey, Rich," I said, leaning my head just slightly into his doorway as if wishing him a sunny good morning. It was probably my eighth attempt to get this done. He looked up stone-faced.

"What's up?" he said without a hint of warmth.

I speculated that he would recoil or scoff at anything that suggested I wanted to speak to him on a personal or human level. Rich was a man's man. He was a slap-on-the-back kind of guy.

I went with this. "I just wanted to see if we could grab lunch this week and talk about some content initiatives."

I chose to keep it short and dispassionate.

"Regal," he said, with more than a hint of irritation. "We don't need to break bread. You just need to do your fucking job."

The conversation lasted less than twenty seconds. But it has stayed with me for twenty-five years.

With that, he looked back down like a sergeant dismissing his private. I was no private; I was the VP of original programming for the entire network.

I nodded my head and left without saying a word. By the time I returned to my office, McKenna had likely forgotten this exchange.

That was the last significant conversation I ever had with Rich McKenna. The chilling effect had devolved into a frozen effect.

We had women in positions of authority, but masculinity was part of CSTV's culture.

During this time, I also developed and produced a documentary series called *Coach*, in which we profiled legendary UCLA Bruins basketball coach John Wooden, among others. As part of that effort, I traveled to Detroit, where Bill Walton was broadcasting an NBA game. He'd agreed to do a sit-down interview about his beloved coach. Bill Walton told touching stories about his days playing for Coach Wooden and their relationship as if he was telling them for the first time.

Two hours after the interview, I got a call on my cell while driving back to the airport. "Hey, Andy, it's Bill Walton. Thanks again for the interview opportunity today. I love talking about Coach. I just wanted to make sure I did a good job for you and gave you everything you need for the documentary you're working on."

I couldn't believe one of my boyhood idols and one of the most admired athletes, a Hall of Famer, a great broadcaster, and an icon, was calling me, checking to see if *he'd* done a good job for *me*.

It was just a two-minute call. But it has stayed with me for twenty-five years.

I join the sports world in mourning the recent loss of this gentle giant.

In the early summer of 2005, Brian Bedol, the CEO of CSTV, called me into his office—a very unusual event. He kept his office dark. The only light in the room came from the numerous monitors he was operating simultaneously. The glow gave him an evil-genius vibe.

Despite the somewhat sinister environment, Brian smiled as I walked in. He motioned me to sit down.

"You and I have known each other a long time, and so I will tell you something in utter confidence. We're selling the network. I can't tell you to whom, but it will happen in the next four to six months. I'm telling you this because when the sale goes through, we will have to let you go, and I want you to have time to look for something new.

I didn't know what to say. I knew I should congratulate Brian, and I did. But I didn't understand why they needed to release me. Certainly, the buyer would want and need someone with my skill set to create and produce quality sports programming. Apparently not.

Rich McKenna never spoke to me in the months before the public announcement of the acquisition. I believe Rich was instrumental, and perhaps even responsible, for my demise at CSTV.

The deal was months away from closing, and even though Brian swore me to secrecy, I sensed everyone knew I was not part of the team going forward.

Humiliating.

I sat in my glass office and felt that not only could my colleagues see right through the glass, but they could also see right through me and see how dejected and worthless I felt.

On November 3, 2005, it was announced that CBS had agreed to pay $325 million to acquire College Sports Television. I was out of a job again, but my options came to $85,000, a sizable if not life-changing "severance" package. At least I had achieved my goal of not being on the outside when Brian sold another company and wondering if I'd missed out on a million-dollar windfall.

I mentioned I never spoke to Rich McKenna again. Well, that's not entirely true. We never spoke while I was still at CSTV. But just days after I left the company—or the company left me—I was sitting in my apartment when my cell rang.

"Hey, Andy, it's Rich McKenna."

His tone was upbeat and cheerful, and he had every right to feel that way. Who knows how much money he made in the sale, and he was keeping his job with CBS Sports.

"I just wanted to tell you how truly sorry I am about how things ended and that Brian couldn't find a place for you within CBS Sports. I wish there was more I could've done. And please let me know if there's anything I can do for you in the future."

"Oh, thank you, Rich. I will. I'm doing fine and looking at some great opportunities," I lied.

"Well, that's great. Good to hear. Listen, I've got to run to a meeting with the CBS Sports execs. Good luck, Andy."

That call took me completely off guard. I was trying to reconcile the kindness he seemed to offer with the disregard and disrespect he exhibited for years. I can't be sure what his motive was in calling, but I must admit that, at that dark time for me, I assumed the worst.

I was sure this sadistic bully was calling me because it wasn't quite enough that I was now out of a job. It was my dream job before he became my manager. McKenna diminished me, humiliated me, and made me miserable—my self-esteem shattered. I believe he wanted to hear my voice in complete and utter capitulation. I think he was getting off on knowing that he'd won. I was on the ground, beaten down, and he wanted to get in one more good stomp.

Mary Lamia, PhD, is a clinical psychologist and psychoanalyst in Marin County, California. In her article for *Psychology Today*, "Why Bullies Don't Feel Bad (or Don't Know They Do)," she shared that "the bully's attacks are projections of their own shame and feelings of inadequacy that are modified to penetrate a victim's vulnerability. Attacking others not only halts any inclination to look within themselves, it also can be exciting as it stimulates the physical experience of power."*

Clive Boddy is a leadership and organizational behavior professor and currently the deputy head of the School of Management at Anglia Ruskin University in Cambridge, England. For the past decade, he has studied the

---

* Mary Lamia, "Why Bullies Don't Feel Bad (or Don't Know They Do)," *Psychology Today*, March 1, 2015, https://www.psychologytoday.com/us/blog/intense-emotions-and-strong-feelings/201503/why-bullies-dont-feel-bad-or-dont-know-they-do.

evidence and effects of toxic leadership and bullying. In a TEDx talk, he discusses why bullies bully. He makes the point that bullies can be "totally ruthless and sleep perfectly well at night." He continues, "Why is it so pervasive in all companies, around the world, and in all countries? . . . [They are] predatory. So they do it because they like it. They do it because they enjoy it. They do it because they like to see people squirm. They like just to hurt people, they want to damage their careers . . . It's enjoyable."*

I'm not always a kind and forgiving person. I carry the hurt and the anger. However, I am fully aware that such negative emotions are only poison in my own system. There doesn't seem to be any antidote for the harm done, and the damage we bully targets live with is distortion of perspective and diminishment of joy.

As targets, we hold on to the grudge, unable to let the memories go. We recreate the factors of distress over and over and over again. It is not so easy to move on.

Workplace bullying can have profound and enduring psychological effects, often leading to long-term trauma that persists even years after the incidents, says Dr. Sharie Stines in her article "The Trauma of Workplace Bullying," on Psych Central. She discusses how such experiences can lead to lasting emotional devastation. She notes that individuals subjected to workplace bullying may feel ashamed and humiliated, making it difficult to share their experiences with others, including loved ones. This internalization can exacerbate the trauma, leading to prolonged psychological distress.†

For those of us who've been bullied, whether in and around the schoolyard or in and around the boardroom, the harm stays with us, in some cases forever. My friend Bill Boggs used to ask me, "Andy, what's in it for you to hold on to these memories and feelings and the depression that results?"

---

* Clive Boddy, "Bullying and Corporate Psychopaths at Work: Clive Boddy at TEDx-HanzeUniversity," TEDx Talk, October 3, 2012, posted December 3, 2012, YouTube video, https://www.youtube.com/watch?v=tlB1pFwGhA4.

† Sharie Stines, "The Trauma of Workplace Bullying," Psych Central, July 30, 2017, https://psychcentral.com/pro/recovery-expert/2017/07/the-trauma-of-workplace-bullying#1.

I had no answer.

Now I do, and I hope it helps other bullying victims understand and address their trauma.

CHAPTER 42

THE BULLY WORE PRADA

I'd been out of work (again) for a few months. It was late spring 2006. My agent Adam called. There was a new show launching in the fall, and he thought I'd be perfect for it.

"Regs, it's taking you back to your daytime talk roots. You'd have to take a bit of a step back in title; it's a senior producer role, but the money will be good. It's Telepictures. It's perfect for you. The target audience is women, and the host is this really compelling guy, Dr. Keith Ablow. I'm putting your name in, and I will pitch you hard."

I loved Adam's enthusiasm.

Wow, Telepictures, I thought to myself. In the early nineties, I'd returned to Chicago for a couple of months to help produce the pilot shows for *The Jenny Jones Show*, which became a massive hit for Telepictures in syndication during the days of trash talk TV.

Telepictures was starting a new talk show, one to compete with and rival Dr. Phil's, which, in not particularly clever fashion, would be titled *The Dr. Keith Ablow Show*.

I met Dr. Keith, as I would come to refer to him, at his hotel suite in midtown Manhattan.

Dr. Keith was the kind of guy who, when you read about him and all that he'd accomplished, makes you feel like an indolent failure, especially if you are the same age. Which I was.

He graduated magna cum laude from Brown University with a bachelor of science in neuroscience. He received his MD from Johns Hopkins and completed his psychiatric residency at Tufts Medical Center. He'd written numerous books and contributed columns to *The New York Times*.

He was even more impressive in person. Keith made an immediate and powerful impression. He had a shaved head, was about six feet tall, and it was clear he worked out. He met me with a wide smile and bright eyes. I was there for a job interview, and within seconds he made me feel as though I was hanging out with a good college buddy who I hadn't seen in a while.

In the hour we spent together, it was clear that Keith was driven and intent on making his show a huge success.

"Andy, if you watch Dr. Phil, and Judge Judy for that matter, they're on high, passing judgment on the poor souls who have misbehaved and now must sit there and be subject to condescension and public humiliation. That will *not* be my show."

He looked me straight in the eye as he said this.

"A core principle of my life and my practice is empathy. My show will be built around and based on empathy for the people who come on the show looking for answers to some of life's most tragic circumstances. I won't be wagging my finger at them, shouting, 'Shame, shame!' I care about people. Deeply. And I can help them come to a revelation about their past that, while painful, will put their life on a new and healthier course they never thought possible. And with this show, we can do that for my guests and for the millions watching at home. The key to the entire show is empathy, Andy. Actually, the key to life is empathy."

I was starting to develop a man crush. Here was a medical minister preaching the gospel to someone desperate to be saved. This was my chance to be cleansed from the decades of work in which I had toiled for bosses who ruled—I can't even say *managed*—with a total and utter lack of empathy.

I wanted to hug Dr. Keith. During the interview, he asked me all kinds of questions about myself. I'd fallen under his spell. He cared about me and was interested in what I had to say. This guy was getting me to trust him, and I'd just met him. He was going to be a star. I could feel it.

As I was about to leave Dr. Keith's hotel room, he said, "Andy, I want you on my staff. We'll have a great time together. And the staff is all women right now, so we need at least one more male perspective."

I could feel my latest unemployment nightmare coming to an end. I could sleep again, feel happy again, and breathe again. And I'd already convinced myself this time would be different as I exited the hotel's revolving doors.

Lynne Radley called a couple days later. She was one of the development executives at Telepictures in charge of *The Dr. Keith Ablow Show*.

"Hi, Andy. We just got off the phone with your former boss, Brian Bedol. We know Brian here at Telepictures and have great respect for him. He just gave you a rave review. Ed Glavin, your friend and one of our top executive producers, also said great things. We want you to join the staff of the *Dr. Keith* show."

I met my new boss, Diane Rappaport, the executive producer of *Dr. Keith*, a couple of weeks later at Telepictures's production offices in New York City. It was early summer 2006. After a few minutes of getting acquainted, Diane looked at me and smiled. "Andy, I'm so thrilled to have you on the staff. I've heard all about you. I can tell we are going to do great together."

Diane, in her late forties or early fifties, slight, with blond curly hair, had the warmest disposition. She had an impressive résumé in daytime television. She'd been in the talk show game for years as executive producer of the *Maury* show, *The Howie Mandel Show*, and *The Montel Williams Show*, and she'd served as executive in charge of production for *The Oprah Winfrey Show*. She was also an attorney. Diane was a very strong and definitive leader.

And she was smart, kind, thoughtful, and fun.

Dr. Keith's premise for the program (and his worldview) was that we're all products of our upbringing. Keith's paradigm was that dysfunctional, often domineering behavior, whether it's violently criminal or simply cruel, is a direct result of one's childhood. No matter what his guests confessed to, Keith was going to show them empathy for the traumas they experienced.

The staff consisted of women in their twenties and early thirties, most of whom had worked on other talk shows. There were around forty people on staff, including production assistants, associate producers, producers, two senior producers, Dr. Keith, and Diane.

Lynne, the development executive, was in from Los Angeles to work with Diane and guide us to the launch. Her geniality from our initial phone interview had faded. Launching a television show is crushing, which is why leadership—*inspiring leadership*—is so crucial. From the outset, it was clear to me that Lynne's often stern and unrelenting, even agitated, management style was beginning to erode Diane's more maternal, supportive, arm-around-your-shoulders leadership approach.

The tension mounted as each day passed and we came closer to the debut.

The greatest pressure with almost every talk show is finding the right guests. Not only did we need to find people with very intimate, even disturbing, personal and family problems, but we also had to find people who could help Keith identify something in their past that could work as an "aha" moment. The show's stated goal was to "offer viewers practical solutions to everyday challenges."*

Keith would conduct the psychological interview, and then at some point in the show, he would lead the guest to something in their past that he could then extrapolate as the reason for the current destructive behavior. On the show, we made it appear that Keith had uncovered this dark secret or long-forgotten memory, even though the booker would've done so weeks before during the lengthy preinterview process.

A bit of talk show sleight of hand.

Finding the perfect "life victim," complete with a ruinous marriage, paralyzing addiction, or destructive behavior—who *also* had family members, friends, or both who were willing to go on national television—was a grind. We were working fifteen-hour days. I got into the office at eight and usually

---

* *The Dr. Keith Ablow Show*, TV Series Finale, accessed March 18, 2025, https://tvseriesfinale.com/tv-show/the-dr-keith-ablow-show/.

didn't leave until eleven. It was draining.

By this time I had a wife, a two-and-a-half-year-old daughter, Sophie, and a newborn son, Lucas. I was rarely at home. And when I was home, I was often in a brittle mood. Somehow, Jennifer recognized and understood the reason for my dark disposition, and she kept it all together without my support. I was not a good partner during this time. I was having just as many meltdowns as baby Lucas—maybe more.

Dr. Maureen Duffy told me toxic work environments are "a public health concern because the impact isn't just limited to the target. The consequences for the target and the family are immense. The health consequences can be very severe. There are often both physical consequences and psychosocial consequences. Especially during the acute period of bullying, you get anxiety and depression, shame, gastrointestinal problems, relationship problems, increased irritability, or just wanting to be left alone."

Check, check, check, check, and check.

Some of the show's episode titles were "Dark Family Secrets," "A Family of Addicts," "The Anger Illness," "My Mother: Does She Love Me?" "Marriages on the Edge," "Sex Addiction," and "Teens with Obsessive Behavior."

Once the guests were booked, the "show package" had to be assembled. This was the bulk of the painstaking preproduction work. The package included all preinterviews, relevant research, video inserts, segment flow, and, most importantly, Keith's carefully crafted questions. This package also detailed whether we needed to supply clothes for the guests upon arrival to the studio if they didn't own attire presentable for television or if any guests needed to visit the show's dentist before filming because they were missing teeth.

We worked frenetically to launch this show and keep it going. Instead of creating a sense of collaboration and shared goals, this panicked pace cast a feeling of dread over the entire production. We began to realize that identifying an agonizing moment in each guest's past that, once revealed, would lead to a life-altering catharsis was a bleak and nearly impossible task.

This was the first time I experienced a female bully in my career. Lynne was irritated, frustrated, and angry with us. She seemed surprised and disappointed that the staff wasn't seamlessly and effortlessly putting each show together.

Instead of working toward a single purpose, Lynne was scornful of our efforts and dismissive of anyone's experience or ideas. It was, "Well, you all are incapable of doing this right, so I guess I'll have to do it myself."

Those who "didn't get it" included me. I was the senior producer, and Lynne had no interest in my concerns, or insights. I was summarily ignored, and she never asked how I thought the team was handling the strain or what I could contribute to improve the environment.

Lynne could be unrelenting. She would change the show materials for each episode to be the way she wanted them. Regularly, she would rewrite every word of the blue reference cards Keith would have on the set during taping. This was laborious and took hours and hours. Lynne would be with us until after midnight as she criticized the work that had or hadn't been done. I gave her credit for her work ethic, but she wasn't improving the show. She was tormenting the staff.

Gary Namie's 2024 Workplace Bullying Institute national survey found that 28 percent of all workplace bullies are women.* Heidi Lynne Kurter, a senior contributor at *Forbes*, explains in "Women Bullied at Work: Here's Why Your Female Boss Doesn't Support You":

> While their intentions for the organization might be good, their own insecurities end up turning them into a toxic leader. Instead of using their power to help women below them, they use it to prey on those they're intimidated by to keep them from advancing. It's also common for toxic women to belittle others while talking themselves up. Dr. Froswa Booker-Drew, founder of Soulstice Consultancy, shared that her former female boss "always talked about

* Workplace Bullying Institute, *2024 WBI US Workplace Bullying Survey: The National Study*, October 22, 2024, https://workplacebullying.org/2024-wbi-us-survey/.

> herself as being someone who did everything and nobody else was ever competent."*

Lynne could be so abrasive and arrogant that nobody—certainly not me, the other senior producer, or Diane—had the mettle to speak up about the challenges inherent in producing this show: why the material was inadequate and what we could do collectively and collaboratively to move it forward more effectively.

Lynne Radley was a complete b-word—no, not that b-word . . . this b-word . . . bully!

Once again, I was confronted with a boss who rarely had a reasonable conversation with a team member to address concerns or used the team's collective experience to solve problems. Lynne was obviously under tremendous pressure to launch this show and make it a success. But she was allowing the tension to flow downhill like a torrent.

Radley would scoff at us and look at us with disdain. The young female staff became dispirited—and they had arrived with so much hopefulness and enthusiasm a few months prior.

I was very fond of the staff and tried to encourage them. I'd been through quite a few startups in my career, and I tried to explain to them that launching a show was always a tough grind but that we'd be gratified once we saw our tireless work on the air. What I didn't express to them was something that was obvious to me.

This production wasn't tense. It was toxic.

Radley was just plain mean to a staff that was 95 percent female.

After reaching fifteen, I lost count of the number of staffers who asked to see me in my office and, once there, couldn't hold it together, breaking down, tears streaming down their faces. Between the long hours and the absolute lack of consideration, communication, and appreciation for what they were being

---

* Heidi Lynne Kurter, "Women Bullied at Work: Here's Why Your Female Boss Doesn't Support You," *Forbes*, updated December 10, 2021, https://www.forbes.com/sites/heidilynnekurter/2020/02/19/women-bullied-at-work-heres-why-your-female-boss-dislikes-you/.

tasked to do, it was too much.

I was the only person they could confide in.

WBI's 2024 poll focused on aggressive behavior in the office but also has a series of questions related to toxic work cultures. Respondents were asked, "Thinking of the most flagrant personal or witnessed workplace harassment or mistreatment incidents reported to an employer, either formally or informally, how did that employer respond?"

- 18 percent reported that the employer ignored the complaint. No action was taken.
- 19 percent stated the employer investigated the complaint to an unsatisfactory conclusion.
- 9 percent said the employer blamed the complainant, who then experienced adverse circumstances.
- 10 percent indicated no negative consequences to the accused harasser.*

So in more than half the instances where a case was made, the victim received no satisfaction.

And where was Diane Rappaport, the executive producer, during this turmoil?

"Can I talk to you, Andy, in the strictest of confidence?"

By now, I was accustomed to staffers confiding in me, but I never expected Diane to do the same.

She looked shaken. I thought a family member was ill or worse. When we started working together, she was buoyant and filled with confidence about her ability to lead the team to a successful launch and a strong premiere season. But now, she looked wan and in distress as she quickly closed my office door behind her.

Diane and I had established a bond, a trust—and I'd like to say a friendship—in the early days of the summer when she and I were the only ones in

* Workplace Bullying Institute, *2024 WBI US Workplace Bullying Survey*, p. 18.

the office before the remainder of the staff had been brought on board.

"Andy, have you noticed anything lately?"

"I'm not sure what you mean, Diane."

"Have you noticed I haven't attended the daily production meetings with Lynne?"

"Well, sure, of course. But I figured you were dealing with Dr. Keith, the director, the studio crew, or the Telepictures people in LA."

"Well, that's just it . . ."

She leaned in toward my desk and spoke more quietly.

"They've stopped inviting me to meetings. I've been ostracized. Why, I have no idea. About two weeks ago, Lynne's tone changed toward me. She was impatient, snippy, and bordering on rude. Then, she just pretty much stopped talking to me. I'm just sitting alone in my office."

She looked ashamed, having to admit all of this to me. I didn't know if she would be the sixteenth person to break down in my presence, but I prepared my box of tissues.

"Do you know a woman named Donna Vellman?" Diane asked me offhandedly.

"Yeah, sure, I know of Donna. Why?"

"I've been told Telepictures is going to bring her in as a consultant, another pair of hands, so to speak, to help us over the next few weeks."

I stared straight ahead. I was now looking at a dead woman sitting. Perhaps Diane didn't know it, but I did. (I recognized all the signs.)

I knew Donna Vellman. She was renowned (a better word would be *infamous*) in talk show circles. She'd be brought in as an "executive consultant" to any production Telepictures deemed problematic.

Donna had been in the talk show game her entire career. She'd been the executive producer for several of Telepictures's failed programs.

I'll never forget the first days with Donna on the team. Following a perfunctory hello when she arrived in the office, she hardly acknowledged my existence. You'd think she'd want to talk with me to get acclimated.

One week later on a Sunday (we worked every Sunday), I was planning our next episode with my team. I had gotten in around eight; it was now eleven in the morning. I heard someone coming down the hallway toward my office—the steps getting closer as they shuffled against the carpeting.

As Donna passed my doorway, I lifted my head from the show material I was reviewing. She kept walking to her office. I could hear her getting settled two offices down from mine—hanging up her coat, arranging things on her desk, and signing into her computer. I waited to see if she would circle back and say hello, ask me how things were going, and ask how she could offer some guidance.

Nothing. Not a word. There were only seven of us in the entire office, and I was the senior person in attendance. I would work another ten hours that day, making it around seventy for the week. But Donna, our new executive consultant, didn't have the decency to acknowledge my existence.

The following Sunday, the same passive-aggressive, bullying behavior was repeated.

I worked not twelve feet from Donna Vellman. Occasionally, she would pass my office to head toward staffers' cubicles to speak with them. I would even hear her joking with them. On her way back to her office, however, she would stare straight ahead and stride right by my open door.

The previously mentioned online piece "Adult Bullies: How to Spot Them, and How to Handle Them" describes the effect that adult bullies have on our well-being when they ignore us: "Isolation comes in two forms: they will either manipulate scenarios to where you create distance between yourself and others, or they will actively tear you down so that others create distance from you. Both have disastrous consequences."*

According to the article, adult bullies don't simply target insecure people—they create them. "The more self-assured, accomplished, and likable person they conquer—the more confidence they can ride until they find their next victim . . . This process comes in the form of insults, cut-downs, backstabbing, gossiping, and anything else that will rattle your self-esteem. In the end, the

* Blush, "Adult Bullies: How to Spot Them, and How to Handle Them."

goal is for you to rely on this person for any happiness you experience in your life. It's controlling, it's manipulative, and it's scary."*

Like the popular kids in high school, the development executives decided who was in and who was out. I seemed to be on the way out. Diane was now a complete outcast. They no longer included her in meetings, but she was still in the control room playing executive producer during the tapings. Diane divulged that they hadn't spoken to her once about any dissatisfaction with her, her work, or the show.

Diane would continue to come into my office periodically, and we'd commiserate about our circumstances and wonder what might happen next.

Despite the tears falling and the tension rising, we produced and recorded two weeks' worth of pretty good shows. It was Friday. A launch party was planned for the staff that evening because *The Dr. Keith Ablow Show* would premiere nationwide on the following Monday. At about 2:00 p.m., Diane came into my office and closed the door.

"I'm done. Donna Vellman is taking over the show. I've never had anything like this happen to me in my entire career."

She looked shell-shocked.

"They still really want me to come to the celebration tonight. Do you think I should go?" Diane looked at me with a surprised, hopeful look.

"Are you kidding me? Your time is done here, but you are more than welcome to come and cheer on Dr. Keith and the team at the premiere party. No, Diane. You need to leave here and go home as quickly as possible. Don't even think about coming tonight."

She lifted herself slowly and exited my office, her shoulders hunched. She left without saying another word.

At about 6:00 p.m., I walked over to the party with my team. I almost wished they'd fired me, so I wouldn't have to attend and pretend that I was in a celebratory mood. The word had gotten around that Diane was out, and Donna was in. I figured I was next. When we walked through the doors, I was

---

* Blush, "Adult Bullies: How to Spot Them, and How to Handle Them."

dismayed to see Diane sitting there.

She was a nonperson now, so nobody dared come and talk to her and appear to be loyal to her. She sat there crestfallen while somehow trying to force a grin.

I was one of the few to have the courage to approach her, wish her well, and show her some compassion and grace.

I never saw Diane after that night. From what I can tell, she never worked in television again.

She'd had enough.

CHAPTER 43

"YOU CAN'T EVEN WORK THE FUCKING CUE CARDS"

I'd always dreamed of producing a show at 30 Rockefeller Center, the home of NBC Studios, *Saturday Night Live*, *Today*, and *The Tonight Show*. That's where we taped *The Dr. Keith Ablow Show*.

Lynne Radley and Donna Vellman continued to treat me as a liability. I was trying to keep the show moving and the team together. They still never asked me for my opinion about anything, even issues related to the episodes I was overseeing.

My colleagues couldn't help but notice. They now kept their distance from me. I was a leper.

Dr. Keith and I were no longer BFFs. On show days at the all-important preproduction meeting to go over the show with Keith, Lynne or Donna took over. They wanted me and everyone else to know that I was incapable of prepping the host, even though I'd been doing exactly that on national shows for twenty years.

I was demoted to running cue cards for Keith, stage left. Like any job, it takes some practice. You must be in sync with the talent.

Keith and I were no longer in sync.

The key for the cue card person is timing. An example is a cue card that says, "Go to break." If the talent sees that message too soon, he might go to a commercial break too early in the show. If I wait too long to show the message and the host doesn't see it until it's too late, then the commercial doesn't run at the proper time, which is also a problem. There is a tight window to keep the commercials on time and not disrupt the host's concentration.

During a break in shooting, I ran to the restroom just down the hall.

Upon exiting, I see Keith coming down the hallway toward me. I planned to say hi as we passed or my usual upbeat, "Great show so far, Dr. Keith." As we approached each other, and before I could utter a word, he said, "You can't even work the fucking cue cards." And he just kept walking.

So much for Mr. Empathy. Or should I say Dr. Empathy?

As I walked back toward the studio, I felt like I was descending into a cesspool of desperately unhappy guests confessing their sins and exposing their shame for all to see on a show whose fundamental tenet was to be understanding.

There was no such sensitivity on air or off. The executives working on the show were the nastiest, least empathetic group of people I'd ever been unfortunate enough to encounter.

Soon after a show taping, Donna approached me in the studio. A decision had been made. I'd no longer be permitted to come to the studio on my show days. I was directed to stay in the office and work on future shows. They thought they were punishing me.

I was relieved and thrilled by this reprimand and demotion.

I often felt racked with tension from the pressure that gradually built toward show day. It was like the moment right after a bully tells you, "I'll be waiting for you outside after school." Everything was dread from that moment on. And living with dread is, well, dreadful.

The bullying, the long hours, trying to attend to the demoralized staff, and still focusing on producing the best episodes possible—it was all affecting my emotional and physical health. I couldn't sleep. I had digestive problems and frequent headaches. The suicidal ideation returned.

I was miserable to be around. Jennifer was kind, thoughtful, and generous not to make an issue of it. She knew I was being tortured.

After nine months with Dr. Keith's show, I started looking for work. Again.

I wasn't the only one this time, though. We were losing staff. A few people found new jobs, while others quit without securing new positions. They told me they couldn't continue working under those conditions.

To keep the show afloat, Telepictures brought in some folks from their Los Angeles office to serve as production support. Much to my delight, Jacqueline Bender showed up one day. I knew Jacqui. We'd worked together for a few months on the *Jenny Jones* pilot for Telepictures years earlier, and we'd stayed in touch. She'd worked as a supervising or senior producer on a few Telepictures productions.

Seeing Jacqui was like being lost in the forest for days, and, just as you are losing hope of ever finding your way out, a ranger appears. Upon arriving at our office, she met me with a smile and a hug. It was the first expression of civility and warmth I'd been shown in months.

Jacqui had been working in our production office for a couple of days when she, too, appeared in my doorway, looked left and right, and said while closing my door, "Can I talk to you?"

At least I didn't have to get my Kleenex box ready. I wasn't concerned that Jacqui was about to break down.

"Andy, we're not just here to help ensure that episodes are produced. We're aware of the challenges in putting the show together, and we know morale is a huge problem. We've been talking informally to as many people as possible here, and we know you're not the problem. We've been told repeatedly that you are working to improve things, help the team, and find solutions. I'm not surprised, knowing you, but we want you to know that we know."

I thought for a moment that I would be the next person to cry in my office. This was vindication. I was being given a reprieve from the role of outcast. I never expected Lynne's or Donna's behavior to change, and it never did. But I now had confirmation. The gaslighting was over. I wasn't the problem.

It was liberating.

I still wanted out. I needed to get out.

I'd been talking to Jim Whitman for a couple of years about a new venture. I'd met Jim while developing and producing *Inside America's Courts*. He was a New Line marketing executive, and he was most often the smartest guy in the room. We both grew up in the Chicago area around the same time.

Jim was one of those guys that I knew would be successful, and I stayed in touch with him.

Jim had an intensity and drive about him. I liked him, and we'd become friends.

He was about to launch an online fantasy-sports media business, and I was talking to him about joining his team in a senior editorial capacity.

Jim didn't know it, but I would have worked for free—even paid him—to get me out of the Dr. Keith morass. My contract was about to lapse in a month. In the meantime, Telepictures was asking me, no *imploring* me, to stay. Their attitude about me had apparently changed. The show was imploding, even though nobody would admit it. They told me, the toughest times were over, and I should stay to enjoy the show's success.

Eight weeks later, Whitman threw me a lifeline, offering me the role of executive vice president of programming and content. I said yes to Jim, hung up the phone, and leaped what felt like six feet into the air, arms raised.

When I floated back down to Earth with a soft, gentle, sublime landing, I was sure this time would be different.

I couldn't wait to quit *The Dr. Keith Ablow Show*. It was the first time in my career that I got the chance to leave before they kicked me out.

This was delicious. I was going to a creative, thrilling, entrepreneurial sports job with a boss and colleague I respected, and leaving a nearly year-long nightmare.

The Dr. Keith Ablow Show was canceled three months later, after just one season.

CHAPTER 44

FANTASY SPORTS AIN'T NO FANTASY

Six of us were walking down Broadway. We were the first employees of a startup digital sports media company, Winning Edge Sports (WES). Jim Whitman, our CEO, had an ingenious idea. Hundreds of independent fantasy sports websites produced daily content for millions of fans hungry to participate in this growing recreational activity. But these site owners, while able to churn out insightful content about football, didn't have the wherewithal to sell advertising and monetize the audiences they were aggregating. Whitman planned to combine these websites into a partnership network and sell advertising against the traffic these hundreds of individual proprietors could attract.

We hoped to create a media company to entice a deep-pocketed broadcaster like ESPN, CBS, or Fox and make us all rich.

We had been in business only a short time when an opportunity arose to move from our cramped, single-room office on the Upper East Side. A hierarchy of offices had never been established. When we arrived for work, we all plopped down on whatever couch or chair was available around this one room.

But now, for the first time, we were heading over to see new and permanent offices in Times Square. As we were walking to our new digs in Midtown, I wondered if Jim had determined who would get which office.

"All I know is that I'm taking the second biggest office," Cole Vance said, finishing the sentence with a maniacal snicker.

Cole felt pretty good about himself. He was in his early forties, with a stocky build.

Like Cole, a few of us had executive VP titles. Until this moment, I thought we were equals.

Nobody challenged Cole on his bold land grab. I certainly didn't, although I thought about it. I feared that if I spoke up questioning his right to the bigger office and lost out, I'd be humbled.

We walked into the new space. Cole quickly spied the biggest office and the next biggest, claiming that one as his own. I remember he walked in, sat down behind the desk with his hands locked behind his head, put his feet up on the desk, and stated to anyone listening, "This is all mine, assholes."

WES grew quickly. We went from 40 website partners to 80 and then to 250. Cobbling together all the traffic these sites brought in, we quickly became a top-ten sports network, even beating some of the major professional sports leagues during their off-seasons. We still trailed the big guys like the NFL, NBA, ESPN, CBS Sports, Fox Sports, and Yahoo Sports, but we were moving up quickly in the rankings.

Cole had worked for the CEO in the past and did a great job of managing up. His top priority was his relationship with Jim. That connection implicitly allowed Cole to behave however he desired, which usually meant a demeaning, belittling, bullying management style, which created tension, dissension, and distress in the office.

Cole is what we call in the anti-bullying space, "a brilliant jerk." He was smart and cunning. He was a good salesman. But the costs of his leadership outweighed the revenues he brought in.

Clive Boddy, a professor of leadership and organizational behavior, has seen this all before in his study of workplace aggression, and he calls it "instrumental bullying." He explains, "It creates a smokescreen for them to get on with what they're really doing, which is gaining power, and influence, and prestige, and money within the corporation."*

One of Cole's many responsibilities was overseeing and managing the head of sales. This was a crucial senior role, as the revenue derived from advertising on our member websites would support the business, incentivize our partner publishers to stay with us, and perhaps encourage additional sites to join us.

We went through three heads of sales in three years, mainly because Cole made them all miserable. Instead of working with them, he undermined them. These were good people with applicable experience and a very tough assignment. Though our business grew, most of the significant advertising dollars—those big-money campaigns for such things as March Madness and the Super Bowl—still went to ESPN, Fox, and CBS Sports. Despite increasing traffic and our top-ten status, ad agencies offered us what was left. We needed strategic discussion, inspiration, and collaboration to overcome this obstacle, which Cole shut down at every turn.

It was usually about four months in before one of these heads of sales would email me about meeting them outside the office for a walk around Bryant Park near our Times Square office. It turned out they were miserable and feared for their job. They each would ask the same question: "How do I succeed with Cole working against me? He dismisses everything I say. In a power struggle between Cole and me, I get crushed."

I had no answer. I'd encourage them to keep working, and when the money started rolling in due to their efforts, they'd have leverage. But in the early days, like most startups, the money didn't come in quick enough or in large enough sums.

All of this caused a great amount of strain on our fledgling enterprise. But Cole wasn't only mistreating the ad sales head; he was that cliché bully who ensured no junior person on the team ever found favor.

We hired Tim, a bright guy out of Stanford University. He was in his early twenties, with dark, messy hair. Tim was as likable, eager, and competent an employee as you could find. He was also tech-savvy. His skill set was precisely

---

* "Bullying and Corporate Psychopaths at Work," TEDx Talks.

what we needed. We had good content, but our leading fantasy portal and the websites in our network lacked the appealing graphic design and upgraded software our fantasy sports competitors were implementing.

It wasn't long before Tim was asking me to meet him outside. His early enthusiasm and positivity had given our small office a lift. Now, he was despondent.

"I'll quit," he said defiantly as we walked outside, blocks from the office. Tim was single and had quite a bit more freedom than the rest of us.

"I'll go back to California. I've had it with being bullied. He stymies every idea and pounces on every mistake. You know, I sit right outside Cole's door. All he does all day is talk to his mother and his hockey-playing buddies."

Tim left the company. Years later he told me, "I can still feel the anxiety of those days. Cole made me feel like everything that went wrong was my fault."

His departure hindered our ability to innovate.

One morning, we had an important meeting with prospective funders. Our CEO was concerned that everything would go just right. Our most junior person, an office manager who was relatively new to the team, made the arrangements for bagels, donuts, fruit, coffee, and juice. The meeting was set for 9:00 a.m., and the delivery was supposed to be made by 8:30 a.m.

It never arrived.

Jim was fuming. He stormed back to his office for us to figure it out. I volunteered to race over with our office manager to the corner deli.

The order was lost. I beseeched them to get it all together as quickly as humanly possible. It was 9:10 a.m. before we ran back to the office, our arms filled with bags of food and drink. We entered quietly. I could see the entire team around the table, Jim at the head. To my delight, our guests were running late. And then, without anyone offering to help us unload, and with my back turned, I heard Cole cackle, "Jesus fucking Christ, Regal, you can't even 'produce' breakfast!" Everyone laughed.

Dr. Maureen Duffy helped me understand what Cole's malevolent attempt at humor was all about:

"Some of these things start as casual comments, and those turn into character assassination. By the end of it, the target has been delegitimized despite his contributions. You become a shell of yourself. This is unethical communication in the workplace. He's saying something demeaning in a public forum. It's nothing huge. It's boorish. It's not throwing a punch at someone's head. But maybe we shouldn't use physical abuse as the comparison. People do understand that kind of damage better than psychological assault at work, which is very corrosive.

"It says something about the target of the nasty comment to the others in the room. The target is worthy of ridicule and doesn't or can't stand up to it."

I wanted to stand up to it. I wanted to push back against Cole's baseless belittlement. But I needed just the proper retort, and, in the moment, I had nothing. It's not the way my mind works.

As Mark Twain once said, "There is no character, howsoever good and fine, but it can be destroyed by ridicule, howsoever poor and witless."*

During this time, Jennifer and I started looking for a house. We were living in an apartment on the Upper West Side. The garbage trucks at 5:00 a.m. and the buses passing every fifteen minutes started weighing on us. Like many other couples with young children, we longed for more space and greenery than New York City could provide. It would be the first time I'd ever own a home.

I needed an oasis from the rancor in the office.

We drove about twenty miles north of the city to see the available listings. I felt like Goldilocks. One house was too big, and the next was too small. This one didn't have enough closet space, and all of them were too expensive. None of them were just right. We were scheduled to visit the final house halfway up a steep hill on a pretty street. The homes at the top of the hill had a view of the Hudson River. This house didn't have a view. It was small and drab brown. It looked in some disrepair and in serious need of a paint job.

"Let's not go in. It'll be a waste of time. There's no way I would live in that

* Mark Twain, *Pudd'nhead Wilson* (Harper & Brothers Publishers, 1903), vii.

shitty little house," I said to Jennifer and our realtor. Our daughter, Sophie, was preoccupied in the back seat.

The sun had started to set on this mild autumn day. I wanted to get back to the city to beat the traffic. I was anxious enough already thinking about the week to come, and the stop-and-go drive back would make me more irritable.

"Why don't we go in just to look at it since we're here?" Jennifer asked.

"I tell you what," I said. "Sophie's been sitting for hours. I'll take her around back. Maybe there's a playset there. Let me know if this place is worth seeing, but I highly doubt that'll happen."

Sophie took my hand, and we walked around the side of the house and into the backyard. There was nothing for her to play on or play with, but I noticed the lot was much larger than I'd expected and was surrounded by beautiful, tranquil woods. Sophie and I stood there for a moment, looking around.

She spotted a white butterfly fluttering a few feet in front of her. She started running toward it as it bounced in the air just out of reach. There were several butterflies, and as one flew away, Sophie found another. She was in absolute glee and wonderment, giggling, laughing, and running about. She was carefree.

We bought the house.

WES grew despite the dysfunction.

Gannett, the owner of *USA Today*, which already had a significant profile in fantasy sports, made a strategic investment in the company. The corporation was confident that WES was a growing enterprise.

We were on our way.

Enough revenue was coming in and money going out that we needed a CFO. We hired Dave O'Neil. Dave was fit and youthful, in his mid-thirties, with short, light-colored, tightly cropped hair. He and I had crossed paths previously at College Sports Television, where he served as VP of finance. I had no doubt he would fit in nicely with our group.

Dave had a biting sense of humor. He was a confident guy. I sensed and hoped he might not be so quick to accept every ill-considered comment and dictate from Cole simply because Cole sat closest to the throne.

In the meantime, I needed Cole's buy-in to move my programming and sponsorship initiatives forward. I would meet with him and suggest an idea that could be pitched to brand marketers using our unique content and broad reach. But without any rational or strategic explanation, he would tell me he couldn't and wouldn't support it.

It felt to me that Cole didn't want me to succeed. What other reason could there be to impulsively turn down revenue-producing ideas when we were in need of them, without even discussing it further with Jim and the team?

"These people spend more time maneuvering than contributing," says Dr. Namie from the Workplace Bullying Institute. "I call this type of workplace aggressor 'the gatekeeper bully.' They manage by omission. They withhold information and opportunity. Anybody who is a threat is going to be sacrificed. The bully is going to destroy that person. And the group goes along."

Luckily, Jim, our CEO, had a deal that would benefit me and the business. Cole had no choice but to support it.

Jim was still holding the cards. He was the boss.

I was heading back to Vegas.

CHAPTER 45

BULLY ON THE BRINK

Jim negotiated a deal with famed broadcaster Billy Packer to do a series of March Madness college basketball events in 2009 from the Wynn Las Vegas. Billy convinced his friend, legendary coach Bob Knight, to cohost.

I would serve as executive producer.

Bob Knight was the most renowned and revered bully in sports in the 1970s, '80s, and '90s. Because of the national championships he was winning, his brutal and brutish behavior toward his players, the refs, and those at the highest levels of Indiana University was ignored.

Knight got away with all kinds of misconduct for years. Decades, even. In 1983, from midcourt, he cursed out the Big 10 Conference commissioner Wayne Duke, who was in the press box. In 1985, he tossed a chair across the court in a game against Purdue. In 1994, he head-butted one of his players but justified the act as unintentional. In 1998, he was fined $10,000 for berating a referee. In 1999, Knight was investigated for battery after allegedly choking a man at a restaurant. And in March of 2000, Indiana University investigated an allegation that Knight choked former player Neil Reed during a 1997 practice.*

* Associated Press, "Events in Knight's Coaching Career," ESPN, November 14, 2006, https://www.espn.com/mens-college-basketball/news/story?id=2661738.

Knight would've gotten away with this unconscionable act, but this time, a video of the incident surfaced.

Indiana University finally slapped a zero-tolerance policy on Knight. They didn't fire him. He was given one more chance. But he couldn't control his temper, and in September 2000, he was fired for, wait for it, a "pattern of unacceptable behavior."*

Now I was Bob Knight's executive producer. I nervously prepared to call Coach Knight for the first time to introduce myself. He was so erratic, and I needed to be careful not to offend him.

"The best advice I can give you is don't ever call him Bobby," Jim said. "It sets him off. He is Bob or Coach Knight. Never Bobby. And don't ever mention *A Season on the Brink* [the bestselling John Feinstein book about Coach Knight]. He hates that book. And if you get through this whole thing and he doesn't throw a punch or chair at you, I will consider it a success."

My first conversation with Coach Knight went something like this:

Ring, ring, ring, ring.

"Yeah, who's this?"

"Coach, hi, it's Andy Regal. I'm the executive producer of *Billy Packer's Survive and Advance* show at the Wynn Hotel. I look forward to working with you."

"Okay."

I could feel some perspiration start to form around my forehead as I continued, eager to fill the uncomfortable silence. "I'll be putting together research material for all the games we'll be talking about on the show during the NCAA tournament."

"This is a basketball show, right?"

"Yes, Coach. Basketball and gambling, Coach."

"Well, I don't know shit about gambling, but I know plenty about basketball. Why the hell would I need your research?" And with that, Knight hung up on me.

---

* Associated Press, "Events in Knight's Coaching Career."

I didn't dare call him back.

I commuted from New York City to Las Vegas for the entirety of March Madness. For six weeks I left on Thursday night and returned late Sunday night. I thought I'd enjoy the solitude of the five-hour flight and the excitement of Vegas, but I missed Jennifer and my two little wonders.

The flights gave me far too much time to reflect on and grieve over my mother, who had died just a month before. Each week, I selected a window seat to hide the tears streaming down my face like raindrops sliding down the aircraft's windowpane as I stared out into the darkness.

The first thing I did each Friday morning was meet with Billy and Coach Knight. But sharing a meal with Coach wasn't always the most pleasant experience. We were at the Wynn having breakfast. Coach Knight and Billy would be heading off to play golf afterward, and I would spend the day preparing for that night's *Survive and Advance* show. This was an opportunity to spend a few minutes with my two hosts going through the broadest details of the program, including which teams and star players we'd feature that night.

Coach Knight had invited one of his best friends who lived in Vegas to play a round of golf and to join us for breakfast. Coach ordered a big, hearty meal. His friend arrived about five minutes after we'd all sat down. He also ordered a full breakfast. Coach Knight's food came first, and he devoured it with the same fervor and ferocity he exhibited toward referees. He was just finishing his food and dabbing the sides of his mouth with his napkin when the server arrived with Coach Knight's friend's food.

"Let's go." Knight pushed away from the table, stood, and walked away.

His friend was about to put his fork in his mouth with a delectable first bite of French toast when Billy summoned up the courage to say, "Hey, Bob, your guy just got his food."

Coach Knight kept walking. With his back to all of us, he said, "I don't give a shit. He was late."

And with that, both Billy and Coach Knight's friend shrugged their shoulders, got up from the table, and started to leave. Coach Knight hadn't paid for his meal, so before Billy left, he threw down cash for Coach Knight.

"I guess I got Bob's breakfast too."

And that wasn't all that Billy "was getting" on behalf of Coach Knight.

Billy Packer and Coach Knight played golf just about every day we were in Vegas. They played two or three rounds per trip, and we produced six weeks of shows during the tournament. Let's say they played fifteen rounds of golf. Billy confided in me that Coach Knight hadn't paid for golf, and it was unlikely he would do so. I was told that greens fees at the Wynn top out at about $500. I know for a fact they were not getting comped. I'm not a mathematician, but I can do this math. Coach Knight's part would come to around $7,500.

"I'm going to have to talk to the hotel and deal with this myself," Billy said with a hangdog look and more than a little frustration. "Maybe I can somehow convince them to comp, Bob."

Knight's ill-mannered behavior, rudeness, and lack of civility were tolerated not because people adored Coach Knight or because he was going through a particularly tough time, but because people feared him. We were all afraid of his temper, even as he approached seventy.

Victims of bullies, who often have no leverage, can't marshal the courage to stand up and say, "Stop! No more."

We all enable the bully.

The shows we produced in front of a live audience at the Wynn Race and Sports Book were fun to work on and watch. We featured basketball icons such as Louisville coach Denny Crum, Celtics great Bill Russell, David Thompson of North Carolina State fame, and Christian Laettner, one of the all-time Duke greats. Everyone was excited for the annual college basketball tournament and thrilled for the opportunity to see and meet Billy, Coach Knight, and their high-profile guests.

John Feinstein titled his bestselling book *A Season on the Brink* because every day during the six months he spent with the coach and his Indiana basketball team, Knight would do something to put himself or the team in jeopardy.

I felt that same sense of dread.

We spent the first half hour of each show doing what is done in almost every sports talk show: talking about the big games that had just been played, the top contests coming up, and the players across the country having the most significant impact on March Madness. Then, for the latter part of the show, we'd go into the crowd for audience questions.

Like the rest of us, the fans were always respectful and careful around Coach Knight to the point of obsequiousness. One night, we'd taken three or four questions about Duke and North Carolina's chances, and we had a question or two about Michigan State, which had a great team that year. A well-meaning fan stood up, smiling broadly.

"Hey, Bobby, it's great to have a chance to meet you. Could I come up there and have you sign my copy of *A Season on the Brink*?"

When I heard the guy call him *Bobby*, I looked up from my clipboard in horror. I saw the fan standing in the audience and then whipped my neck up to the podium. Coach Knight was rising from his seat, clenching his microphone into a fist, and his face was starting to go beet red.

Upon hearing the words "*Season on the Brink*," Coach Knight started moving toward the front of the stage as if he were going to storm into the crowd.

"That book sucks," he snarled into the microphone, pointing at the fan.

The crowd was whooping it up at the sight of the famous bully displaying his most infamous characteristic. Billy was able to corral Coach Knight and bring him back to his seat before he made it into the crowd.

Billy confided in me after the tournament concluded that he paid Bob's golf tab.

CHAPTER 46

AT LEAST WE GOT TO GO TO COSTA RICA

WES continued to grow. Our traffic from nearly five hundred sports sites put the company among the top six in sports media. But our revenues didn't grow to match our position in the market. What grew was the animosity between our CFO and Cole.

When another of our sales heads left the company, Dave moved into the office next to Cole's. I remember hearing heated conversations between them. As the days and weeks wore on, they started working separately behind closed doors.

With the closed doors came an end to any communication between Cole and Dave. In the last six months of our business, the number two and three people in our company didn't exchange a word.

Long ago, I learned how to recognize who the unhappy people are at work: It's the ones toiling with their doors closed (unless you're working at the CIA, that is).

Cole's symbiotic relationship with our CEO was deteriorating. We could hear their arguments.

I'd grown to resent Cole for his bullying and undermining everything we were trying to build.

I needed a vacation.

Jennifer and I had decided years ago to reschedule that trip to Costa Rica and make it so memorable that it would wash away all the hurtful feelings we still felt from the indignity of Henry Schleiff's forcing us off the plane.

We booked the Four Seasons Resort Costa Rica at Peninsula Papagayo. It was the most beautiful hotel I've ever stayed in. And the service lived up to the Four Seasons reputation. The grounds were verdant, and brightly colored flowers burst into view everywhere. And if you looked up at just the right moment, you'd see the howler monkeys gregariously leaping from one branch to the next. They could only make you smile. The weather was spectacular, and every meal surpassed the last. One night after dinner, while sipping cocktails at the bar with Jennifer, a server wandered over and inquired whether we might like homemade chocolate cookies made special for us. The answer was a resounding, "Yes, please!"

Life was good. Really good.

I was finally shaking off what Jennifer and I called the "Costa Rica Curse" from the time we were pulled off the plane.

Everything about this trip was sublime. I couldn't remember a recent vacation that wasn't in some way tainted or downright ruined by the bully in the corner office.

Not this time.

We returned to our room with our warm cookies. It was spacious, luxurious, and tranquil.

And then, I got a text from my colleague. Cole had left the company. There had been some Shakespearean power struggle between Jim and Cole, and Cole had lost. Ding-dong, the bully was dead! Cole was entering unemployment hell as I was experiencing utopia.

Here it was. Sweet justice. Served warm, like the chocolate chip cookie.

Unfortunately, utopia is an imagined place. When I returned to work after the weeklong respite, the pressure to drive revenues intensified. Gannett, the parent company of *USA Today*, which had previously invested in our company, swooped in and bought the remaining equity.

My dreams of riches were dashed. Much more important to me now was to keep my job. I met with the *USA Today* executives, and they were very complimentary. They liked my experience and told me I could help them as they integrated the hundreds of websites we had in our network into their fantasy offering. They'd be sending me a contract over the weekend. All I had to do was sign it, and I'd become a Gannett employee. They agreed to keep me at my current salary. I had to take a lesser title than my current executive VP credit. But I thought *USA Today* might be a solid place to continue my career.

As promised, Gannett emailed me the contract. Everything was in order, but they only offered two weeks' vacation, and I wanted three weeks, given my seniority. So I didn't sign the contract. I figured I'd have a quick conversation with the HR person at Gannett handling my deal first thing Monday morning, and even if they turned down my simple request, I'd sign the contract immediately.

I came into the office early on Monday, and William Lestan, who'd joined us recently as COO and was handling the transition to Gannett from our side, met me at the door and asked me to come into his office. William tended to be an upbeat guy even during this unwinding period, but he looked disturbed.

"Andy, Gannett decided not to offer you a contract over the weekend. They've continued to review our books and determined that they need to make further cuts now, and they have no role for you."

I was incredulous. "You're wrong, William. I have the contract right here." I held it up in my right hand. "They sent it to me."

"I'm sorry, Andy, but they are reneging on the deal, and you need to gather up your belongings and leave the office."

I was jolted.

"William, there must be a mistake. They told me they wanted me. I talked to them at length about what I could contribute. You have to call them back. Let's call them together."

"I'm sorry. There's nothing that can be done." William grabbed my coat and politely ushered me out of the office. I grabbed my briefcase and walked out the door.

I was in a daze.

I ended up at Bryant Park just a few blocks away, the same park where I'd taken my colleagues who were desperate for guidance and support when they feared they'd be tormented for a few more weeks or months and then discarded like the garbage lying in the metal cans situated around the park.

People swirled around me on their way to offices, where I envisioned they'd be met by smiling, supportive colleagues who had piping-hot coffee waiting for them.

I had nobody to talk to and nowhere to go. I couldn't call Jennifer. I was too ashamed. I was alone and out of work. I found a weather-beaten, wobbly, wooden chair. I sat down, hid my face, and cried.

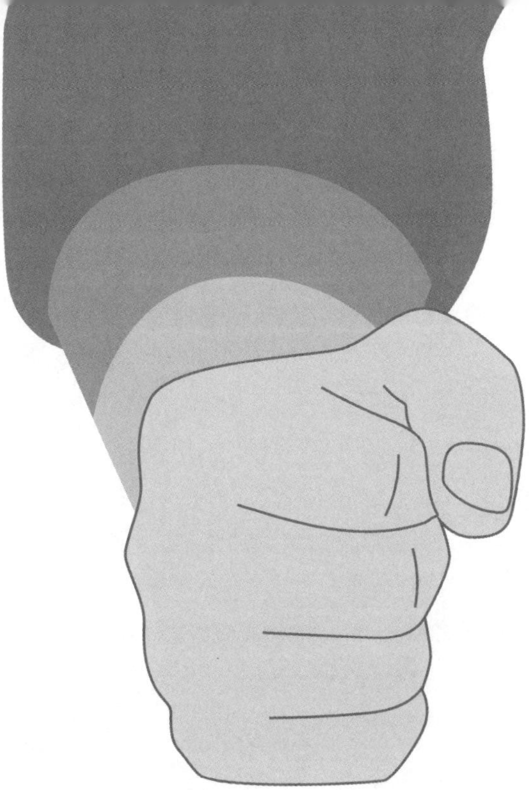

SECTION 8

REACHING THE APEX . . . AND I WAS SCARED OF HEIGHTS

The secret to success is good leadership, and good leadership is all about improving the lives of our team members and workers.

—TONY DUNGY, HALL OF FAME NFL COACH

CHAPTER 47

BUON*JOURNAL*!

Jimmy Harris, a high school buddy, had done business with Aaron Musto, a guy high up at the *Wall Street Journal*. I had no idea what I might talk to him about, but then Jimmy mentioned that Aaron was involved in some way with the *Journal*'s video department. I didn't even know the *Journal* had a video department.

It was now early spring 2012. I was out of work, miserable, and desperate for anything to give me hope. An introduction to Aaron would be a reason for hope.

We met at a Midtown coffee shop near the *WSJ*'s offices at the News Corp. Building on Sixth Avenue. Aaron had a round and serious face. He was maybe five eight and on the soft side. He met me with a warm smile, but I realized Aaron was an intense guy as we started talking. He could laugh but often spoke in a monotone, conspiratorial tone.

We'd been talking for about fifteen minutes, mostly about our families, upbringing, career paths, and people we knew in common. Then he mentioned a woman named Naomi who ran the video department on the production side. Aaron explained that he was in charge of video from the business side.

"We don't talk anymore. I don't think I've said a word to her in months," he said triumphantly. I wasn't sure why this was something to be proud of, but I liked that he trusted me enough already to confide in me about the personal dynamics of the *Journal*'s video department.

"You could help us. And Naomi needs the help. She doesn't know what the fuck she's doing."

Aaron liked the f-word. He liked it a lot. This meeting was turning out much better than I'd anticipated. I thought it was simply a friendly informational interview as a favor to Jimmy. Now, Aaron was scheming how he might get me in as a consultant.

"Let me think this through. I want you to meet Alan Murray. We'll have to get him on our side to get you in the door."

"I'd love to meet with Alan. I'm a fan of his work."

Aaron and I parted ways.

I started walking along Sixth Avenue and headed east on Forty-Third. I thought about what it would be like to work at the *Wall Street Journal*, one of the last true bastions of great journalism. It would be the pinnacle of my career. The pinnacle of anyone's career. I read the *Journal* often with interest and admiration. The business and political reporting were unparalleled, and the writing was stellar, especially the feature writing on music, movies, the arts, real estate, wine, cars, sports, and science.

I was in Alan Murray's office two weeks later. At the time, he was deputy managing editor and executive editor of online content. Alan spent twenty-nine years at the *Journal*, including a decade as the *Journal*'s Washington bureau chief. Under his leadership, the bureau won three Pulitzer Prizes. However, I was most familiar with him from his frequent appearances on CNBC.

Alan was upbeat and gregarious. He laughed frequently and seemed comfortable in his elevated station in life. I found myself immediately drawn to him.

"I'd like to work for you, Alan, and I know I could significantly contribute to the video team in any way you see appropriate."

I was surprised at my own candor. It was rare for me to speak up for myself.

"I just don't think I have a spot for you right now, Andy. I already have a consultant working for me in video, and I have no further budget and no open slots for full time."

We shook hands. More than a bit dispirited, I headed out into the Diamond District on my way home.

I feared this opportunity, such as it was, would dissolve like so many others. But unlike so many others, I so wanted this one. I wanted to be a *Journal* guy. I wanted to say to people, "I work at the *Wall Street Journal*."

I worried I didn't have the proper *WSJ* pedigree. I hadn't gone to an Ivy League school, and I didn't have an MBA. I wondered if I knew a highly respected journalist who had a connection to the *Journal* and might be willing to write to Alan on my behalf. In a moment of clarity, it dawned on me.

Steve Brill.

I hadn't spoken to him in a couple of years and hoped he would be impressed that I was being considered for a position at the *Journal* and that he might like to help one of his own gain employment there.

I emailed Steve, and when he responded promptly, I felt validated. I called him a couple days later.

"Hi, Steve, it's Andy Regal. Thank you for taking time."

My heart was thumping.

"Andrew, how nice to hear from you. You said in your email that you have an opportunity with the *Journal*."

"Well, not yet, Steve. I'm talking to Alan Murray about a possible opportunity."

"I know Murray. Good guy. Really knows his stuff."

I envisioned him biting down on a cigar, leaning back in his chair, his suspenders snug against his body.

"I had a great meeting with him, Steve. I was wondering if you might mention me to Alan. A positive referral from you could make all the difference."

"Andrew, I'm working on a new venture, and I might like to hire you. I still need some time to dot the i's and cross the t's, but whatever you do, don't you dare take another job until you hear back from me. Got that?"

"Thanks, Steve, that sounds great."

We hung up, and I felt elated. I had another job prospect. And then, just as quickly, I realized Steve had made it clear that speaking to Alan on my behalf wasn't in his best self-interest. Steve was nothing if not self-interested. And why would I ever work for Steve Brill again? As forlorn as I was and desperate to find someone eager to hire me, I would have accepted a role if Steve had offered.

Pathetic.

I still yearned for his approval.

Pathetic.

I never heard back from Steve about hiring me for his new venture. Nor did he ever help me secure employment at the *Wall Street Journal.*

I was at a dead end with my prospects. I'd wake up early each morning after a tension-filled night's sleep. Self-pity coursed through my every thought as I watched my neighbors heading into the city to start their busy day.

I'd stare at my computer or glare at my phone, trying to will them into activity. It's so demoralizing to go through an entire day receiving six emails, five of which are junk and one from your sister imploring you to "hang in there."

And then, I caught a break. Alan Murray's name popped up in my email inbox. We hadn't spoken in a couple of months.

"Andy, why don't you come back in if you're still interested? I might have some budget available in the video department after all."

I spent the next twenty-four hours watching *WSJ* videos and preparing to meet with Alan.

"Andy, the best I can do is give you three months," Alan told me bluntly.

Three months! This would give me somewhere to go in the morning, and I could put the *Wall Street Journal* on my résumé. For the rest of my days, I could say I'd worked at the *Wall Street Journal.* And maybe, just maybe, I could turn three months into four months or even six months.

I bounded out of the News Corp. Building. I was so happy. I started dialing Jennifer to tell her the great news.

Before she could pick up, I'd convinced myself this time would be different.

On my first day, I walked into the building filled with pride and trepidation. The *Wall Street Journal* occupied several floors. The lobby was teeming with bright, well-dressed people coming and going with important things to say and do. And now, I was one of those people.

I met Naomi, the head of video production. She had a bright smile and a sturdy handshake. She was doing a great job concealing it if she held any animosity toward me, and I wouldn't have blamed her if she did. (Nobody likes a consultant.) We spoke in her office for about an hour about the strong team she was managing. She played some of the most recent pieces that the team had produced. We discussed the strategy and her desire to develop new programming, in which she hoped we might collaborate.

I told her it all sounded great, and I was eager to get started.

And then, an hour later, Aaron emailed me.

"Let's meet outside. We'll grab coffee. Fifteen minutes."

The nature of his note was intriguing. I hoped this would be a "How's the first day going?" type of get-together.

"You've got to start reviewing the team immediately," Aaron said with urgency and a sense of gloom. "They aren't very good. Naomi doesn't have it in her to fire people. There are people on that team who've been here forever. They have no sense of how to tell a video story in a contemporary way. You're going to have to shake things up."

I'd been on the job as a consultant since nine o'clock. All the hallways looked the same to me. If I dared make my way to the men's room, I couldn't even find my way back to my little cubicle near Alan's office, and yet Aaron was already demanding that I "shake things up."

"I'll be working with staff members very soon and evaluating each of them."

I was trying to placate Aaron.

Alan Murray had mentioned nothing about this being one of my responsibilities. If I found producers lacking in their skill set or work product, I'd certainly discuss it with Alan and Naomi. But I wasn't inclined to suggest wholesale changes until I'd observed the team over a few months. I knew all too well how it feels to lose your job, and I'd never fire anyone and send them into the street cavalierly.

My first three months flew by, and I hoped I'd provided enough value to somehow outlive the freelance budget I'd inherited. Alan Murray called me into his office and asked if I wanted another three months and whether I'd oversee the video team's long-form documentary work. I accepted eagerly.

I was creating meaningful relationships with the most senior members of the video team: Becky, Jill, Mark, Nuna, Wendy, and Joanne. This was a hard-working group toiling long hours, very experienced, and devoted to carrying on the tradition of great print journalism into the *WSJ* video world.

Aaron was wrong about this team.

I found that the *WSJ*'s reputation for journalistic excellence was hard-earned and spot-on. More than anything else, the people I worked with throughout the newsroom cared most about getting the story right.

I came into the office one day near the end of my second three-month stint, and it became immediately apparent that something had happened. I wasn't sure if it had occurred the night before or early that morning. As it was relayed, Naomi had engaged in a vitriolic shouting match with Aaron. I knew the animus had continued to mount between the two, and the fact that Aaron was engaging with me and not even talking to her could only have contributed to the foreseeable blowup.

I was playing an off-screen role in this acrimonious drama. Naomi's downfall, if it came to that, would likely lead to my advancement.

Alan was furious with both Aaron and Naomi. He demanded that they work out their differences. That was never going to happen. Soon, it became clear why Alan didn't want to get involved in mediating this bitter conflict.

"Andy, I'm leaving the *Wall Street Journal*."

Alan had invited me out to lunch. Just my luck, one of the best bosses of my career spends a generation at the *WSJ* and takes off the minute I show up.

I pretended I was more interested in his future than my own.

"Why are you leaving, Alan? Where are you going? I thought you were vying for the editor-in-chief job?"

"You can't tell anyone. Very few people know, but I wanted you to know. I'm not getting that job. It's going to Gerry Baker. I've taken a job as president of Pew Research," he revealed before taking a forkful of his salad. I did the same and sensed we were both considering our futures as we chewed.

The next set of rumors circulating was that exit negotiations were underway for Naomi's departure. She didn't come to work the next day, or the next. I was sure Naomi thought I was in cahoots with Aaron the entire time.

I struggled with the notion that maybe she was right.

It was a matter of days before Alan came to me and asked if I'd like to become staff at the *Wall Street Journal*. My title would be senior executive producer, and I'd be the interim global head of video.

Aaron had already notified me that I was the heir apparent before it all happened, and he sent me a short note of congratulations when it became official.

Aaron was responsible for this promotion. We both knew he'd dictate whether the "interim" tag would ever be removed. He also had the power and the cunning to orchestrate my undoing.

Once I started the new job, Aaron's WTF emails began to drip.

One such email came after I had held the interim job for precisely one week. On New Year's Eve 2012, Jennifer and I decided to go see *Silver Linings Playbook*, the hit movie at the time. I was exhausted from taking over the department and the rigor of twenty-four-hour global news coverage. Jennifer and I, two suburban parents with young children, planned a wild New Year's Eve celebration. We went to an early-evening movie and expected to be home by eight.

There was much to be grateful for. Our kids were cute and healthy, and I had a job.

It was an interim position but a good job with great promise.

We were feeling gratified and planned to open a bottle of something when we got home. I took a deep breath and settled deep into my seat. I had my favorite moviegoing companion in my arms. No, not my wife. A big box of Junior Mints. And I knew Jennifer would never finish that jumbo box of popcorn.

I was a happy man.

The opening credits rolled. I don't remember much about the movie other than the very start is about the main character's psychological problems. We were about twenty minutes into the film when I experienced my own trauma. My phone buzzed. It was an email. I looked at the sender.

Aaron.

I can't quote it exactly because I hadn't started printing his mean-spirited emails, but I remember what he said and my reaction.

It went something like this: "What the fuck is wrong with your department? You promised change. And you promised swift change. I see no difference between what you are doing and what Naomi was doing. Please make me happy we put you in charge. You might start with figuring out who you are getting rid of."

I had been in the job for a week. One week.

My heart dropped to the floor and then started beating through my chest. This guy wasn't even my boss. I feared he'd already decided I couldn't do the job. Naomi had been eliminated, and I feared Aaron was already planning to do the same to me. I made some lame attempt at a response: I was on it and had many plans and needed some time.

I was dispirited. I couldn't focus on one frame of the movie. I dejectedly tapped Jennifer on the shoulder. "We have to leave."

"Is it Aaron?" Jennifer whispered indignantly.

I nodded.

We stood up and excused ourselves profusely as we tripped over numerous moviegoers in our row, all wondering where we were going when the movie had just started.

"I can't do it. I can't enjoy the movie," I said, looking over my shoulder as we headed out of the theater and into the parking lot. A blast of biting-cold air hit my face and invaded my body. "He's hounding me about not doing enough to turn around the department."

"You started five days ago!" Jennifer exclaimed.

We drove home in silence. We never opened that bottle.

Like every other bully before Aaron, I let him take the joy out of my life. He was leasing space in my brain.

I was familiar with the axiom "With great power comes great responsibility" from watching numerous superhero movies with Jennifer and my son, Luke.

At the *Journal*, it was more like "With greater power comes greater hostility." That hostility was coming straight from Aaron's email account.

The email hits kept on coming. I started printing them out for my protection.

"What the fuck happened?"

"Who's in charge of this shit today? Maybe I should suggest a new #2?"

The answer to that was a resounding no. I had an extremely valuable number two by the name of Wendy Bounds, who'd been at the *Journal* for twenty years. Wendy was highly accomplished and one of the best people I ever had the good fortune to work with. Everyone respected Wendy, except Aaron.

Then this:

"There's a fucking article on that on *HuffPo*, and we had it on video weeks ago."

Aaron was upset that we'd failed to get our video placed or embedded into the *Huffington Post*'s article, thus presumably driving huge traffic. This was not easily accomplished with an outside—and many would suggest a *competing*—media outlet.

And this:

"Watching the game video. Fucking 10 minutes are clips of his music videos. Jesus."

Aaron found issues with everything my team was doing. He didn't like the titles we gave our videos.

"Who the fuck is clicking on that title?"

Under the email subject line, "Let Me Know When You Are Free," he said, "Not happy at all. It's a clusterfuck down there." (Aaron sat on a floor above the video department.)

And if it wasn't WTF, it was WTH.

The subject line of the email is "What the Hell": "What is the point of this 9-minute video . . ."

Aaron didn't like the way I was running the department. I'd been in the role one month when he started sending emails like this one:

"Are you free at 11 as I would like some deliverables taken care of on process and structure?"

By this, he meant individual assignments and who I planned to fire.

Did I mention Aaron was not my boss?

I was under a great deal of pressure, trying to prove I was the right person to run a global video news team of fifty people in New York, DC, London, San Francisco, and Hong Kong. I was responsible for all video journalism across the *WSJ*.

Aaron's torment was affecting my mental and physical health. I wasn't sleeping. I wasn't digesting. I was suffering from extreme anxiety. The suicidal ruminations were flashing through my head again.

In a 2023 *Psychology Today* article titled, "Is It Natural to Respond to Bullying with Anxiety?" Jennifer Fraser argues that bullies are lashing out due to their own emotional issues. Bullies, in essence, have significant self-doubt and translate that into aggressive conduct to relieve their own insecurity and stress.

"Targets of bullying may feel a great deal of anxiety in response to aggressive, hurtful, unjust, and threatening behavior. They may find themselves mirroring the emotion concepts of the bullying individual: namely fear, humiliation, or shame (or all three). Psychologists refer to this phenomenon as 'identifying with the aggressor,' which is an escape mechanism designed to survive the onslaught. As most know, bullying is a cycle, a transfer of harm."*

I finally politely and deferentially asked Aaron to stop the cursing in communication with me. That prompted this email five days later, listing everything I'd failed to do that day:

"Didn't tweet at christian siriano and his 300k followers. Didn't put $apl or whatever apples symbol is for iphone video. Didn't go @digits. Didn't check to see what was trending for Valentine's day. Didn't tweet out this evening walts

---

* Jennifer Fraser, "Is It Natural to Respond to Bullying with Anxiety?" *Psychology Today*, June 23, 2023, https://www.psychologytoday.com/us/blog/the-bullied-brain/202306/is-it-natural-to-respond-to-bullying-with-anxiety.

review. Thanks (streak of no curses may end soon.)"

I responded to all of Aaron's WTFs with alacrity and fealty. But I reached the point where I could no longer function effectively in my role with his bullying and not-so-veiled threats. I don't have an official record of his specific phone call early on February 14, 2013, six weeks into my tenure as interim head of video at the *Wall Street Journal*, but I'd been taking verbatim notes on my interactions with him. Aaron was sending his version of a Valentine's Day bouquet to me when he left this menacing voice message:

"If things don't turn around soon, it's going to get ugly down there."

At 10:13 a.m., I responded to our Valentine's Day heart-to-heart in an email: "I'm always willing to continue the conversation with you. But when you tell me 'It's going to get ugly down there,' I need to understand what that means. If you are threatening my job or that of my staff, I will need to discuss this further with others. I am happy to work through this with you. Your call."

Aaron's response was dripping with unctuousness.

"Thank you for your note. I think you may have misunderstood our conversation. There was no insinuation of any kind related to people's careers. I simply requested that we continue to be accountable for key deliverables as we look to improve the overall quality of our product."

Aaron had figured out that I was keeping a record of our communications. Thus, his condescending and officious tone.

The invectives just kept coming in person, on the phone, or via email.

Monday, March 4, 3:41 p.m. email: "I specifically called to ask you to fucking send. They had a meeting with their leadership team."

The following day, Tuesday, March 5, 2012, 5:57 p.m.: "Did he not fucking check?"

And then, there was a phone call from Aaron on March 12. I don't even remember the context. I remember that he was in London for a presentation, and he called me ranting, and I wrote down exactly what he said.

"You are fucking up my show!"

In each instance, I'd try to respond as quickly and sometimes as apologetically as possible. Securing my dignity was not an option. I'm sure, at times, my team and I hadn't executed perfectly. I managed a global team that was producing thirty to forty videos per day related to breaking news, politics, terrorism, the economy, the arts, sports, science, and more.

While trying to please and appease Aaron, I was also looking for an opportunity to develop programming unlike anything *WSJ* Video had ever done. That moment arrived when the Nasdaq market site was interested in partnering with the *Journal* on a lucrative content sponsorship.

Startups were all the rage in 2014. Along with two of my favorite colleagues, Vanessa O'Connell, a deputy US editor, and Gabriella Stern, deputy managing editor and editor for strategic initiatives, we came up with a concept titled "*WSJ* Startup of the Year."

Over a six-month period, we documented and judged how startup founders and their employees from around the country stacked up when handling challenges involving scalability, utility, startup culture, team building, customer acquisition, the elevator pitch, and fundraising.

We planned to capture the highs and lows of entrepreneurship and track the companies' journey as they battled it out for startup supremacy.

We also were able to enlist celebrity judges and business tycoons to assist us, such as Sir Richard Branson and will.i.am.

I served as executive producer on the project and oversaw every aspect of the documentary series. For our efforts, Vanessa, Gabby, and I were awarded the Associated Press "Innovator of the Year" Award.

The *Herald-Tribune* reported on our achievement on September 17, 2014: "The Wall Street Journal won for 'Startup of the Year,' a multimedia project that selected 24 entrepreneurs and paired them with noted business leaders for guidance. The project involved extensive use of video, including online video chats between the participants. The innovator award recognizes bold, creative efforts to improve products/services and grow audience."*

---

* Michael Pollick, "Wall Street Journal Prevails," *Herald-Tribune*, September 17, 2014, https://www.heraldtribune.com/story/news/2014/09/17/wall-street-journal-prevails/29270285007/.

During the few months that I was the interim head of video, I heard periodic rumors that Gerry Baker, the editor in chief of the *WSJ*, had a consultant in mind to come in to run the video department. It was an open secret and not something that concerned me. It didn't seem to be based on my performance. The word was he was going to bring in a longtime friend and colleague who he thought could contribute to the overall video strategy of producing extraordinary visual journalism and increasing views and revenues.

And then he showed up.

Chris Cramer.

He had to be in his mid- to late sixties. He was almost bald, with a bright red nose and ruddy cheeks. Chris had been in the States for decades but had held on to every nuance of his very heavy British accent. I learned he and Gerry had been close colleagues years ago in the UK and had remained close friends when both men came to the United States to forge their journalism careers.

Chris rose to become executive vice president and managing director of CNN International. Before that, he'd spent twenty-five years at the BBC.

Once Chris arrived, people couldn't help but show up at my doorstep and tell me they heard Cramer was "tough, blunt, and uncompromising." Former colleagues from the BBC said he was "rough in manner, looked uncomfortable in a suit, and never deferred to anyone." He was also described as "decisive to the point of brutality."

I feared the next bully in my long line of bullies had found me.

Chris was inquisitive in our first meeting. He wanted to know how things were going—what was working, what was not.

He was a good listener. He told me he heard I was doing excellent work and that he was here to help me and the team continue on that track.

My biggest fear was that Chris, wanting to secure his own standing early on, would learn that Aaron had quite a bit of power, and he'd look to align with him.

CHAPTER 48

MY BODYGUARD, MY PAL

"Aaron is a complete arse."

Chris had been in the job for about three weeks when he called me into his office and gave me the assessment of my nemesis.

I sat down to hear more of his delicious views.

"I met with him," Chris said dismissively. "Do you know what he does? I mean, what does he really do?"

"He spends most of his time demeaning the video team and discussing who should be fired," I said, feeling suddenly emboldened.

At that moment, I couldn't help recalling one of my favorite movies, *My Bodyguard.**

The plot involves a teen boy, Clifford, living in a Chicago luxury hotel with his father, the hotel manager. Clifford is attending a new school, Lake View High School. He quickly becomes the target of bullies and enlists Ricky Linderman, a physically imposing, taciturn, brooding, and troubled student, rumored to be a murderer himself, to protect him against the bullies. Clifford and Ricky become close friends. Ricky protects Clifford, and Clifford helps

* *My Bodyguard*, directed by Tony Bill, produced by Melvin Simon Productions and distributed by 20th Century Fox, 1980.

Ricky deal with a traumatic family tragedy, which ultimately eases him out of his hardened shell.

I had found my Ricky. I hadn't asked for Chris's help. I didn't want to appear vulnerable or needy, but I was both.

"People know that I can walk into Gerry's office anytime," Chris said. "Decades of friendship give me the right to do that even if he is the editor in chief. But I don't think Aaron will be involving himself with the video department much, if at all, any longer."

And with that, the bullying stopped. I rarely dealt with Aaron anymore. He took on new responsibilities within News Corp, the parent company of the *WSJ*, well away from the newsroom, and shortly thereafter left the company to take a new job.

And so began the most fulfilling, challenging, and rewarding year and a half of my career. I could now focus on the news, the journalism, and the needs of my team.

Chris treated each staffer as a person with feelings, not simply someone to be manipulated, used, and abused to help him get ahead. He instinctively recognized what people wanted and needed and whether their intentions were honorable.

Chris was empathetic to those people he found to be right-minded. He was my oasis in a desert of self-involved, self-aggrandizing, unreasonable, sadistic bullies.

Oh, and he was funny. Chris, like veteran journalists of his day, had a lifetime of stories, which he reveled in telling and, at times, even retelling. He was a terrific raconteur, and when the inevitable punch line came, nobody would laugh harder than Chris himself.

I loved working for Chris. He left me alone to do what needed to be done. He was appreciative, trusting, understanding, and direct but never demeaning, disrespectful, or demanding. He listened. He was commuting weekly from his home in Atlanta, so there were days he worked from home, which was somewhat unusual for this type of work in the pre-COVID days. There were fewer laughs on those days. And there was less alcohol consumed. It wasn't unusual for Chris to walk over to my office before five, grab my coat, and announce louder than necessary, "Andy and I have a meeting. Email us if news breaks." And with that, we'd head off to one of his favorite watering holes.

I learned a lot about red wine on those days.

Chris ran interference for me. He let me run the department, even though he was ultimately responsible. He wanted us to focus on driving video views and revenues. Under his direction, that's what we did.

There were innumerable stories for us to turn into compelling video journalism. We had the Ebola outbreak in 2014. Malaysia Airlines Flight 370 vanished in March of that year with 239 people on board. The rise of ISIS was a constant story for us with our Mideast print colleagues on the ground.

On Saturday, May 24, 2014, a gunman opened fire at the Jewish Museum in Brussels, Belgium, killing four people. Three of them, an Israeli couple on holiday and a French woman, died at the scene. The fourth victim, an employee of the museum, later died of his injuries.*

On that day, I was playing with Lucas, my then eight-year-old son, at a nearby park. We had a special game of tag, which he adored. I'd chase him around the large playset, and somehow, he climbed or slid narrowly out of my reach every time, much to his absolute delight.

We had a rule that Dad had to interrupt playing every fifteen minutes to check his phone for any emails or news reports that required his attention. I was obsessed with never being out of touch. Once again, I narrowly missed touching him as he gained sanctuary in a lion's mouth, and I called a time-out to check my phone.

Lucas hated the time-outs.

I read the bulletin about the terror attack in Brussels. I looked up at Luke's expectant face.

"C'mon, Daddy, let's play. You haven't caught me once."

"Lukie boy, Dad needs to go home right now. I have to go to work, buddy."

Luke's brilliant smile turned to a gloomy pout. I knew that look. This was

---

* "Brussels Jewish Museum Murders: Mehdi Nemmouche Jailed for Life," BBC, March 11, 2019, https://www.bbc.com/news/world-europe-47533533.

not the first or last time breaking news would break his spirit. Luke burst into tears. He cried all the way home as I held his little hand.

Views were skyrocketing thanks to these compelling news stories and, I trusted, our journalistic creativity. We were gaining an audience on WSJ.com and what is called "off-platform," in other words, other online spaces where people could view our videos, such as AOL, Yahoo, YouTube, and MSN.

One of the department's stated goals was to produce videos for mobile devices, given that more people, particularly younger people, were starting to consume video content on their phones and tablets. This form of visual journalism aimed to introduce the younger demographic to the *WSJ* brand. Our editorial strategy was working. According to a Nielsen report provided to me, from 2014 to 2015, the percentage of mobile video traffic grew from 1 percent to 31 percent. The growth in 2015 alone was from 19 percent to 31 percent.

We were expanding viewership to the most sought-after consumers where they were.

By early 2015, Chris mentioned that the commute from Atlanta was becoming arduous. He hinted that his consultancy might be coming to an end in the next few months.

Shortly after Mr. Trump came down the escalator at Trump Tower to announce his candidacy, just nine blocks south, Chris Cramer went down the elevator at News Corp for the last time after announcing his retirement.

"You deserve to be the global head of video, pal," Chris said one evening over a few glasses of pinot noir. There is something very special about affectionately being called pal in your fifties. It reminded me of my best days with Mort.

"I have spoken to Gerry and the other stakeholders. I'm pretty sure this is going to happen. I've made it clear that you're the guy. Gerry wants to meet with you to discuss the role. I'll be just a phone call away if you need me," he said thoughtfully as he left the office.

I knew serving as the global head of video for one of the world's leading journalistic enterprises would be the pinnacle of my career. I was also keenly aware that my bodyguard could no longer protect me once he'd departed the premises.

CHAPTER 49

"LISTEN, DON'T JUDGE"

A few weeks later, Gerry Baker and I met for lunch on a sun-kissed late-spring day in Midtown Manhattan. We sat outside at one of his favorite Italian restaurants. The owner came over to say hello, and the servers approached Gerry with reverence. It was a proud moment, sharing a meal with the editor in chief of the *Wall Street Journal*. He asked me where I saw the department going, what I thought of the video team, and my views on American and European football. Gerry was a big sports fan. He was impressive in his fit frame, shaved head, and expensive, bespoke pinstripe suit. He was also warm, brilliant, gracious, collegial, and commanding—befitting his position.

As we walked back to the office, I couldn't help but feel like my six-year-old, first-grade self, driving back to school with my teacher, Ms. Levine, after having her over to my home for lunch. We did that in those days. My mother would dress up, set the table, and make a special meal for this occasion. As my fellow students looked on, I got to walk back into school with Ms. Levine, the prettiest teacher at Wayne Thomas Elementary.

Well, I got to walk back into the News Corp. Building with the editor in chief of the *Wall Street Journal*.

He got off the elevator on the floor below mine, and I quickly thanked him for lunch as he headed into the newsroom and back to his office.

He had an empire to run.

By the time the doors closed and Gerry was out of sight, I'd convinced myself that this time would be different.

I was named global head of video for the *Wall Street Journal* in July 2015. My name was added to the masthead. It was small print, but it was there.

I was now officially in charge of a global team of fifty.

Shortly thereafter, I received an email from human resources offering a series of one-on-one "management seminars" with Christine Glancey.

Christine was a no-nonsense journalist who was running things from the center of the newsroom, known as "The Hub." The video team was off in a far corner on the same floor as the news hub but not near the newsroom hub, which might tell you something. Christine was direct, commanding, and confident. In her late forties or early fifties, Christine's dedication to the highest standards of newsgathering and reporting were inspiring. Still, you knew she had survived and thrived through many years fighting daily deadlines and the extraordinary demands of competing against the top media organizations in the world.

Christine had a thoughtful, generous, and caring side. She loved talking about her teen daughters, whom she adored. She was also keen on improving the management skill set of those taking and holding leadership positions at the *WSJ*.

In my first meeting with Christine, she explained that she wanted to become certified as an executive coach. I was one of her guinea pigs/customers/students/patients.

We met in a glass-enclosed conference room. Christine explained her mission was to boost her educational designs and provide me with tools to navigate the "matrixed environment" at the *Wall Street Journal*. She described the topics we'd be discussing such as conflict resolution, nurturing talent, effective communication, the delegation process, managing complaints, providing performance feedback, supporting change, and setting up my team members for success.

Each week, I would bring in a different problem or crisis I was confronting, and we'd discuss how to broach it and work through it. Christine was a terrific counselor. I became fond of her, and I sensed the feeling was mutual. As I got to know her better, I would stop by her office to say hello. She'd invite me in, talk about the pressures of the day, and gradually turn to our personal lives. I sensed she felt she'd missed quite a lot by choosing a life and career in the newsroom.

We met at least a dozen times, but one lesson especially resonated then and sticks with me still: "If you remember nothing else from our training sessions, Andy, remember this. *Listen, don't judge.* If you listen to what people are saying before judging them or their motivations, you'll be a better manager than most."

I felt like crying. If only the people who had bullied me all these years had just listened.

As I reached my office, looking out at my team with their heads down, hard at work, I was suddenly starkly aware that I wasn't a good listener. And that I was judgmental. I needed to get better, and I vowed that I would. I was forced to think about my own treatment of others. I realized I may have—no, I had definitely—caused distress among people who had worked for me over the years. I yelled. I pounded on a few tables and a wall or two. I became exasperated, and I interrupted people whose opinions I disagreed with.

I didn't listen. I judged.

Christine had provoked a shocking and dispiriting question—one that terrified me to my core: Had I been a bully boss to my team members?

"Andy, you have to remember the definition of workplace aggression," Dr. Namie explained to me in his reassuring voice. "Repeated, health-harming mistreatment of one or more people by a manager or supervisor. It's a repeated behavior. And repeated harm. We are not talking about a boss blowing up on a bad day and then apologizing for the behavior. You're not a bully if it's out of character."

He asked directly, "Andy, how often did your outbursts happen?"

"A few times a year, I suppose."

"Was the person you were angry with the same person each time?"

"No."

"How did you feel after these episodes?"

"I felt awful and ruminated over it. I have to admit, I don't think I apologized every time for my behavior, but I often did."

"Andy, you aren't and have never been a bully boss. Get that self-blaming attitude out of your head."

CHAPTER 50

TOTAL PARANOIA IS TOTAL AWARENESS

With Chris Cramer gone, I remember feeling for the first time the weight of being wholly responsible for the video team, our coverage of events, and traffic and revenue growth. I realized how much I liked and missed having an appreciative and protective boss. As the new global head of video, there was nowhere to hide.

Our on-platform goal was to achieve ten million monthly views. Under my leadership, which began in July 2015, we hit these numbers:

- 11 million in September
- 10 million in October
- 11.9 million in November
- 10.2 million in December
- 13.7 million in January 2016
- 11.6 million in February 2016

I was pleased and proud of the quality of our journalism and the upward trend of our traffic. We were getting results in producing *WSJ*-worthy videos and driving more people to our brand. And I was confident that if our numbers were going up, we must be making more money.

And then Alexa Moore, a new person from the business side of the *Wall Street Journal*, descended upon me. Moore had little or no inflection or energy when she spoke, and she rarely smiled. I was aware that the *WSJ* valued her, and that she was on the rise.

My heart is beating faster even now as I type these lines, reliving the beginning of what would become the bleakest period of my career. It seemed to me that Moore was on a mission (or was she doing the bidding of someone else?) to prove that the video department was a losing proposition, and in so doing, she was determined to prove I was ineffectual and dispensable.

While I oversaw video journalism, with some responsibility for increasing revenues, she was responsible for monetizing our video work product and the website. She was not my boss. She was on the business side; I was in editorial. But she had expanding influence, power, and authority.

We never met to discuss a revenue-driving strategy. We would pass each other in the hallway, and she'd stop me and eagerly say, "We're losing money in video; we have to do something about that. We should be making three times what you guys pull in right now."

That was a frequent trope.

I was eager and anxious to make ten times what we were bringing in. But I couldn't do it alone.

Alexa seemed more interested in hammering home that we weren't getting it done than in helping to address and attack the problem.

At the *WSJ*, no other top editor had direct revenue responsibility, not the markets and finance editor, tech editor, politics editor, sports editor, or the US editor.

For some reason, though, the video department was treated differently. I often wondered why nobody in the entire ad sales and business side was explicitly assigned to figure out how to make money from video. But there was absolutely nobody. Not one person. So I accepted that it was my job. I liked the idea of being a department head who could impact revenues.

I was grateful and relieved when Chris Moran from the business side was assigned to work with me to identify revenue-producing video opportunities.

Finally, a dedicated liaison between ad sales and video.

This was progress.

Chris Moran was unremarkable. He was British, having come from the Dow Jones office in London. He was maybe five foot eight, in his early to midthirties, with blonde, floppy, unkempt hair. He dressed casually—*shabbily* would be more accurate.

I liked him. He said he just wanted to help and was eager to work with my team and me. That's all I needed to hear. I was elated.

Moran was touted as an expert on video analytics. He examined how people engaged with our video and how to monetize it more effectively.

We agreed to meet once a week to discuss the numbers. Then he would devise a business strategy and set up meetings with other ad sales stakeholders to develop an overall plan that would ultimately lead us to make "three times the amount of money." Or more.

And meet each week we did.

"So, Chris, how much money did we make off the videos we uploaded last week or last month?"

"Oh, I'm working on getting those numbers," he would respond on cue.

"And when can you schedule a meeting with the sales team to discuss how we can all work better on finding brand marketing sponsorships for video?"

We would look at more graphs and charts every week, but we never made any actionable progress. I didn't want to be too outwardly frustrated with him because he was my only ally.

"Okay, Andy, I got us a meeting with the sales team," Moran said about three months after we started working together. I was thrilled. It would be my chance to present directly to those selling *WSJ* ad inventory and tell them that video was a great place for advertisers to allocate their budgets. I spent hours putting my presentation together, detailing our captivating international and domestic coverage and our creative work utilizing animation and graphic design.

I knew that when the ad sales team members finally understood the value of all we were producing and the millions of eyeballs we were attracting, they'd be incentivized to reach out to their best clients, and the money would roll in.

The day of the meeting finally came. That morning, Moran sent me an email that said, "The meeting has been postponed."

That was it. He didn't even mention trying to get it back on the calendar. So I called him to find out what had happened. I left him a voicemail imploring him to do whatever he could to please get the meeting with his business colleagues back on the schedule.

I went off to deal with the day's news events and get my team started on their story assignments. I returned to my desk an hour later, and the voicemail light was on. I hoped it was Chris telling me it was just a postponement, and he'd rescheduled our sales meeting for the next day or two.

Instead, I got a voicemail dripping with vitriol.

"Andy. I'm not your assistant. I don't have time to schedule your meetings. If you want to reschedule something new, do it yourself." *Click*.

He felt no compunction about speaking to me in that tone.

I wondered where his newfound audacity came from. I could only surmise that Alexa Moore had emboldened him somehow.

Following that meeting cancellation, I started noticing a disturbing trend. Whenever someone from a department outside editorial asked for a meeting with me, I'd respond yes. Then, a week or two later, they'd cancel the meeting.

At first, I didn't think much of it. These were generally unimportant meetings, but after it happened four or five times, I started wondering what was happening. As best I could, I dismissed it as workplace paranoia. And then I recalled that I was fired every time after I'd suffered from workplace paranoia.

The fear of losing my job intensified. I had lost any feeling of psychological safety at work. Every morning during my ten-minute drive to the train station, I'd tune in Don Imus, an infamous and popular New York radio shock jock, on WFAN-AM. One morning, weeks after the Chris Moran incident and a day or two after the latest person canceled a meeting with me, Imus started talking about "how you know or should know when you're about to get fired."

"There is one surefire way to know if you're on the way out, and I should know," Imus said in his gravelly voice to the millions listening across the country. "When they stop talking to you, you know you're out. They just stop talking to you."

I was pulling into my parking space at the station. I turned off the engine and put my head on the steering wheel.

Oh my God, oh my God. I'm being set up to fail. I'm getting fired, I said to myself. I was sweating and hyperventilating. I couldn't move. I wept. I finally looked up to see my train pulling out of the station.

Psychologist Maureen Duffy has seen the damaging effects of workplace trauma in her family practice. She told me, "As a bully target, you become an outcast. It's the scarlet letter, but instead of an *A*, you have a *T*. You are marked a target. Everyone in the workplace knows it. We react so strongly to this sort of workplace aggression and adversity because our identities are tied up in our work. Alongside that, you make a huge investment in your work but often with very little control of what happens to you."

Hymie Anisman is an author and professor of neuroscience at Carleton University in Ottawa. He takes an evidence-based approach to understanding the role of stress on human health and identifying characteristics and behaviors that render people more vulnerable or resilient. The principal focus of his research involves the influence of "stressors on neurochemical and neuroendocrine systems, and how these influence psychological (anxiety, depression) and physical (immune-related and neurodegenerative) disorders."*

Professor Anisman has found that bullying taxes coping resources and can have a cumulative effect. He adds that the distress created by workplace degradation can metastasize, like cancer, so that victims develop symptoms of depression and anxiety, sleep problems, and, in some instances, post-traumatic stress disorder (PTSD), with symptoms persisting for years.

The *Journal* was going through a difficult time with diminishing print newspaper sales and an aging subscriber base.

We were invited to a meeting about a new and expansive program to

---

* Hymie Anisman, *Stress and Your Health: From Vulnerability to Resilience* (Chichester, West Sussex, UK: Wiley-Blackwell, 2015).

"modernize newsroom operations." Given the digital revolution throughout the media landscape, a "newsroom transformation" was necessary to compete and thrive. The *Journal* would focus on digital newsgathering and publish web stories faster than ever. That was the priority. The newspaper was still vital, but the emphasis would be on getting accurate information out to the world as quickly as possible.

I understood from older staffers and union members that *newsroom transformation* was a euphemism for *layoffs*.

Jason Sachs, who had served in several top editorial positions and was leading the newsroom "reorg" from the content side, was discussing the changes and which senior editors would be responsible for overseeing various aspects of the newsroom reorganization. I was quite fond of Jason. We weren't close, but we'd shared a meal or two over the years, and I always enjoyed my conversations with him when the rare issue arose that required an in-office meeting. He was thoughtful, focused, and an accomplished journalist. He had the respect of the entire newsroom.

My favorite moments with Jason occurred when Chris Cramer was still around; he would see Chris hanging out in my office and swing by to join us for a laugh or three. After Chris left, Jason never stopped by my office again.

All the reorganization responsibilities were given to people on the editorial side. I was not among them. Then he said, "And I'm pleased to announce that our highly regarded colleague from the business side and a trusted colleague of mine, Alexa Moore, is being promoted to chief transformation officer, and she will be leading this new effort to enhance our multi-platform digital efforts."

I slumped in my chair, and my heart started beating out of control. I walked back to my office, certain I was once again a dead man walking. I was wondering when the verdict would come down.

And then again, maybe I was being paranoid.

I was focused desperately on saving my job if it needed saving. What award could we win? What amount of traffic could we pull in? What sponsorship might we attract that would keep me in the job I had worked my entire career to attain?

I thought maybe a top technology company's virtual reality platform might provide a reprieve or perhaps even an acquittal. The top companies were investing heavily in virtual and augmented reality (VR/AR) technology. Without compelling content to watch on the headsets, the hardware was "virtually" useless.

We could bring our readers and viewers closer to worldwide events like never before through VR technology. It would be an immersive experience. With the actual help of a colleague on the ad sales side (ironic, no?), we negotiated a highly lucrative deal to produce VR content shot around the world.

I was too valuable to be discarded.

We produced some fantastic VR journalism as part of that deal. We went into the hills of Colombia to cover the FARC communist rebels who lived in the jungle and fought for social justice. The government had accused this guerrilla army of rape, bombings, and murder.

We traveled to the Bonneville Salt Flats in Utah for a unique attempt by a female cyclist to break a land speed record, traveling over 130 miles per hour. Our cameras made you feel as though you were right next to the rider herself.

My favorite story in the VR series took viewers to Hollywood and onto the set and behind the scenes at the award-winning prime-time comedy *Modern Family*. Director Steve Levitan and his cast couldn't have been more welcoming as we placed our camera right next to Steve to get the director's POV. Then we set up our cameras in the soundstage to get the actors' perspective. We also put our cameras in the writer's room. For viewers, it was like sitting at the table as the script was coming together. We provided a 360, up-close view of how an episode of one of the most celebrated shows in television history was conceived and executed.

I decided that with this success, I could no longer wait and hope that those "transforming the newsroom" would identify me as part of the solution, not the problem. I thought I'd start with Editor-in-Chief Gerry Baker. Even though he was my direct supervisor, I didn't deal with Gerry that much other than attending the weekly meeting of his direct reports. And that meeting was often demoralizing. Each of us would have a chance to discuss recent issues and successes. When I talked, I noticed Gerry on his phone, reading or responding to emails and paying no attention to what I was saying. He routinely did this to others as well, but at a time when I was feeling vulnerable, it seemed to be another indication that I was on my way out. But Gerry was my boss, the big boss, and I was going to get in front of him and make sure he was fully aware of my most recent significant editorial and revenue-driving contribution.

Trying to meet with Gerry would be a good indicator of my standing. Within minutes, his assistant emailed me back. I was elated. My job could not have been in immediate jeopardy if Gerry agreed to meet with me just minutes after my request. In fact, for nonemergencies, it often took days to get on his calendar. Maybe he valued me after all. My previous encounters with him had been positive. Perhaps he looked forward to seeing me, given we hadn't spoken much in recent months.

I took a deep breath.

This was a very good sign.

At 1:57 p.m., I left my office to head down the hall through the newsroom to the editor in chief's office. Once I got to the main newsroom, I could look across and see Gerry in his glass-enclosed space. I was pleased to see nobody in there with him. His meetings could often go long, and with my heart racing, I was anxious to go right in. Gerry was reading something pensively.

I stayed out of his line of sight and let his assistant know I was there for my two o'clock meeting. She said I could go right in. I walked up to the sliding glass doors and opened them. I was inside by the time Gerry looked up.

"Hi, Gerry," I said as upbeat as I could. I stood in front of his desk, waiting to be told to take a seat. He finally looked up.

"Andy, what are you doing here? Do we have a meeting? My assistant didn't tell me."

And with that, Gerry looked around me and glared at his assistant.

My knees went weak. I had to steady myself.

"Oh, sorry, Gerry. Yes, she gave me the two o'clock slot. I can make this quick," was all I could think of saying to ease his apparent annoyance. Was he perturbed at my mere presence or his assistant's lack of proper coordination?

I couldn't tell.

I told him about our deal with Google and even gave him a headset to put on and view some of the VR material we'd shot. He watched for about fifteen seconds and said, "This is making me nauseous."

I decided to move on quickly.

"Gerry, just one more thing. Thank you for your time. It seems like a lot is going on with the newsroom transformation. And I know video is a big part of that transformation. But nobody is talking to me about how the video department might be impacted. I want to make sure I have a chance to contribute to the ongoing dialogue."

"Don't worry. Nothing is going to happen without your knowledge, Andy."

Gerry never looked up at me when he said that. He was looking down at his papers. I wanted to tell him about all I'd done for the *WSJ* over five years—how hard I'd worked, all I was doing, and what I could do going forward. Instead, I walked the few steps over to the sliding doors, opened and closed them, and headed back toward my office.

Out of the corner of my eye, I saw Gerry snatch his phone off the receiver and put it up to his ear. Then, just as I passed his assistant's desk, I heard her pleading into her phone, "I am so sorry, Mr. Baker. It won't happen again."

Maybe he was just busy and had little time to talk to me. Or maybe Don Imus was right that they don't speak to you when you're on your way out . . . and if they do, it is because the assistant screwed up.

CHAPTER 51

THEY COME TO GET ME

I had one more move to save my job. I had to get a meeting with Alexa to make sure she understood all that my team was doing and could do as the transformation was taking shape.

I hoped spending time with me would make her realize how devoted I was and that she'd learn to like me.

I could think of no better plan.

I wasn't sure she'd meet with me, but then she had no reason not to. We simply disagreed about whether the video team was making money. I didn't see that as insurmountable in our ability to work together. And yet, as the person heading up the newsroom transformation, Alexa held all the power.

I sent the email invite. In the note, I said, "I'm eager to tell you all that video is accomplishing and my specific approach to driving future revenues." Similar to my thoughts about meeting with Gerry, a no to my invitation—or worse, getting no response—would mean I was getting fired. A yes would mean she cared about my opinion and experience, and maybe she didn't hate me.

Most importantly, I'd still have a job.

Once again, I stared and stared at my email. Nothing.

Throughout the day, I thought, *She must be very busy with all that transforming she's doing.* Then, hurriedly, I'd return to my desk and scroll through all the emails. Nothing. A second day came and went. I was despondent. I couldn't eat or sleep. She was going to spurn my invitation.

When bully targets fear for their jobs minute by minute and day by day, it's debilitating and traumatic. I had been a confident, experienced, industrious, loyal, and productive executive overseeing a global team. I was reduced to a hypervigilant, anxiety-ridden individual yearning for any sign that I was still wanted, still needed, still respected, and still secure in my position, a role I had worked my entire career to achieve.

But then . . . there it was. Her name popped up in my email, and I quickly clicked into it. Did she accept? Yes! She did! I was elated and relieved.

Why would she meet with me if I was on the way out? Silly paranoia. I knew when I got in front of Alexa, she'd recognize all that the global video team had accomplished and all that I could do to contribute to the newsroom transformation. Whatever that was, exactly.

I had my assistant find a meeting room for Alexa and me. All the meeting rooms were booked. There was a small one, more like a phone booth than a conference room, where two people could comfortably fit. I was anxious to finalize the details of the meeting. I thought a smaller space would mean we'd be able to relate more personally than across a big corporate-style boardroom table meant for twenty people.

I had no idea what Alexa might be most interested in talking about, but I was prepared with my list of achievements, current initiatives, and future revenue opportunities.

I was ready.

I got to the cozy, glassed-in conference room early. I sat with my back to the wall, facing the little door that opened to the space. There was just a tiny table with enough room for two people to sit down with a couple laptops. At the top of the hour, right on time, Alexa came around the corner. I stood as she reached out to open the door.

I smiled.

I said, "Hi, Alexa, thank you so much for taking the time—" and then stopped mid-sentence. Following five feet behind her and entering the now-too-crowded space was Chris Moran. I was stunned. After our last encounter, I vowed never to meet or speak with Chris Moran again.

I almost said, "What is he doing here?"

New plan: Don't look at Chris. Don't acknowledge Chris. Do not speak to Chris.

At least that part of the plan went off without a hitch. During the hour we were together, I never so much glanced over at Chris Moran. Alexa got 100 percent of my focus.

She listened intently, asking quite a few questions about decisions regarding which stories to cover, who'd cover them, how many resources to devote to each story, and how much time to give to a particular video news package. I was pleased to show off how much I knew and what it took to orchestrate this grind every day and every night. It was cathartic. I was gratified that she was so attentive. I tried not to lose my focus, but I couldn't help wondering why she'd brought Chris to the meeting. Perhaps, as her number two, she wanted him to take notes. He was scribbling mightily. I could see that out of the corner of my eye.

The only real point of contention during our meeting was when I mentioned the VR deal with Google.

"This is the kind of deal we should look to replicate," I said. "I can help negotiate these deals, and we've proven we can deliver the content. Google is thrilled with the stories we produced. The deal we struck with Google should help video move toward profitability this year."

Alexa looked at me. No smile. "That money is not going into video," she clarified. "That goes to ad sales. That's ad sales revenue."

I wasn't about to argue with her. I needed to keep Alexa on my good side. I thought I'd successfully communicated my worth and that of the video team.

We concluded the meeting positively and amicably.

As I returned to my office, I took a deep breath and thought, *That went well.*

I decided to visit Christine Glancey, my executive training coach, colleague, and friend, to tell her about my successful meeting with Alexa and let her know I was proactive in making my case to those overseeing the newsroom transformation.

Christine had taken on new responsibilities herself in the last few months. She'd been promoted to deputy managing editor for news operations and talent. She welcomed me into her office, which was adorned with colorful flowers. I always felt better in Christine's presence.

I told her about my conversation with Alexa, and in passing, I mentioned, "This guy Chris Moran, who seems worthless to me, also attended the meeting." I asked her if she could provide insight into the newsroom transformation. I still didn't understand the goal and how it might impact the video department.

Christine smiled and listened, but this time, she didn't display her usual compassion. I could also tell her smile was forced, and her response was curt.

"I don't really have much insight, Andy. It's a process." Christine then abruptly changed the subject.

I wondered if her new job was so challenging that she, too, might feel at risk during this transformation.

And then it happened. Christine, the hard-nosed newsroom lifer, started to cry. She apologized and grabbed some tissues. She wiped her eyes and composed herself. Christine then mumbled something into her tissue: "Everything is just so hard at the moment."

I don't remember what else we might have talked about before I left her office. I'm sure I tried to console her. I didn't stay long. After closing the sliding doors, I took about five steps from her office, and an unwelcome thought popped into my head: *Is she crying over her situation or mine?*

Jason Sachs, the head of the newsroom transformation, was the last person I was determined to speak with to plead my case. I had devised a plan to save the *Journal* hundreds of thousands of dollars and wanted to share my thoughts with him. If I got traction around my idea, it could save my job.

The *Journal* was hosting more live conferences around the country and around the world, spending a fortune hiring local video production services for these events. I had a plan in which my video team would use its resources and expertise to provide the same services for a fraction of what it was paying third-party providers.

I called Jason's office a couple times. I left a message on his answering machine. I waited a day. Nothing. Then, I called and reached his assistant. I told her I was hoping to get on Jason's calendar. I waited two days. No response. The week was almost over. It was getting late on a Friday afternoon. I was coming out of the men's room, and Jason was walking directly toward me. He was reading news copy with his head down.

"Jason, hi."

I startled him. I could tell he was uncomfortable. I must've interrupted him in deep thought.

"Could I just get you for five minutes before the end of your day? I have a plan to save the *Journal* hundreds of thousands of dollars, if not millions," I embellished. "I'll be happy to wait. I'm working late again tonight."

It was my weak attempt to impress him. Jason looked fatigued and forced a slight smile, not dissimilar to the one Christine gave me before she broke down.

"I can't, Andy. I don't have time."

He still seemed immersed in whatever he was reading, and with that, he walked away from me down the hallway. I was crestfallen. He didn't even have five minutes for me. I felt beaten down and ostracized. Jason became yet another person who wouldn't meet with me, and worse, wouldn't look me in the eye.

I knew too much by now about what that meant.

I didn't work late that night. I went home dejected.

Nathalie Martinek, PhD, a leadership and workplace Dynamics Coach in Melbourne, Australia, writes extensively about scapegoating in daily posts on LinkedIn:

> At first, you're celebrated.
> You're positioned as capable, collaborative, even exceptional.
> And then, without warning, the tone shifts.
> The invitations stop.
> The narrative turns.

And you're left wondering what you did wrong.

That confusion isn't accidental.

It's designed to protect power, not people.

This is the Scapegoating Playbook—a series of predictable stages that competent professionals are pushed through to preserve a fragile structure.*

According to Dr. Martinek, the devaluation stage of the Scapegoating Playbook is excruciating. Your credibility is rewritten so the system can justify turning on you. The shift is rarely announced. It happens quietly, through meetings you're excluded from, whispers you're not part of, and sudden changes in tone from people you thought were allies.

What makes scapegoating devastating is not only the loss of your role, but the collapse of trust. Your credibility has been rewritten in real time, and colleagues you collaborated with, now turning on you. This is why scapegoating leaves people reeling even after they've left. It's not just the exile. It's the disorientation of seeing your strengths turned against you and your belonging revealed as dispensable.

I spent a fretful weekend wondering and obsessing over what it meant that Jason couldn't find five minutes to hear my proposal.

At nine o'clock, on Monday morning, sitting at my desk with my heart beating out of my chest, I saw an email from Jason come in.

"Hey, Andy, do you have a few minutes for us to catch up this morning? Perhaps 10:30?"

I could've thought, *Oh, this is great. He found time to meet with me! I must've just come upon him at a bad time last Friday.* But while I'd occasionally met with Jason over the years, he'd never emailed me to "catch up" in the nearly six years I'd worked at the *Wall Street Journal.*

I was about to get fired. I didn't know what to do. Or who to call. I was panicked. I reached out to the friendliest voice I could think of, my former boss, Chris Cramer.

---

* Nathalie Martinek, "Scapegoating Doesn't Begin with Blame," LinkedIn, May 26, 2025, https://www.linkedin.com/posts/nathalie-martinek_scapegoating-doesnt-begin-with-blame-it-activity-7332737330623012864-pXKC/.

"I think I'm about to get fired," I said over the phone, trying to compose myself.

"Oh rubbish. What makes you think they're getting rid of you?"

"Jason Sachs just called and wants to 'catch up.'"

I felt myself trying to make air quotes. I was having trouble breathing.

"Wait a minute," Chris said, trying to be helpful. "Who do you report to?"

"I report to Gerry."

"Well then, Jason wouldn't be letting you go. That just wouldn't be proper. Gerry would have that talk with you."

Gerry Baker was my boss, and given that I'm about to report what transpired, it's imperative at this crucial moment (call me defensive) to share Gerry's last review of my job performance.

> Andy has managed video effectively through a challenging year. It has been a period marked by considerable upheaval-changes in some of the working practices of video team staff and the separation of Dow Jones Media from the *Journal* which has created a fresh set of challenges.
>
> But Andy's team has focused on producing quality video in the areas that are of most value to *Journal* subscribers and readers. The team has also accelerated the pace of innovation, as noted in our review of Andy's goals and achievements below. He also managed costs well; even as demand for video increased, he cut overall expenses for the video department. There have been some setbacks, notably our declining traffic on some off-platform channels, *and he needs to work with the business team to develop an effective strategy for this* [my emphasis]. But Andy is a supremely confident manager, with a good feel for the opportunities of video and a willingness to take risks and successfully innovate. He is also a highly congenial colleague, and I greatly appreciate his experience, wisdom, and counsel.

I received a 4 rating out of 5, which corresponds with "Exceeds expectations."

At 10:28 a.m., I exited and walked toward Jason Sachs's office. The glass door was closed. He looked up and signaled for me to come in. I was just about to sit when he uttered these exact words.

"We are making a change at the top of your department."

It took me a split second to absorb what he was saying, and in that split second, I remember thinking, *Hey, wait a minute, I'm at the top of my department.*

I sat down, and set my forehead on his desk. I kept repeating, "I can't believe this. I can't believe this. I've worked so hard." I'd been thinking about this very moment incessantly for months. I'd even calmed myself in those moments by foolishly thinking that with the *Wall Street Journal* on my résumé, I'd find good work . . . easily.

I was stunned. It occurred to me, I was being scapegoated for the video department not making more money.

While I was trying to take it all in, Jason shared the most staggering news.

"Chris Moran will be taking over as head of the video department."

I was so dizzy from trying to comprehend what was happening that I couldn't laugh or cry or debate the suitability of my successor. I couldn't quite grasp what I'd heard, and I was so unnerved by my demise that I couldn't focus on who was taking over for me. As far as I knew, Chris Moran had never produced a single video during his career. And he'd never managed anyone and certainly not a global team of fifty people. In fact, from what I'd observed, he had enough trouble managing himself.

If I'd been tasked with evaluating his job performance, I would've given him a 1 out of 5: "Never Meets Expectations."

They'd also egregiously bypassed Joanne Po, my now–number two, who'd been at the *Journal* for years and was doing a stellar job helping me manage the video team. Everyone liked Joanne and had the utmost respect for her as a leader and journalist.

In his excellent novel *Restless*, William Boyd states, "In the end, they come to get you."*

"I have to get off the phone, my darling. The doctor is coming to get me." Those were the last words I ever heard my mother say.

They come to get us. Before they do, we work ourselves to exhaustion.

My rule never to adorn my office with any personal effects—no family photos, no posters, no diplomas, no knickknacks, and no awards—was again proving an effective strategy.

When they come to get you, you want to be traveling light.

I got on the train. It was nearly empty. Who goes home at 11:24 a.m. except for some loser who just got canned? Sitting there in my befuddlement and despair, I had time to realize that Alexa Moore had duped me. She met with me and brought along my heir inapparent so they could download as much of my knowledge as possible on running a global video department because neither of them had a clue how to do it.

The leaders of the newsroom transformation had decided months ago that Chris Moran was better suited to lead the team than me.

I've had people tell me, "Get over it; that's just what you have to contend with at work." Remember when discrimination and bias based on gender, race, age, disability, and sexual orientation were just "part of the workplace"? Remember when sexual harassment was just something women had to deal with? It's time to say workplace bullying and the resulting psychological and physical harm can no longer be one of the challenges that comes with the job.

There are many definitions of workplace incivility and degradation. I argue it's time to adopt this one:

Workplace bullying involves repeated behaviors—such as undue criticism, exclusion, withholding of opportunities, subtle undermining, and threats—that affect an employee's well-being and work performance and provide no benefit to the worker or the business.

This interpretation highlights how psychological harm can occur even in

---

* William Boyd, *Restless* (Bloomsbury USA, 2006).

the absence of overt aggression. Scheming, belittling, and ostracizing to the detriment of the staff member and the organization can no longer be considered just "part of the workplace."

And as I have described in these pages, talented employees leave toxic environments, driving up costly turnover and recruitment expenses. Teams suffer from poor morale and reduced collaboration, and reputational damage makes it harder to attract new talent. In the end, unchecked bullying drains both human potential and financial resources, undermining growth and long-term success.

It was now clear to me that I had been targeted, set up to fail, unduly criticized, scapegoated, ostracized, and discarded. I walked through the front door of my home and tried to make it up the stairs. Nobody was home. Everything was heavy, from my shoulders to my feet to my heart. What would I say to Jennifer, Sophie, Luke, and my friends and family?

I decided to go into our home office. I sat at the desk, my laptop open. My impulse was to check my work email. Oh, right. No reason to do that anymore. I was becoming more irrelevant with every passing moment. I sat there, slumped over. The months of trying to overcome the inevitable, and the even more enervating attempts to convince myself that it wasn't happening—it was all now engulfing me like a crashing wave coming ashore.

As I saw it, three hours after being fired I'd already been forgotten by those who had orchestrated my departure at the *Wall Street Journal.*

I stared straight down; I couldn't even support my head. So very, very tired. I slipped off the chair and lay down on the floor. My abject depression joined me. I fell asleep. It was an anguished loss of consciousness. I woke up thirty minutes later, and my heart immediately sunk to my stomach.

Yes, it happened.

Yes, it was over.

"The loss of a job following months or years of bullying can result in a feeling of shame and grief. So much of our soul is wrapped up in our work, and we are at a loss when that is unceremoniously and unjustly ripped from us. When you meet people, you often immediately tell them what you do. After job loss, you are unable to define yourself. You have lost your identity," Gary Namie explained to me.

Jerry Wainwright, my senior year high school basketball coach, mails inspirational messages about leadership and dealing with life's inevitable hardships to his former players across the country. He's been doing so for more than a decade. I thought it was such a unique way to stay in touch that I convinced the *Wall Street Journal* to write a story about it.

My favorite message Coach Wainwright ever sent was this quote from the bestselling novel *The Alchemist*, written by Paulo Coelho: "The secret of life, though, is to fall seven times and to get up eight times."

And that's what I did. I struggled to my feet, then sat myself right back down at my desk and started thinking about who I could call who might console me or, better yet, provide me with a job lead.

I started with Coach Wainwright. He'd been a very successful high school coach and went on to coach in the college ranks, leading the University of Richmond and the University of North Carolina Wilmington to spots in the NCAA basketball tournament. But I also knew he'd been let go from his job as head coach of the men's basketball team at DePaul University in Chicago after five unsuccessful seasons.

"Nobody at the *Wall Street Journal* cares that you worked your ass off and you were devoted to the job. And they shouldn't," Coach Wainwright said after I explained my situation. It wasn't exactly the uplifting, empathic, galvanizing, impassioned locker room speech I desired.

"Did they pay you?"

"Yes, Coach."

"Did they pay you fairly, even generously?"

"They did."

"Then they have fulfilled their end of the deal. You weren't on the Supreme Court. This was not a lifetime appointment. They don't owe you anything. The people at the *Wall Street Journal* are not your family. Maybe you were fired because you did a lousy job. And then again, there may be other factors out of your control that led to this. You'll never know, and it doesn't matter. So, stop with the woe is me, and get up. Stand up strong," he said in his bass, booming voice, the one I so clearly remember screaming at me in the Highland Park High School gym my senior year.

"Regal, you're the dumbest fucking smart kid I've ever coached!"

He was right then and he's right now. During my entire career, I never learned. Every time, "I thought it would be different."

But the problem was, *I* wasn't different.

I never adapted to the personalities and the politics in each office. Sure, it's about effort and results. But as in kindergarten, it's how well you play in the sandbox with others, especially those holding all the digging tools and the toy trucks. I kept digging my own holes without the necessary tools.

Ultimately, I just dug myself deeper and deeper.

Let me be clear. This is not about self-blame. It's about self-realization, understanding, and coping. It's about nurturing your self-worth, and the light that resides in each of us, and not allowing someone—a bully boss—to darken your light.

I needed the experts who I only recently encountered and who have given me context, awareness, compassion, and relief.

As Coach Wainwright hung up the call with me, I tried to straighten up and stand taller.

And then, I once again began the grind of searching for a new job.

CHAPTER 52

HER KINDNESS KNOWS NO BOUNDS

I spent my days sending out résumés and staring at my phone trying to will it to ring. I'd gone from a couple hundred emails per day and fifty people who needed my attention to nothing and nobody. The winter of 2017 was harsh, cold, and lonely.

I reached out to someone who understood my situation better than anyone else, Joanne Po, my former number two at the *Wall Street Journal*, who was now a dear friend. After being snubbed herself, Joanne decided to take her talents, reputation, and experience and return to the Fox Business Network. They were thrilled to have her back.

On March 15, 2018, Joanne and I made time for dinner in the city. I was in better spirits, but the hurt remained, and one overarching issue lingered: To the question, "What do we need to do to drive three times the revenues and vitalize the video department?" why was the answer, "Get rid of Andy Regal and replace him with Chris Moran"?

I have always loved being in Joanne's company, no matter the circumstances. However, I feared that she was still in touch with much of the team and would have news about how well everyone was doing—that the department was thriving in my absence.

Joanne was facing me in a booth as I walked through the restaurant door.

She was beaming. Joanne has a beautiful smile. I hadn't seen her since the day I was fired. We hugged.

I wasn't even settled in when she exclaimed with eyebrows raised, hands flailing, her face brightening, "Have you seen the news?"

"What news?"

She handed me her tablet.

The headline of *The Daily Caller* website screamed: "Exclusive: WSJ Video Editor Fired for Sexual Misconduct." Just below the headline was a picture of the *Wall Street Journal* newspaper. The article read, in part:

> A *Wall Street Journal* spokesperson confirmed to *The Daily Caller News* Foundation that their top video editor, Chris Moran, has been fired for sexual misconduct allegations following an internal review.
>
> "Dow Jones takes allegations of misconduct very seriously," the spokesperson said in a statement to *The Daily Caller News* Foundation. "Following an internal review, Chris Moran is no longer employed by The Wall Street Journal."
>
> The spokesperson did not provide any details about the allegations against Moran.
>
> Three sources, including a member of the WSJ video team, a Dow Jones employee, and a senior media executive with knowledge of the firing, all told The Daily Caller that Moran was recently let go from the newspaper for misconduct.
>
> The Dow Jones employee and senior media executive both confirmed that Moran was removed after being accused of sexual misconduct . . . Moran was appointed to chief video and audio editor in September of 2017.*

---

* Amber Athey and Joe Simonson, "EXCLUSIVE: WSJ Video Editor Fired for Sexual Misconduct," *Daily Caller*, March 14, 2018, https://dailycaller.com/2018/03/14/wsj-video-editor-fired-sexual-misconduct/.

Other media organizations picked up the story, including *The Wrap*, which added this tidbit under a goofy picture of Chris Moran smiling and pointing to himself: "On his now-deleted Twitter account, Moran described himself as 'bossman of video, documentary films and podcasts' for the Journal."*

I wasn't at all surprised that Chris was more taken with the job's trappings, title, and perceived prestige than the in-the-trenches deadline work necessary to produce top-quality twenty-four-hour journalism.

I sympathized with anyone who Chris Moran might have sexually harassed. I was also crushed once more at the thought that executives at the *Journal* thought he was better suited to lead the video team than I was.

Joanne also shared the identity of one of the other co-conspirators who had worked to oust me.

As a senior leader, I was encouraged to explore opportunities for my best team members beyond raises and bonuses, such as allowing them to attend conferences and conventions. I tried to do this as often as budgets would allow. One of my valued reporters begged me to attend a major climate conference in Paris. I approved the request. He had earned it.

A week after arriving, he asked to stay longer. I said no.

We needed him back in the newsroom.

He was frustrated by my decision and displeased with me about it. I thought that was the end of it. Months later, he joined those from other departments in the coordinated effort to discredit and isolate me.

They sabotaged me, gaslit me, and cut me off from allies before dismissing me.

As for work prospects, I turned to another one of the absolute best people I'd ever met in my career. Prior to Joanne, Gwendolyn Bounds had served as my number two for a short period of time at the *Journal*. Gwendolyn, or Wendy as she's known, had spent twenty years at the *WSJ* when I took over the department. She and I joined forces. Her official title with our video team was managing editor and deputy of *WSJ* Video.

---

* Jon Levine, "Wall Street Journal Senior Video Editor Exits After Misconduct Investigation," *The Wrap*, March 15, 2018, https://www.thewrap.com/wall-street-journal-senior-video-editor-exits-misconduct-investigation/.

Wendy is a star. I always feel elevated after being in her presence. She's a terrific listener.

I remember the day she came into my office to tell me she'd accepted another job. I was surprised and saddened.

"I'm going to be head of video at Consumer Reports," she said proudly. Shortly thereafter, Wendy rose to the position of vice president and chief content officer for Consumer Reports.

I was happy for Wendy at the time, but I couldn't help thinking, *Who in their right mind would leave the esteemed* Wall Street Journal, *covering the most important people and world events, to go to an old and nearly irrelevant media brand like Consumer Reports? Is there anything more boring than reviewing toasters, refrigerators, mattresses, and lawn mowers?*

I didn't know much about Consumer Reports. I'd never even opened the magazine. But as Wendy sat in front of me, excited about her new opportunity, all I could think was that Consumer Reports would be the last place I would ever work.

The absolute last place.

Wendy, to my everlasting gratitude, followed up soon after and hired me to work for her as the head of video for Consumer Reports.

Would my career finally be free of bullies and bullying?

By the time I thanked Wendy profusely for the opportunity and ended the call, I was absolutely, positively certain that this time would be different.

And it was.

CHAPTER 53

GOOD ADVICE, THEN REALLY BAD ADVICE, THEN THE BEST ADVICE

To lead people, walk behind them.

—ATTRIBUTED TO LAO TZU,

ANCIENT CHINESE WRITER AND PHILOSOPHER

I began writing this book in response to existential questions I kept asking myself: What was the point of my career? Why had it turned out this way? Why did people treat me with disdain? Most importantly, why did I always expect it to be different, only to be smacked down again and again?

There are many articles on how to deal with a bully boss. And they all have this type of ridiculous and useless advice:

- **CALL ATTENTION TO THE BOSS'S VALUES:** Try "I know that you really care about everyone feeling valued, and when you do *X*, it undermines that intention. Maybe we could try *Y* in the future?" They're kidding, right?
- **SAY THEIR NAME A LOT:** Try "Jim, I hear what you are saying, but, Jim, I need you to stop doing *X*. I treat you with respect, Jim, and I need you to do the same." I'm laughing now. My bosses would likely

have responded, "Andy, I hear what you are saying, Andy. Now, please, Andy, shut up and get back to work, Andy."

- **DON'T FORGET POSITIVE BODY LANGUAGE:** Yes, *do forget* to change your body language to solve your bully boss problem.

There are also these recommended strategies from the many articles I read:

- **CONFRONT THE PERPETRATOR.** Good luck with that.
- **ASK THE PERPETRATOR'S BOSS FOR HELP.** Seriously? That's his power base!
- **COMPLAIN TO HR.** Do you really think the HR department will support you over the boss when the boss signs the checks?
- **HIRE AN ATTORNEY TO FILE A LAWSUIT.** Unless you are in a legally protected class, you'll be throwing thousands of dollars away and ensuring you'll be out on the street soon.

And, of course, there is my favorite useless pop-psychology advice for dealing with your bully boss problem:

> Keep your cool and remember that sad bully's punishment is that he or she has to be himself or herself. What an unhappy life to lead! You will move up and out of that situation and never look back.

Oh yeah, we targets always get a better, higher-paying job after being bullied, and we never look back. We just stay calm and carry on.

The truth is, I never thought to look for answers to guide me during my career-long bullying experiences. I didn't even identify it as bullying at the time. I thought the treatment I received was part of the job. And to a significant degree my doing, my fault.

I knew that I needed to purge myself of this ache. I hoped writing would be more satisfying, productive, and healthy than throwing up in the nearest waste can or contemplating ending my life.

I was gratified but unfulfilled when I finished my fifth or perhaps sixth draft. Reliving the most devastating moments from the safety of my back porch or my living room, knowing that I'd survived, did help. But it wasn't enough.

It finally occurred to me to use my journalism background to find experts who might provide some insights.

The first expert I contacted on this journey changed my outlook forever. My conversation with Dr. Gary Namie from the Workplace Bullying Institute, the forefather of the anti-workplace bullying movement in the United States, was transformative on many levels. It allowed me to stop bullying and blaming myself for not standing up to my bosses.

It's time for all bully targets to stop blaming themselves.

I couldn't help but laugh and cringe when Dr. Kenneth Yeager, director of the innovative Stress, Trauma and Resilience Program at The Ohio State University, told me, "Andy, I see all kinds of patients in my practice who have suffered from bullying. But I've never seen a bully looking for help."

It's time to raise awareness and find an antidote for the bullying and toxic workplace epidemic.

Through interviews and research, I learned that the fact that bullying is legal delegitimizes any complaint victims might make.

Unless an organization writes specific guidelines about workplace decorum, and few do, bullying is not actionable in any way, unlike harassment. Harassment—where someone creates a hostile work environment—hinges on being mistreated based on a protected class, such as sex, age, race, religion, disability, or national origin. If the bad behavior is unrelated to one of those, it might be soul-crushing and debilitating, but it's not against the law. There's no protection against bullying. As a target, you have to take it or leave it. If you leave it, or it leaves you, you suffer.

There must be a reckoning.

David Yamada, law professor and director of the New Workplace Institute at Suffolk University, has devoted much of his adult life to writing workplace bullying legislation and lobbying to get it passed.

I found comfort in his compassion for me and all victims of workplace aggression in our conversation:

> PROFESSOR YAMADA: This work has been career- and life-defining for me. You can't immerse yourself in this subject matter and not have it affect and change you. Hopefully, soon, we will be more aware of the trauma these behaviors bring. And be more sensitive to how people experience the workplace and how they cope.
>
> ANDY: It never occurred to me that what targets sometimes experience could be considered illegal. I always thought that's just how it is, and I must suffer. After all, I was never hit or threatened with bodily harm.
>
> YAMADA: Early on, Andy, I found that this type of workplace mistreatment deserved its own label. I teach employment labor law, and I started to ask, what legal protections are available to someone severely bullied at work? I was looking for something that would provide legal incentives for employers who engage in preventative measures, protect employees who report abusive work behaviors, and compensate targets when repeated bullying causes harm.
>
> ANDY: Even as a target, I can see it's difficult, I suppose, to discern or delineate incivility from illegality.
>
> YAMADA: I looked at ten years of cases where people had brought these types of claims against their employers for bullying, and the courts dismissed these claims even before they got to trial. The behavior described in those judicial decisions as being just awful bullying still wasn't enough to rise to the level in the court's eyes

> to the claim of intentional infliction of emotional distress.
>
> ANDY: Was there any legal research on this at the time?
>
> YAMADA: No, there wasn't. So, I started researching potential legal protections with a hypothesis that a personal injury tort law claim, intentional infliction of emotional distress, would be the legal remedy that people would have in a severe case of bullying. [As a response to that void, Professor Yamada drafted the Healthy Workplace Bill.]

I wrote the first version of the legislation in 2003. It has been my mission to get state legislators to understand the issue. We had to alert people about the severity of workplace bullying. The Healthy Workplace Bill provides for standard forms of compensatory and injunctive relief, such as lost wages, medical expenses, and reinstatement, as well as for punitive damages and attorney's fees. These allowable damages largely mirror those commonly awarded in successful employee discrimination cases.

> ANDY: But you still have the problem of defining what rises to the level of unlawful?
>
> YAMADA: In this context, an abusive workplace would be defined as the "conduct of an employer or employee, in the workplace, with malice that a reasonable person would find hostile, offensive, and unrelated to an employer's legitimate business interests."

I liked that definition. The opposition to the proposal, not surprisingly, has been from the corporate interests who are concerned about fighting off lawsuits. They're worried about spending money defending their bullies in and out of court.

More than thirty states have considered a version of this legislation.

In the Workplace Bullying Institute's 2024 national survey, conducted by Zogby Analytics, 87 percent of respondents supported the enactment of new laws to protect the interests of bullied workers and that view transcended ideological and political party differences.

New laws are needed to address the failure of nondiscrimination statutes to address these more common and sometimes more harmful forms of misconduct. The United States remains the sole Western industrialized nation not to have laws or health and safety regulations that address bullying, outside the narrowly defined criteria of status-based, civil rights harassment.

Martin Luther King Jr. famously said, "Morality cannot be legislated, but behavior can be regulated. Judicial decrees may not change the heart, but they can restrain the heartless."

I endured twenty-five years of bullying with zero understanding of it. During the last six years, when I mentioned this project to friends, family, and colleagues, almost without exception they couldn't wait to share their bullying stories. And they, too, could not comprehend why their bosses had treated them disrespectfully.

As Dr. Namie told me, "Remember, not one of us asked for it, and not one of us wanted to be treated this way. In the history of work, no employee has ever asked to be mistreated at work."

Ever.

It's not simply the act of bullying that is traumatizing, but also everything that goes on in our minds afterward . . . beating ourselves up continually over why it's happening to us, ruminating over every occurrence, including when the next harsh criticism will come, whether via Zoom, in person, email, text or phone.

For decades, I felt ashamed by my inability to speak up and defend myself. Dr. Namie's counsel was reassuring:

> It likely won't work, Andy. The bully is more powerful than you. The bully has been ingratiating himself above him, and he or she has protection. Plus, you likely waited a long time to confront the

> bully. It is so delayed it will likely be ineffective. You would have if you could've fought it off from the start. If you tell the bully how his behavior affects your work, health, and personal life, you will come off as weak. No. You can't be so vulnerable.

I then spoke to Dr. Maureen Duffy, a leading therapist, consultant, and author on workplace bullying. When I admitted to her how alone and exposed I felt at work during all those years of being bullied and ostracized, she helped me understand power dynamics in the workplace during an impromptu session.

> ANDY: Dr. Duffy, I was a confident leader to my team members. But when it came to how I felt on the inside, I was always fearful of the boss and terrified that he would destroy all I was trying to build personally and professionally.
>
> DR. DUFFY: It's a shared experience. We are all so vulnerable at work. The combination of vulnerability and uncertainty brings about a tremendous amount of anxiety and trauma. It can be terrifying when you have a mortgage and a family to support.
>
> ANDY: Unless you're imprisoned, nobody has more power and authority over you than your boss. And when you believe that person not only doesn't have your welfare in mind but is trying to diminish you or hurt you, it feels like you're in prison.
>
> DR. DUFFY: You're right. This issue is nothing to trivialize. It's a form of psychological terrorism. We haven't begun to have a constructive and worthwhile conversation about these issues in this country. It's happening to too many good people in too many places with too many harmful consequences.

Reflecting on my career now, I'm kinder in my self-talk and self-reflection instead of castigating myself. I'm no longer alone and no longer hurting.

There is hope now for targets still in the midst of their crises and for those needing to recover their emotional and physical health. It's possible, perhaps likely even, that specific types of bullying will soon become illegal and targets will have more options than "take it or leave it." Organizations will have to take consequential action when bullying claims arise to avoid costly legal fees.

Steps must be taken to address this now.

Dr. Yeager agrees that there can be a role for the courts here, but so much strife can be avoided if people, especially bosses, focus on civility and understanding.

"It's pretty simple. And it's not that difficult. If the message is sent to everyone at work to treat each other with basic dignity and respect, that will be the environment. If someone doesn't abide by that rule, they need to be held accountable, and if the employer doesn't do it, the courts should provide a remedy. But in most companies, that general message is never communicated."

I only wish I'd visited Dr. Yeager's office years ago. I confided in him that what stayed with me, in my long-term memory, was the anxiety, shame, and feeling of failure, not the great people I worked with, the friends I made, and the important work we did together.

I asked him how I and other targets might be able to change the narrative. I was still self-chastising for believing throughout my career that this next time would be different.

"Andy, there's a reason we call it the 'Stress, Trauma and Resilience Program.' The idea of resilience is what you do during and after the bullying. Resilient people learn from their circumstances. But it's not an all-or-nothing situation, where you respond with great resilience and you never get bullied again. If you look for an all-or-nothing situation, you will always feel as if you have lost because the next situation won't be perfect. You have to look for incremental growth. And only resilient people can get another job. You didn't sit home and cower. You didn't drink yourself into oblivion. You didn't let it destroy your marriage, your family, and your life. That's resilience. You have to take the small wins with you. Resilient people understand you won't get it all. But you can get what you need."

Dr. Yeager's insights provided an epiphany that brought me to tears. For the first time, I considered that my career was not futile. I am not a failure. I did it. I was resilient.

And Dr. Namie's words were foundational to my healing.

He provides this advice for targets who are the focus of their boss's vitriol: "Focus on restoring your physical and emotional health. You've been damaged. You need time to heal. Stress affects the brain and the organs. It's a full-body effect. You need time to heal."

For all of us, healing starts when we focus on positive self-care, transforming our brain function. We can't make the bully boss into our best friend. But we can be our own best friend.

For those who have experienced workplace bullying and aggression, effective self-care and other methods of coping and recovery will change the way your brain works—the way you think and the way you feel.

In doing the work for this book, I've spoken to hundreds of bully targets and identified six core principles or tenets of self-care, which are crucial to healing and growth.

I know these steps can help bully victims begin to cope and heal. I tell people to start with the first principle because it is critical.

PRINCIPLE 1: REESTABLISH YOUR PSYCHOLOGICAL SAFETY IN THE MIND AND BODY

When subjected to prolonged mistreatment—whether through verbal abuse, gaslighting, or exclusion—our nervous system remains in a constant state of high alert. We feel unsafe, not just in the workplace but in our own minds and bodies. This chronic stress rewires our brain, making us hypervigilant, anxious, and unable to trust others, and even ourselves.

Without psychological safety, no other healing mechanism can take hold. If your body is stuck in fight-or-flight mode, focusing on rebuilding confidence, reclaiming joy, or finding purpose is impossible. Your mind and body must first understand that you can breathe, think, and reason through this traumatic time. This involves grounding techniques, mindfulness, and establishing safe spaces, both physically and emotionally.

Reestablishing safety means reconnecting with yourself, validating your experiences, and breaking free from the internalized fear and self-doubt that bullying creates, helping you step out of survival mode and into recovery.

I spoke to a woman in IT. Her coworkers cyberbullied her relentlessly. She didn't feel safe at home or work. She quit her job and moved away at the height of the aggression. It's been devastating. However, in achieving psychological and physical safety, her heart has stopped racing; she is focusing on peace of mind, gratitude, breathing, and meditation. She negotiated a reasonable severance package and is now ready to pursue new opportunities.

PRINCIPLE 2: RESTORE YOUR SELF-WORTH

When workplace bullying erodes our self-worth, the consequences are devastating. It doesn't just affect our job performance—it destroys our sense of identity. The workplace, where we once felt capable and valued, becomes a battleground where our confidence is shattered, each insult, passive-aggressive remark, and exclusion chips away at our belief in ourselves. We start questioning everything. *Was I ever competent? Did I deserve that promotion? Maybe I really am the problem.*

This relentless psychological assault seeps into every part of our life. We stop speaking up in meetings, hesitant to offer ideas because we anticipate being dismissed or ridiculed. Imposter syndrome tightens its grip, convincing us we're a fraud who will soon be exposed. Even outside work, the effects linger—we avoid social interactions and isolate ourselves. Motivation evaporates, replaced by a sense of hopelessness. We stop dreaming about the future because we can't even survive the present.

Worst of all, when our self-worth is gone, we tolerate the abuse. We stop believing we deserve better, allowing the cycle to continue. Workplace bullying doesn't just damage careers; it destroys lives.

I met an accountant who experienced psychological harassment at work so severe that he lost his self-worth. His entire identity was wrapped up in pursuing validation from the bully.

We are working to restore his self-worth by shifting his focus away from the bully and back to himself. We are working to limit the time the bully's words are in his head, replacing those thoughts with affirmations of his worth. I encourage him to reach out to people who remind him of his strengths: mentors, trusted colleagues, friends, and family. Their perspectives can counteract the bully's false narrative. We also set small, achievable goals: accomplishing even one meaningful daily task builds momentum and restores confidence.

Instead of allowing the bully to define his reality, he focuses on his core values, the people who love him, and the person he is outside of work. Every step toward self-worth is a step away from the bully's control.

PRINCIPLE 3: RECLAIM YOUR SENSE OF JOY IN INDIVIDUAL MOMENTS

This is a lifeline in the throes of severe workplace bullying. When bullying strips away joy, it feels out of reach. Negativity consumes everything, making it difficult to see beyond the pain. But finding small moments of joy—whether through laughter, nature, music, or meaningful connections—becomes an act of defiance against the toxicity that seeks to control you.

These moments act as anchors, reminding you that life exists outside the bullying and that you are more than your suffering. They interrupt the cycle of fear, offering mental and emotional relief from constant stress. Even fleeting joy helps reset your nervous system, grounding you in something positive and life-affirming.

Healing isn't just about recovering from trauma; it's about rediscovering what makes life meaningful.

During my coaching work, I met a woman in public relations who was given a new role and then set up to fail. She received no guidance, no support, and only harsh criticism. She cried every day on the way to work. During the incivility, she had no joy, lost her sense of gratitude, and couldn't enjoy the things she loved—a glorious hike, mint chip ice cream, and the companionship of others.

In her new approach, she understands her boss is bullying numerous employees. She doesn't take the criticism personally. The bully boss still bullies, but she's found a collaborative senior colleague to confide in and answer her questions.

Ice cream tastes good again!

PRINCIPLE 4: REIGNITE YOUR PURPOSE IN LIFE AND WORK

This is crucial when enduring severe workplace bullying because the bully thrives on making you feel powerless, small, and directionless. When daily attacks on your character, competence, or contributions pile up, they can erode your sense of meaning. You begin to question, ***Why am I even here?*** *This is a dangerous and demoralizing place to be.* A toxic workplace or cruel manager does not define your value. Whether through mentoring, a creative passion, volunteering, or reconnecting with professional goals, reigniting purpose reframes your mindset. It shifts the focus from victimhood to empowerment, helping you see beyond the immediate pain.

Having a sense of purpose keeps you moving forward, reinforcing that you are worthy of a fulfilling life beyond the psychological harassment.

I met a head of HR who was bullied by the CEO. He felt irrelevant, powerless, and defeated. Now, he has a spark in his current efforts to find purpose in life and work. He values writing, taking his son to ballgames, and fitness. He's decided he cares deeply about his colleagues' welfare, is grateful for the role and the work, and looks to protect and support other bully targets in his organization.

PRINCIPLE 5: PRACTICE POSITIVE SELF-TALK

This concept is pivotal when coping with and healing from a bully boss because bullying warps your perception of yourself. Constant criticism and belittlement can make you internalize false narratives that you're incompetent, weak, and unworthy. Over time, these external attacks become your own inner voice, reinforcing self-doubt, shame, and despair.

Positive self-talk is the antidote to this psychological damage. It helps rewire your thinking, replacing the bully's toxic messaging with your own truth. Work to avoid absorbing the cruelty. Shifting this internal dialogue restores confidence, strengthens resilience, and prevents you from accepting the mistreatment as normal or a part of the job.

By reclaiming control over your thoughts, you break free from the mental grip of the bully boss.

I will use myself as an example here. During my career, no one bullied me more than I bullied myself. I let others' words and actions weigh on me, leading to a painful road of digestive problems, incessant negative self-talk, catastrophic thinking, and suicidal ideation.

People have asked me why I am so hard on myself. Someone recently said to me, "Andy, give yourself grace." I like that. I am permitting myself to do so. It's become a chief goal of my current, healthier way of life. Where I was once my worst bully, I aim to be my biggest cheerleader.

PRINCIPLE 6: FORGIVE YOURSELF AND THOSE WHO'VE WRONGED YOU

This is the final step in recovering from severe workplace bullying because it releases you from the grip of the past. When bullied in a toxic environment, it's common to blame yourself: *Why didn't I stand up more? Why did I stay so long?* and *What did I do to bring this on?*

This self-blame deepens the wounds, keeping you trapped in guilt and regret.

Forgiving yourself is an act of self-compassion. It acknowledges that you did your best in a hostile situation and allows you to move forward without unnecessary shame.

For some, forgiveness is letting go; for others, it's acceptance. It's the knowledge that it happened and it's over. It's in the past.

Forgiving the bully and toxic workplace doesn't mean excusing their behavior; it means refusing to let their malice continue to poison your mind and future. Holding on to resentment keeps you emotionally tied to them, while forgiveness frees you. It shifts the focus from what was done to you to what comes next—your healing, growth, and renewed strength.

It's a gift you give yourself.

I can't change the past, but I can change how I view it. It is my life story, and I now take pride in it. I may have been damaged, but I am not broken. The pain and shame of my career will always be a part of me, but the memories no longer overwhelm or define me.

I finally have what I need. And if you are a target of workplace bullying, you too can get what you need.

There is a movement, and laws may soon address workplace aggression and psychological harassment.

Until then, there can always be resilience, coping, sharing, AND HEALING!

You are not alone!

In the possibility and pursuit of a more understanding, healthy, and productive workplace for all.

ANDREW REGAL

ACKNOWLEDGMENTS

Unlike the bullies in my life, these people treated me with care, compassion, and love. They shed their light upon me.

Barbara and Seymour Regal; Susan Regal; Fern Jacobson; Donald Regal; Aunt Jean; Uncle Dick; Doug Calisch; Peter Litt; Fred Breyer; Robert (Bid) Kritt; Coach Schramm; Debbie Hoffman; Gus, my grade school custodian; Ms. Levine, my first-grade teacher; Marc Bogan; Mr. Brooks, my fourth-grade teacher; Mr. Olber; Teri Witt; Jon Marks; Elie Elbogen; Bruce Mason; Howard Katz; Ana-Jo Mounce; Brenda Belrose; Siobhan Reynolds; Cathy Hunt; Sol Feldman, my creative partner; Steve Lyons; David Kahn; Gary Belsky; Bill Boggs; Ed Glavin; Johanna Dejesus; Desiree Alvarez; Meredith Lubitz; Gerry Boyle; Jennifer Friedman; Debby Crystal-Rosenberg; Paul Rosenberg; Elaine Friedman; Sophia Friedman Regal; Lucas Friedman Regal; Richard Crystal; Bryan Crystal; Maya Grosz; Siddhu Noncarni; Robert Schweitzer; David Issacs; Leslie Bennetts; and Dr. Michael Canter.

ABOUT THE AUTHOR

Andrew Regal is a seasoned media executive, workplace bullying expert, and speaker. He worked his way up to executive producer, executive VP of programming, and VP of original programming at major media organizations such as Court TV, CNBC, and MSNBC. He served as global head of video at the *Wall Street Journal*, overseeing journalists in New York, Washington, San Francisco, London, and Hong Kong.

He garnered honors, including the Loeb Award for Excellence in Business Journalism, and the Associated Press Media Editors Award, "Innovator of the Year." Regal has created and executive produced multiple Emmy-nominated programs.

He lives in Westchester, New York, with his wife, Jennifer, and his kids, Sophie and Lucas.